Please, Jesus, Give Me
Three More Minutes to Live

Dr. Harold Hammil

VANTAGE PRESS
New York

FIRST EDITION

Published by Vantage Press, Inc.
419 Park Ave. South, New York, NY 10016

Manufactured in the United States of America
ISBN: 0-533-14699-2

Library of Congress Catalog Card No.: 2003095222

0 9 8 7 6 5 4 3

This book is dedicated to our beloved P. & A. platoon leader, 2nd Lieutenant Kenneth Blake of Montevideo, Minnesota, who was killed in action (K.I.A.) June 18, 1944 in very fierce enemy infantry attack while we were attempting to capture Leghorn, Italy from the Germans. He was the greatest person and the finest soldier that I ever knew. God bless him.

Official seal and shoulder patch of the 34th Infantry

Contents

Preface

In this book I am relating only combat incidents that I was personally involved in, and I can verify all of them, one hundred percent. There is not one incident in these writings that I have embellished, glamorized, or improved upon to make them seem more than they were. This book was not intended to be a novel of any kind. They are absolutely true personal experiences during WWII of my platoon in the Italian campaign as ordinary infantrymen. We lived and experienced the same dangerous, life-risking battle incidents that all other unlucky infantrymen, marines, and any soldier or sailor in front line did in combat duty. They were the "queen of battle."

We were in the real front lines, where few officers and absolutely no photographers, politicians, or entertainers were allowed to be.

We were just young, innocent, high-school-aged boys doing a job that no one else wanted to do.

We are not natural-born killers any more than you are. We were just like you until we received our draft notice. None of us volunteered for the infantry. No one volunteers for the infantry, you have to draft them into this dangerous job. I personally volunteered for the Coast Guard and Air Force before I was drafted so that I would not get caught up in the infantry. I'm just like everyone else. The infantry was my last choice, and then I failed the physical examination three times in one day at the Chicago Dearborn station. Technically I should not have been in any service, but I don't think that my pride would have permitted me to stay out during the entire war. I would have been too ashamed. Which is probably why I think that I was a good average infantryman, a lucky survivor of WWII combat.

Now I am very proud to be a survivor of a great combat infantry division to have known these fine brave soldiers. God bless all of them. This was the greatest experience in my life. Everything else

vii

that has ever happened to me since, then I consider very anticlimactical.

This is not a love story, a mystery story, or a Western novel. It is a historical account of the way that so many brave American soldiers had to live to survive and, possibly, return home to their families and loved ones while in the combat infantry and other branches of service that were in actual combat during World War II.

Every incident here is the truth as I, and the other soldiers of my platoon, experienced them. There has been no attempt to glamorize or falsify anything here to make the stories more interesting. These stories are as they actually happened, so help me God.

There are many other soldiers, who could write about their own experiences in detail. I can write only about what I personally experienced, probably no more dangerous battles than many ex-service men and women experienced in WWII, Korea, and Vietnam. I am certainly not a hero. Most of my platoon saw more dangerous action than I did. I was not the leader or the last one in line when it came to these dangerous details. I was in the middle of the detail, just where I wanted to be and wanted to stay until the war was over, if it was to ever end. I can only write about what I saw and what my extra brave platoon did in 1944 and 1945 in Italy. They were the bravest and finest bunch of boys that I have ever met. God Bless all of them.

The servicemen who are in the killing branches of service must keep reminding themselves that this is a "just war and that it is in God's hands." Otherwise it will bother them for the rest of their lives.

I said that this was not a love story. I was very wrong stating that. This is probably one of the second greatest love stories ever told. These combat soldiers so loved America and their families that they willingly risked and gave their lives for America the beautiful. No greater love has any man or woman.

I knew many of them personally, and this is a very sad book for me to write. But at least I can write, as I will soon be eighty years old. So many of those young boys never lived long enough to be twenty or twenty-one years old. May God have mercy on their souls and bless them and their families forever.

Some of you may find this book disturbing, un-Christian, and horrible. Yes, it is. I agree with you, but this is the way a few thousand young American boys had to live, fight, and die in order for you and your families to live in freedom and luxury that you have now and have always had here in America. So I offer no apologizes to anyone. In fact, it is you who should apologize to all the combat men who ever served in our wars. There were a few of us that were able to survive and return home to enjoy some of the freedoms that we so bravely fought for. God bless America.

[**Author's Note:** The tri-state Veterans of World War II organization, under the direction of Senator Richard Lugar of Indiana, had his office personnel interview many veterans of all the wars.Their stories were recorded on tape, to be played in the Veterans War Wing of the Smithsonian Institute in Washington, D.C.

A person can push a button there and hear these actual voice recordings made by the Veterans themselves. My voice, recording some of the material from this book as well as memories of actual combat, is among the recordings available being played now.]

Greater love hath no man than this, that a man lay down his life for his friends.

—*The Bible*, John 15:13

Acknowledgments

I was first encouraged to write my memories of combat in Italy by my two nephews from Tucson and Scottsdale, Arizona, Gary and Rod Hammil. They were both Vietnam veterans. Their father, Arlie Hayward Hammil, my late and only brother was in the South Pacific all during WWII as a Navy Seabee for three years. They both finished college on the G.I. Bill and are both college professors in Arizona.

I also owe much to my late and only sister, Juanita G. Richards of Sugar Grove, Illinois, for her constant encouragement to write this book. She had also written a book on religion but passed on before she could get it published.

I am also very grateful to Phil and Mary Sivert of Lawrenceville, Illinois, for their months of tedious work editing this manuscript. Phil was also a WWII veteran. They are both retired school teachers and very much involved in the First Christian Church and civic programs in Lawrenceville.

I would also very much like to thank my late mother, Flossie, who was once a rural, one-room school teacher, for her persistent teaching to us three children the great and wonderful world of reading and writing.

Please, Jesus, Give Me
Three More Minutes to Live

1

Entering Service—Basic Training

When I was called into service and took my physical examination February 17, 1943, I had just graduated from Fairfield Community High School the previous May 1942 at the age of nineteen. I was six foot one inch tall and weighed one hundred ninety pounds. I had participated in all high school sports at the varsity level, and I was considered fairly strong physically.

From Fairfield, there were exactly one hundred of us boys, on buses, that went to Chicago for our physical exams. They called me back for re-exam three times. I could not figure why, as very few of the boys had to be re-examined.

After the last exam, the army medical doctor spoke to me.

"Hammil, you have failed the exam three times. You don't have any ear drums, a congenital defect. You wear glasses. You have bad varicose veins in both legs, third-degree flat fleet, and one ruptured testicle." He added, "But you are just too damn healthy-looking to be walking the streets while others are in service. I am going to pass you anyway and put you on restricted army ground forces only, the infantry."

That was the last time I ever heard the words "restricted duty" for the next three years. I was never restricted from any duty. I was often given extra heavy duty because of my size and strength. Legally I should never have been inducted.

Of the one hundred boys that went up, they passed ninety-nine of us. The only one not passed at that time was another boy from Fairfield. He was passed and inducted into my division a few months later. That made it one hundred out of one hundred boys who were passed at our time. Normally, fifteen to twenty percent were rejected at all of these exams.

All boys, on their eighteenth birthday, had to register at their

1

local draft board. This became a federal Selective Service law after the surprise bombing of Pearl Harbor and our declaration of war on Germany.

I was a senior in high school on December 7, 1941, when Pearl Harbor was bombed. They called all the students at Fairfield High School into the study hall, and we all listened to the now-famous speech of President Franklin Delano Roosevelt, in which he said, "this day will live in infamy." I can still remember sitting in the study hall, listening to his speech but not realizing at the time how this World War II would affect my life and the millions of others. Our nation would recover, as other nations would eventually, but the lives of many people would be lost, forever scarred, disabled, or mentally ruined.

No one born after WWII knows what bad times, hunger, fear, or poverty is. They are the postwar baby boomers, the lucky ones. I think it will about 2025 before all veterans and their families will be gone and the personal scars and physical disabilities are all gone and forgotten. The same thing happened in the Civil War, World War I, and other wars. Those who fought or were directly affected by the wars are gone and partially forgotten and now reduced to a few paragraphs in history books.

The WWII people are now all called the great generation, because we survived the Great Depression of the 1920s and 1930s. The WWII factory jobs brought the Great Depression to an end. We also survived WWII and the Korean War. The American veterans who were not wounded were not given any compensation for their services—not a dime. I know that personally.

During my stay at Camp McCain, Mississippi, I often drove the jeep for my company commander. One day, he said, "Hammil what in the world are you doing here in the infantry? You are a high school graduate. We have very few high school graduates in the infantry. Most of these boys dropped out of school or never even went to high school. We have seven boys in M company here who cannot even read or write." He went on to say that some of these lesser educated boys will probably be some of our best soldiers in combat under pressure and enemy fire. They are young and unafraid, and that is what it takes in combat. And they were good soldiers!

The Eighty-Seventh Golden Acorn Infantry Division, which we were in then, was called upon three times to send many thou-

2

sands of young infantry boys to Europe and the South Pacific, where death in combat was routine, daily occurrence. Our was the first all-teenage division formed in WWII, and other divisions wanted them desperately for their replacements. That was one of the reasons that I and many of these soldiers were sent to Europe, as replacements for those already killed in action (KIA).

Months later, we would hear about some of the boys that had been in our platoon, squad, or even in our barracks, being killed or wounded. This was sad for us to remember their parents when they came to camp to visit their son, and when sometimes, we went out to eat with them. I personally know of about seventy-five or eighty boys from my original Company M that were killed. In the Battle of the Bulge, in December 1945, one German artillery shell came in and killed five from my squad, including the jeep driver, which was my job earlier. The sergeant that was killed was my sergeant in Fort Jackson, North Carolina. At one time, we were planning on having a double wedding. He was killed, and my fiancée mailed me a "Dear John" letter, so neither one of us ever got to marry. I have remained a bachelor these eighty years.

A fine soldier boy of Italian ancestry who I was training with was killed when an enemy shell came in and got five of them. I used to give him driving lessons with my jeep. He had never driven a car, and he wanted to learn how so badly. So when it was possible, without getting caught at it, I would let him drive some at Fort Jackson, South Carolina. He was eighteen years old then and had never before driven a car, never dated a girl, never smoked a cigarette, and never had to shave his face. Yet, he died for America and all the free world as we know it today. God bless all of them—they deserved a longer life.

Other than our 87th Infantry Division, the first all-teenage division formed in the United States, all other teenagers were sent to other infantry divisions and were among older soldiers. However, new recruits that were twenty-five years older were not usually kept in the combat infantry divisions very long before being transferred to a noncombat support service of some kind. The army thought that most men of that age or older could not keep up, day after day, the strenuous conditions as well as the younger boys could.

We did not know at the time we were training that we were

meant to be used first as replacement division for the combat infantry divisions in the South Pacific and the European theater of operations.

Right after our basic training was over, many of our young boys were called to replace the killed and wounded soldiers in both fields of combat, Europe and the South Pacific. A few weeks later, word got around the camp that some of them were already killed in action. We wanted to stay together and go overseas together.

A few months later, another call came for a lot of privates only to report for overseas duty. I was a private first class, so I escaped the first two replacement drafts for overseas duty. However, I was called in the third call for all privates and privates first class to be sent overseas, March 30, 1944. We were in a very serious situation then, fighting on two different fronts so far apart.

After this call, the government took the R.O.T.C. boys out of college. They had been on an exemption list for awhile, as they attended college. Now the army needed them badly, and they were called to replace us early draftees who were ready for overseas combat duty.

There were no four-lane highways going into this area of Mississippi, and refrigerated trucks were not invented yet, so we had a very meager diet. We ate at squad tables. So if anyone got a package from home, he would wait until he got to the mess hall to open it for his entire squad to get some home cooking, usually cookies or fruitcake. We got so that everyone would take his turn at going to the local PX nearby for a pint of ice cream for each member of the squad at their table.

For breakfast, we usually got dry cereal in a small, individual box with some watered-down milk that had been poured into a tub and thinned with water because there was not enough milk to go around for every soldier. No sugar at all. One morning, each of us got half an orange for our entire breakfast. One of our boys was doing extra duty KP that day, and he ate one whole orange for his breakfast, and the head cook caught him at it. So on his time off the next two nights, for his punishment he had to dig a "six-by-six," a foxhole, six feet in each direction and six feet deep.

The head cook, or mess sergeant, said, "When you get this six-by-six dug call me. I want to inspect it." Two nights later, the hole was finally completed, and he called the mess sergeant to inspect it. As soon as the mess sergeant looked at the hole and had inspected it thoroughly, he said, "Now put that orange peeling that you stole and ate into the bottom of this six-by-six and cover it back up in your spare time." The poor soldier did it. This hole was dug behind our wooden latrine and shower house. I saw it. This soldier was in my company, and he dug the hole in his time off.

We were losing the war the first year that we were in it. We were losing to Germany in North Africa and to the Japanese in the South Pacific. I think that was one of the primary reasons that all military troops were trained and disciplined harder at this particular time of the war. This made the training in the States that much harder on us. America was embarrassed, and the training became much harder and more intense.

Every morning after breakfast was eaten and our bunks were made up and inspected with a bounce of a quarter off the top blanket, we lined up for our daily water ration. We had to stand at attention, with the lid off our canteen, which was full of water. The second lieutenant then came to each canteen and put three salt tablets in each soldier's canteen. We were training to go to the Sahara Desert in Tunisia, North Africa, as replacements for other infantry soldiers that had already been killed or were expected to be killed by the time we arrived there.

They did not trust us to put the salt in the canteen ourselves. The canteen of drinking water was made very salty so that we would not drink much of it at a time, because in desert fighting, a soldier would be lucky to get a canteen full of water every day. That canteen of salt water had to last a soldier in the States training in the infantry, enough drinking water to last all day and still have enough water left to shave by that night.

I learned never to take a drink of salt water in the morning before noon. If I did, I would want to keep on drinking water. But if I never started until noon, I could make it through the rest of the day on my canteen of water. Sometimes we had to share with another soldier. Basic training was tough on all of us young boys, but I think that the city boys from New York, Philadelphia, and Chicago had a much tougher time than did us rural country and small-town boy who were used to being outside in the woods, rivers, and fields quite a bit.

My brother, Arlie Hayward Hammil, and I were both very ac-

5

tive in our local Boy Scouts, which helped us both to adapt to outdoor living. He was in the South Pacific as a member of the Navy's Fiftieth Battalion Seabees. He was there for three years on Tinian, and Marianas and Midway, Guam, and Okinawa, and Fairfield, Illinois, was very helpful to him.

The city boys had never had chiggers on them before they got to our camp in Mississippi, and they really suffered from them because they didn't know how to treat them. We would camp out in the woods and open fields overnight and sleep on the ground where chiggers live. These city boys would scratch them too hard and make open sores on their legs and around their waistline where their belt was. The belt always stops chiggers. They bore in there and suck blood right away. I saw one young boy from Brooklyn, New York, get a handful of sand from the ground and try to scratch his legs to get rid of the chigger itch. He ended up in the hospital the next day.

Another thing that was about as bad as those chiggers was heat rash on our backs where the thirty-pound, full field pack rubbed against our back in the ninety- to one-hundred-degree heat and dust in the summertime during a twenty-five mile hike that we often took.

To combat this terrible heat rash, we were told to wash our one-piece fatigues after every hike by wearing them in the showers in the latrine shed. This would wash out the perspiration and dust from the long, dusty hikes in the Southern, hot summer weather that we had down there in 1943.

Our barracks were built of local lumber covered with black tarpaper. For heat, we had one potbellied stove in the middle of each barracks. The coal fire would go out every night about 2:00 A.M., and the soldiers would get very cold. So we soon learned to go to bed with the same clothes on that we wore in the daytime. Sometimes, we would always put on our heavy G.I. overcoat and knit cap to help keep us warm in the wintertime. The bunks were all double bunks, and the top bunks were always colder in the wintertime than were the bottom bunks; the cold night air circulated more under the mattresses up high than it did under the bottom bunks. But the top bunks were cooler in the summertime due to that same amount of breeze moving under the bed mattresses.

When a person sat down, he had to sit on his bunk or his footlocker beside his bed. Sometimes a soldier would sit on the bottom bunk when he was assigned the top bunk. Man, would he catch it from the soldier who was assigned to the bottom bunk, because if there was an inspection soon, the boy on the bottom bunk would have to remake his bunk all over again, and the boy on the top bunk would be in good shape. The rule was never sit on any bunk that is not yours, or you could be invited outside behind the latrine barracks. There were a few fights in basic training before all the new boys would learn that they were all in the same boat and there would be no favoritism there as they had at home. Fights were usually with the new boys from large towns.

The officers said, "As long as the boys argue and fight, it is a good sign in the combat infantry. It's when they all get quiet and sit around and mope that we have a morale problem that we must attend to immediately, because we could be in trouble."

Our company commander was 1st Lt. Lichtenfelt, an attorney from Ypsilanti, Michigan. Our second lieutenants were Lt. Johnson (KIA, Germany, 1944), Lt. Sperla (KIA, South Pacific, 1944), and Lt. Petoski (unknown). They were all well liked by the enlisted men and served their beloved country with great dignity and bravery.

After we left Camp McCain, December 1943, we went near Nashville, Tennessee, for three months of winter maneuvers in the mountains and woods without benefit of any buildings to shelter us from the cold and very rainy winter.

Each soldier had half of a pup tent as shelter, which he and another soldier put together to form a small two-man pup tent to sleep at night. During the day, our division was divided into two armies, the red and the blue. From Monday morning to Friday evening, we had mock battles, to decide the victory. I was a jeep driver then for the 87th Infantry Co., 347th Regiment M Company as a machine gunner and mortar man. This was the great Golden Acorn division that served with distinction in the Battle of the Bulge under General Patton. Most of these boys in my squad were killed by German artillery shells December 3, 1944. All were killed by just one shell as they were standing near their jeep. The jeep driver who took my place was also killed then. I knew them all, as I had been with them for one year in training. I was transferred out of that division March 1944, and I sure hated to leave that fine division. But I see that my life was saved by my transfer to another division. I would have been that jeep driver that was killed. I knew him well, and I liked all those boys so much. God bless all of them in that 87th Infantry Division. I have the greatest respect for them. I still consider them my home division, and I am a member of the activated newspaper that they put out regularly.

While I was in basic training in Camp McCain, I would wake up in the middle of the night and hear some young GI crying under his blanket at night. Most of these young soldiers had never been away from home overnight before they were drafted into the infantry. And I say drafted, because no one volunteers to be put in the infantry. The infantrymen have many names: dogface, doughboy, foxhole rat, desert rat, queen of battle, foot soldier, cannon fodder, front-line soldier, combat soldier, grunt, and a few more that I cannot think of now.

Once in a while during basic training, I would hear the bunks squeaking at night, and I would look down the rows of bunks and see two young soldiers in one of the bunks performing an act of sodomy. This was rare, but it happens in any branch of service. About a year later, I saw one of these two boys in action against the enemy, and he was a very brave and fine soldier. I watched him in action the day that he was killed in one of our major attacks, and got his share of Germans before he went down. I went over to him lying on the ground and spoke to him. He didn't hear me. He was younger than I was, probably nineteen or twenty years old by now, after a year and a half in infantry service.

Camp McCain was a brand new, makeshift infantry training camp. Our 87th Infantry Division was the first division to ever occupy it, and it was not finished when we arrived there February 13, 1943. In order to finish building this camp, they would gig twenty percent of each company every Friday so that we would have to do extra duty, such as building board sidewalks, picking up trash in the yard, and cleaning out ditches so that the water would drain out properly. We would have to do this on Saturday, our day off.

I tried to remember who these boys were, later on in Italy, when we would come across each other in combat, taking a town, and they were all just as good soldiers as the rest of the boys.

I am not sure that they were homosexual. Little was known about them then, and they were all in the closet, but the ones who I thought were were just as good fighters when the chips were down

8

as were the straight boys. I could tell no difference in combat. They bled and died just like us.

I am sure that some of them could have avoided the draft if they had come out of the closet and declared themselves homosexual. I do not know if the army draft boards allowed deferment from service then or not; probably not.

Our infantry training was so strenuous and demoralizing at Camp McCain that one night a young soldier hanged himself from the rafters of his barracks with his tent rope tied around his neck. Many went AWOL.

They of course were court-martialed and put in the stockade as soon as they were captured. However, they were all let out before going overseas in order to fight. That which they wished to avoid was now their destiny—forever for some.

Infantry was like the marines and paratroopers, a very strenuous and dangerous branch of service that most young recruits try to avoid.

When you first enter the infantry during basic training and other training programs, such as combined, advanced, and invasion training, you are restricted to the camp at all times without any passes for the weekend or furloughs. Consequently, most of us had not seen a woman or a girl for many months. So after all these training programs were over, the army in Camp McCain decided to have a U.S.O. dance in one of the large buildings on the base. So I decided that I would go to it, even though it was a long walk across to the other side of this large camp of about twenty thousand soldiers.

The free dance had been advertised in all the local newspapers, so most of us figured there might be some local girls there for us to see. When I got there, I saw about two thousand G.I.s, and about eight or nine girls dancing with the young soldiers about eighteen and nineteen years old, like myself. We didn't know that most of the parents of the local Southern girls had forbade them to attend this dance or to associate in any way with those damn yankees.

As I stood there wondering how I was going to get me a girl to dance with and talk to, I noticed that the guys who were getting the girls were standing at the front door, and as soon as a girl entered the building, before they could sit down, they would ask her to dance right then. I decided to try that. I got at the head of the waiting line, and I promised myself, "The next girl that comes through that door is mine. No one is going to beat me to her."

Soon a young, plain-looking girl entered, through that door, and I grabbed her and said, "Wanna dance?" She looked at me and said, "I've walked all the way here, and I am tired and gaulded but that is what I came for. Let's dance." So I put my right arm around her, held her right hand in my left hand, and we took two steps on the dance floor, when another G.I. cut in and took her away from me. I was mad and disappointed as I walked away in utter disgust. This soldier that cut in on me had another soldier tap him on the shoulder and cut in before that first soldier got to take one step with the girl on the dance floor. So I felt better.

Modern American history tells us that before WWI, America was a rural, agricultural nation. Most people lived on small farms and made a very modest living. Very few held down a second job in town. There was very little money to be made in town unless you had a small mom and pop business. The machine age did not exist yet.

Most people ate what they grew and bought very little from grocery stores. Their main worry was to grow and can in fruit jars enough to get through the winter without going hungry or depending upon relatives or neighbors for help with food or clothing. They all depended on wood and coal for heating the house and cooking the food.

Rural America didn't have plumbing for running water or inside toilets. The family took their bath behind the pot-bellied stove in the living room, one at a time, on Saturday night. All dirty clothes were washed by hand on a corrugated washboard or hand-operated washing machine that had a corrugated washing paddle on the bottom that someone had to push back and forth. I remember these things very well and write this from my own personal experience.

These children in rural American attended one- or two-room schoolhouses with one or two teachers teaching all eight grades. My mother and a few of my relatives were among these teachers. If there was only one or two students in a single class, the teacher would often advance them or hold them over in another class to make fewer grades, regardless of the student's age or their parents' wishes. Many of these schools were very successful in the education process. Later on, they advanced to one year for each student and age bracket.

After WWI, 1914–1918, America went into an economic slump called the Great Depression. This was partly due to the fact that when WWI ended, so did all of the jobs requiring all of the able-bodied men and all of the young girls and women who had left their country farms. They were now idle, as they were no longer needed in the sewing factories, steel mills, and other areas that had previously needed them for the war effort. The factories themselves closed down. Some went bankrupt as many banks holding what little money some people had in them. Franklin D. Roosevelt, President of the U.S.A. then in 1933, '34, '35, took over federal control of the banks, which were up to that time privately owned with no insurance or auditing whatsoever.

Also our American soldiers were coming home from France after winning the war and they were looking for a job also. They were given some preference in job applications if they were academically capable, such as in the post office department and as rural route carriers.

During WWI and WWII, history tells us, we had the lowest rate of unemployment in the history of America and the greatest period of moral decay and promiscuity, resulting in a great amount of venereal diseases and illegitimate children.

The infantry and mounted horse cavalry bore the brunt of the dangers and death as usual in WWI. Eighty-seven percent of all deaths in WWI were in the combat infantry, and what small percent of men were in that fighting branch, I don't know. Over 224,000 were killed in WWI, and over 195,000 were in the infantry. In WWII, over 823,000 were killed, and over 661,000 of them were combat infantryman. That doesn't sound like a place to be in war time. No wonder most men volunteer for other branches of service. These figures do not include the wounded and maimed for life, or the nervous breakdowns.

2

North Africa—Tunisia

There were about 5,500 of us privates and private first class infantrymen headed to an unknown destination and a more unknown future as we rode in a WWI railroad passenger coach train, dirty and crowded. A seating section for four people contained three G.I.s and three large duffel bags, one for each soldier in that seat.

In order that enemy spies could not detect our destination, at night we would travel in the right direction, then during daylight hours, we would travel for hours in the wrong direction so as to throw them off as to our final destination. We slept sitting up in our coach seat for two days and one night before we arrived at our final destination, Hampton Roads, Virginia, or our port of embarkation (P.O.E.), which was the same P.O.E. for many troop ships during WWII. I came back to the same port to disembark after the war was over, two years later. We had just finished one year of basic infantry training before P.O.E. As our troop train was pulling into the station at Hampton Roads, I heard one of the soldiers on our troop train say, "There goes my sister walking over there on her way to work at the bank, and I am going to see her before I go overseas."

We had to march single file between machine guns and military police (M.P.) to a long loading ramp to the ship.

When this young shoulder said he was going to see his sister for the last time, an M.P. said, "You step out of file, and I will shoot you."

Just then another M.P. spoke up and said, "It's okay. I will go with him and watch him." The young soldier, about eighteen or nineteen years of age ran to his sister and hugged and kissed her. I was a witness to this. I hope he made it back. He was a fine boy, but I never knew him personally.

All 5,500 of us young American infantry boys were loaded into a Henry Kaizer, all-aluminum, small troop ship and were headed for combat somewhere overseas. We didn't know until eight days later where we were until we landed at Oran, North Africa, where earlier there had been some very bloody battles between American forces and General Rommel's forces, who were good soldiers and well trained in desert warfare.

General Rommel won the earlier battles at Fondouk Pass but eventually lost the battle in Tunisia and the Sahara Desert, He retreated to Sicily and Southern Italy, where he eventually lost after two more years of heavy fighting, which I and all the other 5,500 young infantry boys were to experience. Many of these boys were killed or wounded before their twentieth birthday. I personally knew and served with many of these unfortunate boys. May God bless all boys who gave their lives for our country. Most free Americans never knew any of them or ever heard their name. If they were to be reincarnated, I hope they would still be proud of America.

When we arrived at Oran, they put us in a villa, named Camp Canastell, where the Duke and Duchess of Windsor of England spent their honeymoon in about 1936. The house was now a first-aid station for our American medics. I received three shots in both arms there. We were to stay there about two weeks awaiting shipment as replacements on Anzio beachhead for the other soldiers that had been killed. This is when you start to worry about our own chances.

When we arrived at Oran, they told us to get in line for chow, which we did without getting a chance to wash our newly issued mess kit, which was coated with a rust preventive called cosmaline.

Cosmaline is a compound made up of axel grease or hard oil with graphite mixed in to prevent all iron or metal from rusting. Our rifles especially were coated with that when we first got them to prevent rusting in storage.

We went through the chow line without a good scrubbing, which is required to removed the cosmaline coating, as it is very toxic to eat.

About midnight that same night, I woke up with a terrible cramping in my lower bowels. I immediately recognized it as a diarrhea attack. I headed for the outside latrine. As I went outside of my four-man tent, I could see hundreds of dark shadows, squatting on the ground, evidently relieving their bowels as I was going to do.

13

All soldiers who did not get to wash their mess kits had this diarrhea. I went into the wooden latrine, and all of the holes were covered with agonizing G.I.s, just like me. Then I went to the urinary trough, which was two one-by-six boards nailed together and extending about fifteen feet long. To no avail, as the boys were standing, straddling it and gushing bowel movements.

I then went outside and squatted on the sandy desert as hundreds of others were doing. The cosmaline had irritated the colon, and nature was trying to get rid of it, which it did the only way it could.

The next morning, the camp director had us all get our trench shovels and dig a hole and clean up the entire area, which we did.

The nights were very cold there. The daytime temperatures would be about 110 to 120 degrees, then drop to 30 to 32 degrees at night. Due to heat expansion in the daytime and cold contraction at night, the large mountain rocks would split with a terrific boom about midnight, waking us up. The hotter the day and the colder the night, the greater the noise at night. It sounded like German artillery coming in on us every time a rock split and shattered.

We stayed here about two weeks. They then shipped most of us up to an old abandoned dairy farm near Naples, Italy, on L.S.P.T. boats (landing ship personnel troops), which could travel in shallow water to shore. At night, we could see the lights flash from our artillery guns on Anzio Beach, near Rome. We could also hear the distant rumble of our artillery pieces firing at the Germans and the noise of their shells landing and exploding on our infantry troops, incoming artillery shells make a quick and short whistling sound. In a few days, all but absolute battle gear was taken from us and we were standing where these terrible artillery sounds were coming from. Deadly combat, to kill or be killed.

In a few days, we were all sent to different outfits. I was sent to the Thirty-Fourth Infantry Division, 135th Regiment 3rd Bn. Hq. Company.

In the P.A. platoon, I was a demolition, booby trap, and land mine-sweeper. I had some training in land mines in the States, and I figured this was about as good as I could get now. I had to take it. You do not get a choice in the infantry.

As I look back at it now, I think that this platoon I was assigned to was a lifesaving assignment for me.

In this platoon, I met the greatest, bravest, and most unselfish group of boys that I have ever met then or since. I still send Christmas cards to the ones who are still alive. We all remember the great dangers that we went through and still respect each other dearly. I pray that God will bless every soldier that I ever served with and all other men who have ever been in combat for their country. Our own lives were in each other's hands all the time, day and night. God must have blessed all of us that made it back alive. These young boy soldiers were the greatest.

The city limits of Oran and Casablanca were off limits to the enlisted men; the officers had their own clubs.

We didn't have any, so some of our very enterprising young men would test the off-limits section and usually got caught and court-martialed the next day. The court-martial only meant a reduction in rank, as the army needed these poor G.I.s up front for the Germans to shoot at. One M.P. judge in Oran had a favorite speech at his court-martial hearings. He would say, "Stand up, sergeant, sit down, private." Then he would take both hands at the same time and rip the sergeant's stripes off his uniform. This judge was a colonel, and we all hated him, even the other officers around him did not like him. I met him later on in combat, and I did not like him either. He was the only one that was right; everyone else was wrong. Their opinion wasn't any good, only his.

From January 24, 1944, to May 23, 1944, our division and the entire Fifth Army lay on Anzio-Nettuno beachhead on the narrow, sandy coastline along the Tyrrhenian Sea, which is a part of the Mediterranean. The Germans had all the high ground and all of Italy behind them. The enemy could look right down our throats and watch our every move during the day. Most of our activity had to be done at night.

When our soldiers had to urinate or defecate during daylight hours, they had to do it in an empty C ration can or K ration box. When they were finished, they had to check to see from which direction the wind was blowing and quickly, with one arm, pitch the waste with the wind from the foxhole. This was standard practice for three months on the beachhead.

The first thing, when a young recruit from the States came and joined the outfit, was to explain this to him. One new recruit didn't believe that this was necessary, so he stuck out his entire arm, with his waste in a C ration can, from his foxhole and emptied the can slowly. He got shot right through the elbow by a German bullet. He had to stay in the foxhole until nighttime so that the medics could evacuate him back to the beachhead hospital and then back to the States. Sometimes we thought that maybe he was one of the lucky ones. He would probably get to go home with a small medical disability pension and would not have to go through the rest of this terrible war, and he knew for sure now that he would make it home alive. None of us knew what our future would be, possibly much worse than this bullet in the elbow for him. But if we all went home when he did, we would have lost the war.

As soon as darkness arrived, the boys could get out of their foxholes and relax and talk some. However, we had to have search-and-destroy patrols out every night to locate and kill the enemy. Oftentimes, there would be orders to capture a German prisoner if possible instead of killing him so that G2 (intelligence) could interrogate him for possible information.

Our platoon P.A. (pioneer and ammunition) had the regular job of taking food, water, ammo, and mail to the line-company boys in the foxholes at night.

To deliver anything to a combat man, always approach him from the rear, or the American side. You never approach a foxhole from the side or, most certainly not from the front. Only Germans were to approach from the front. A few Americans got killed by friendly fire for not knowing exactly where the next foxhole was when he was delivering ammo and consequently was killed upon entering from the front by our own American soldiers.

Even though you knew who was in the next foxhole to deliver supplies to, you never call out his name in order to find him in the darkness, because a German soldier might hear you call his name and, later on, that German might call his name in order to get him to show himself and make an easy target to get shot instantly.

The German soldiers would often try to foil an American soldier by calling out common American names, like "hey, Joe," or "hey, Mike," just to get the American to answer. Sometimes, it would work, especially with a new soldier from the States who was not combat-wise as yet.

The Americans had very little ground on Anzio Beach to move around in. Every vehicle was bumper to bumper. MPs had to direct traffic day and night in order to keep things flowing as smoothly as possible. There was a high death rate among the MPs; they had to stand in the middle of the intersection without any protection at all day or night.

According to the Geneva Convention, no country at war is allowed to bomb or shell any structure of another country that has the Red Cross sign on it, such as hospitals or first aid stations. But Germany shelled and bombed our American hospital on Anzio and killed eleven nurses and many soldiers who were patients and their doctors.

The United States filed an official complaint at that time with the Geneva Convention on this violation of bombing an American hospital that had a very large Red Cross sign painted on it in plain view of the Germans.

The Geneva Convention replied that the Germans had contacted them that the Americans had violated the Geneva Convention law first by piling army ammunition directly against the outside hospital walls, which is a direct violation of the law that says that no country can store ammunition, gasoline, or any military supplies with in 150 yards of a hospital or aid station.

The Americans, besides being short of space, had piled the ammunition against the hospital walls, hoping that it might prevent it from being destroyed and maybe the Germans would not see it. But the Germans did see it, and we suffered the consequences.

In America, the news that the Germans had bombed our hospital and killed eleven nurses made great propaganda in our newspapers. They did not mention that it was we who initiated the attack by storing our heavy ammunition against the hospital's walls. War news is always controlled propaganda slanted to favor one's own side. What we do in error is never put into print. The newspapers try always to print that we are virgin pure in wars, but that is not always the truth. We are as capable of doing anything to win a war as any country that we have ever fought. I know of a few instances that I am not going to put in print here.

When Axis Sally put out her famous words "and we shall take no prisoners," some of the front-line boys who had prisoners and were taking care of them shot and killed them before the Anzio push-off, then in the push-off, which was spearheaded by the First Armored Division and the Third Battalion of 34th Red Bull Infantry

Division. This was our battalion. This was the same combination of fighting forces that helped spearhead the attack in North Africa and all the way through the forty-five fighting days in Sicily under General George S. Patton. Incidentally, our infantry boys did not like General Patton one little bit. In fact, they hated him, the ones who had served under him and knew his battle tactics. I did not serve under him. He was relieved of his command when our boys were fighting in Naples, Italy, before I joined them as a replacement at Bloody Gulch.

Axis Sally must have had some spies or information leak somehow, and knew what was done to their soldiers, because she never used that phrase again during the entire next year of the war. The Germans lost more than we did on this breakout at Anzio, and sometimes, we were outnumbered three or four to one. This was over a month before D day and the second front opened up. Our boys began to wonder if there was going to be a second front; the pressure would be less from the Germans, as they would have to divide their forces more and take some of the pressure off the Italian front. We had been carrying the entire load in Europe for America until June 16, 1944. Our division went overseas in 1942 to North Africa and had been keeping the Germans at bay for two years before D day. But the D day boys had a terrific battle on their hands, as now the Germans were defending their homeland and were expecting the second front to be made by the Allies. But they did not know exactly where or when or how many troops would be involved.

A few days after our breakout at Anzio on May 11, 1944, the infantry boys and the first Armored Tank Division were leading the main attack on the Germans during the breakthrough the same as this combat team, working together, had done in North Africa and Sicily when they came to the famous Mussolini canal just off Anzio.

Mussolini had this canal built during his regime to irrigate the valley from the Arno River. The canal was very wide and had very sloping concrete walls and bottom that was easy to cross for the infantry boys, as it was not deep at this time. This was about when I joined the platoon as a replacement from the States.

After the first bunch of fighting boys and the First's armored tanks got across the canal, one of the tank drivers spotted a young German soldier who could retreat no further without having a bowel movement right then. The German soldier got on the front porch of an old, small, deserted peasant's house and pulled his pants down and squatted to relieve his bowels. One of our armored tank boys said to the other boys around him, "His butt is about as low to the ground as it can be. I'm going to see just how high I can blow it up into the sky." With this, he turned his tank at the young German boy and fired his 75-mm cannon right at him in the squat. After the soldier was hit with that cannon shell, they went over and looked at him to see how much of him was left. There were very few pieces of flesh near the spot of impact, but they found some pieces a few yards away from the house. The tank driver got a big kick out of telling this story many times in the next two years. I heard it many times.

Most of the foxholes on Anzio were two-men foxholes. Since their stay in that static condition was over three months, the boys had dug some very elaborate foxholes. They were mostly two-man foxholes, so that one man could rest or sleep while the other kept a sharp lookout for the enemy. But the one on lookout had to keep his head and shoulders down low, as the Germans were on the high ground, always looking down on him, just waiting for some soldier to make that fatal mistake and stick his head or arms out of the hole.

These two-man foxholes had a cave dug back from the upright sentry hole and usually had a burlap sack over the entrance if there was a candle lit in it so as not to show any light to the enemy at night. These two-person caves were about five to six feet down in the ground then dug back about six feet so that one soldier could lie down completely and sleep. Some had Marilyn Monroe's and Betty Grable's pictures stuck to the sand and dirt walls, pinned with wire or nails into the dirt. They also had a Coleman stove to heat their C rations and provide some light and heat when necessary.

One of our soldiers even invented a small radio by using some communication wire wrapped around a long nail and actually got some voices on it. Some of the boys got some coil tubing from the motor pool and heated a canteen can full of Italian wine until it became steam and went up the coil tubing into another canteen at the other end. What dripped into that canteen was about one-hundred-percent-proof alcohol, which they had to share with the motor pool boys for giving them the coiled tubing. It really worked, but there was not enough to go around to everybody. These boys were very popular as long as they made the alcohol.

19

They would put a piece of hard candy from a C ration into it, and with some water in their canteen cup, they had a very good potent drink. However, they had to drink slowly. Oftentimes, this one cup had to be shared with three or four soldiers. There was never enough to go around. The ones making this alcohol never let it be known when they were brewing it.

In North Africa near Oran, Casablanca, Tunisia, and the Sahara Desert in 1943 and early 1944, our division fought General Rommel, the German general who was credited for being probably the smartest general of all in WWII. He was nicknamed the "Desert Fox" because he was so sly. He defeated the Allied forces in their first skirmish of the war at Fondouk Pass. My division fought there.

General Rommel fought a very smart retreating war, mostly through Tunisia, North Africa, Sicily, and Italy. He strung out the war and made it last almost four years. Had America and its allies been as prepared for this war as was Germany, this war should have lasted only about one-half as long as it did and many of our boys would not have been sacrificed.

In Tunisia, the country's Arab citizens did not always trust the city banks, so the father of a family carried their money in his baggy pants. Some of our American soldiers heard about this, so when they would see an Arab, they would shoot and kill him and go through his pants pockets to find his money.

Soon our Fifth Army general heard about this slaughter of the Arabs. He put out the order, "Any soldier who kills an Arab must dig a six-by-six foot hole in the desert and bury him there or he will be court-martialed and given a dishonorable discharge." This stopped the Arab killings, as it was usually about 110 to 120 degrees every day in the desert. If a family father died or was killed, the eldest son carried the family money with him in his baggy pants.

Our Fifth Army general then was General George S. Patton. When he was relieved of this command, he was replaced by General Mark Clark, who continued as our general for the rest of WWII.

The chief means of transportation in Tunisia was usually by small donkeys. The wealth of the family among the Arabs was determined by the number of animals the family owned. The entire family always stayed together. When a son got married, his bride came to live with him and his family. They never left the family. Three and four generations would be living together in their tents.

As many as twenty or thirty people or more all living together, working together, as well as eating and sleeping together in a few tents, like a small tribe.

The burro or any beast of burden, was a very desirable product there. The United States and the local magistrates worked out a standard payment plan early in the war because our army trucks would often run over a donkey. The United States agreed to pay the owner forty dollars for every beast run over and killed. Some of our G.I. drivers drove very fast, and I am not sure that they worried much about avoiding hitting the beasts or not.

If any army vehicle hit and killed an Arab's child or an adult, the U.S. government had an agreement with them also. They would pay the family of the victim thirty dollars a person. Human lives with the Arabs were cheaper than that of the beast of burden; they could get another child easier than they could another beast of burden.

I was not personally involved in any Arab's death. Neither did I ever have any dealings with them, as I was only in North Africa about thirty days waiting for my transfer to the dairy farm replacement depot, then on to Anzio—Nettuno, Italy, across the Mediterranean.

I did not fight on the Anzio beachhead January 22 to May 23, 1944. I came to this division May 12, 1944, my twenty-first birthday.

When the original American soldiers landed the first wave of combat infantrymen on the beach, the officers gave the order to "grab a piece of the sandy beach and keep pushing, as there is no way to retreat. The LSPT boats that you came on will all be destroyed by our own navy, so you have to fight to survive. There is no way to escape. So grab a piece of sand and keep pushing."

The first year of WWII, America was losing the war on both fronts: the South Pacific, where General MacArthur lost the Philippines, Bataan and Corregidor, and the first battles with General Hermann Goering at Fondouk Pass in the Sahara Desert in Tunisia, North Africa. The Thirty Fourth Division was involved in their first battle there, suffering some loss of life and their first battle of the war. They returned and fought many more battles there and eventually forced the Germans to leave North Africa and retreat to Italy, which they had occupied for five years and knew the terrain and best advantage ground. We stayed there two full years and suffered

21

twenty-five thousand young American boys lost in the entire Italian campaign.

I personally did not fight in North Africa but arrived there April 1944 to guard a few German prisoners of war. We didn't know it, but we were to be sent up on the big push-off from Anzio to Rome. I think most of us made that. That was where we ran into some of our stiffest German opposition of the entire war, Bloody Gulch.

During the short time that we infantrymen were in North Africa, near Oran and Camp Canastell, we were given the duty of guarding the German POWs, who were enclosed behind a wire fence and played soccer all day.

At night, when the day's duties were over, the army had a movie on a large 6-by-6 truck with a white sheet mounted on it for a screen, which we watched every night. Many times it was the same movie over and over, as they could get very few movie films fast enough from the States. I think that I saw the *Song of Bernadette* at least six times, then I quit going even though they told us that they had new movies from the States. They very seldom did get new movies from the States, unless the rear echelon troops kept them for themselves. We were always second.

The reason we were told that the Arabs wore such baggy pants on the men was that "some day, Allah, our God, is going to send another prophet to earth to guide our people, and a man could possibly give birth to this new prophet, so his pants were to have enough room in them to receive the birth of this new prophet." This story was told to me exactly in these words.

At night, while we were at the Oran replacement depot, not knowing that we were being processed to go the Anzio breakout attack, we could hear the weird, high-pitched voices of the Arabs as they were singing their prayers. Some of our American soldiers who had been there for some time working as camp guards would get tired of hearing this weird, monotone singing and would fire their rifle at the sound in the darkness. If they heard a cry or a noise from the direction of the rifle shot, they would take their pocket knife out of their pants pocket and carve another notch in their wooden rifle butt much, like the Texas gun slinger we read about in our Western books. I did not personally approve of the shooting at the Arabs. But I thought it was about time that I learned to mind my own business. I might live longer this far from home, and everybody had at least one gun of some kind.

There was also a black market there, with the Arabs trading, usually at night with our soldiers, who were support troops and had been there for a few months and knew all the illegal ropes of how to obtain extra supplies and sell them to the desert Arabs. G.I. pants would bring forty dollars; a shirt, thirty dollars; a blanket, forty dollars; and a new pair of G.I. boots, seventy dollars. The support troops usually had someone at the ships' docks who would steal boxes of these goods. The soldiers on guard duty would sell them at night to the Arabs in the desert for a large amount of money. They would then split the money.

Later on, I was to discover that this black market system flourished in Naples, Rome, and Florence. Through the entire war, there must have been millions of dollars of goods stolen that was supposed to go to our boys up front. I personally witnessed thousands of dollars exchanged on the black markets there. Most of the black marketers were noncombatant support troops.

Oftentimes we would say, "I wish that I had a chance to make some money in the black market like those lucky noncombat soldiers." Instead, we received about sixty dollars a month for overseas.

Everybody said whatever they did was "for the boys up front." I was up front; we didn't get anything except a cold can of C-rations and sometimes we had to steal even that.

The black market soldiers could always tell when an Arab was out in the brush in the desert wanting to buy black market goods. He would strike a match that would glow enough to be seen from our camp. If there were four or five men out there wanting to buy, you would see four or five lighted matches in the night that resembled our American fireflies. I would sit there in my tent and try to count the flickering lights in the dark.

Some of the American black marketers got very smart and brave. After they sold their goods to the Arabs, they would walk a short distance away, put an M.P. (military police) band on their arm, and arrest the ones that they had just sold the G.I. goods to and confiscate the same goods that they had just sold to them and sell them again to another Arab and possibly arrest him later also.

Many times I have been ashamed of our American soldiers' actions overseas.

After we were all seated at a movie, sitting on our army helmets for seats, they let the German prisoners that we had been guarding all day come in, unguarded, to sit in the back rows and watch the movie with us, when the movie was over, the prisoners then walked back to their barracks for the night. Their wooden barracks were better than our canvas tents.

These German prisoners of war were the lucky ones, we think, because they had done their duty for their country, had fought the enemy, us, and gotten captured and were now safe and knew that when the war was over, they would be able to go back to their homes and loved ones. That is about as lucky as you can get in the combat infantry.

We were just new, green, recruits going up to the front for the first time to do battle with the enemy. Our fate was not determined yet. About a third of us would be killed in action (K.I.A.). Before the war was over and another third possibly missing in action (M.I.A.) or unidentified on the battleground and mistagged because they were unable to find the dog tag due to severe mutilation of the body by artillery shell's direct hit on their body.

The Tunisian Arabs near Oran and Casablanca had their own criminal laws, one of which a few American soldiers were to learn about first hand. If an American soldier was to have sex with, rape, or molest an Arab girl or woman and the Arabs were to catch them, they had their own laws for a sex crime.

If it was any sex crime involving an Arab woman, the Arab men would catch the male offender, cut his entire scrotum off with a knife, put this entire scrotum, which included his penis and both testicles in his mouth and then sew the lips together with a thin string of leather—all this while the offending person was still alive. Then he was taken out into the desert, also still alive, and staked down, spread-eagled, with his arms and legs in all four different directions. The four stakes that were driven in had the leather strings soaking wet, so as the sun dried out the leather, it shortened and drew them tighter. He usually died from the extreme 110-degree heat or he bled to death. If it was a very serious sex crime, he may also be spread-eagled over an ant hill. In my opinion this would be the worst way to die that I can imagine. I don't fear death. I have

24

narrowly escaped it many times in combat before I was twenty-two years old. But I personally cannot stand pain or suffering, and I don't like to know that anyone else is suffering, either.

I lived through many death-defying combat situations when I was nineteen, twenty, twenty-one, and twenty-two years old. Sometimes I think that the rest of my long life has been anticlimactic and unimportant, since being so near death so many times in two years of deadly combat with the enemy. Death soon becomes a very common thing in your life while you are in combat. Death seems so cheap when you see it on someone else.

3

Anzio, Italy

On the first day of combat in Italy, an officer said, "All right, you boys, I want you to walk along this trail and pick up all the dead soldiers that you see, throw them over the small bank of the ravine, and I mean German and American soldiers both. We will be having some new recruits from the States coming up this trail soon to go into combat, and we do not want to scare them before they get into combat." I had never seen the officer before or ever again, to my knowledge.

This officer did not know that I had just arrived in the combat zone and that I was one of the new recruits that was not supposed to get scared this soon.

Just about dark that night, I said to myself, "Hey, this is May 12, 1944, my twenty-first birthday. Today I am a man." Little did I realize how much I was to grow up that day. I have often been asked, "Where were you born and grew up?" I always reply, "I was born in Fairfield, Illinois, and I grew up on Anzio, Italy, in WWII." So on my twenty-first birthday, I did not have any cake and ice cream, but I had plenty of fireworks.

During WWII, there were many young boys in combat and in all branches of the service who had their twenty-first birthday while in service. And many young infantrymen did not live long enough to have a twenty-first birthday, especially those young boys who had lied about their age so that they could enlist before the age of eighteen. Those who lived through the war then had trouble with the Social Security office when it came time for retirement if they had lied about their age.

I knew many soldiers who did not live to reach their twenty-first birthday. I served in the first all-teenage division, formed in WWII at Camp McCain, Mississippi, near Granada. I was

26

nineteen then. That was the Eighty Seventh Infantry Division, Golden Acorn.

It was my first day of combat just off Anzio Beach and the breakout May 23, 1944, that I had my first experience of what combat and the real war was all about. It was dark at night except for the ever-present American searchlights that were always on at night to help us watch out for a sneak enemy attack. These lights were like the large movie premier lights in Hollywood. They were situated about ten miles back of the combat front lines. They were very helpful to us combat men at night.

The first dead soldier that I helped pick up must have been dead a few days, because as I picked him up by his thigh muscles, the muscles came off in my hands and the worms and maggots were traveling up and down through his arteries and veins eating out the dead and rotten blood. They were crawling on my hands and arms, so I shook them off and then picked him up by his ankles, as I thought there would be less flesh and blood there.

The other soldier and I carried him over to a small ditch where they told us to deposit them. We slung him over the edge of the ditch, the poor dead soldier landed on top of some other dead soldiers that had already started to decay and their body parts to break down by protein petrification, which is normal for a body that is not embalmed right away.

As I was looking over the edge when he landed on top of the other dead soldiers, I received a large splash of blood and dead body fluids directly in my face, on my helmet, and all over my arms, chest, and shoulders. You cannot imagine what a smell that was!

I learned a lesson very quickly there. From then on, when I helped put any more bodies in the ditch, I jumped back and ducked. We put quite a few dead boys in that ditch. They were to be picked up later by the boys from the G.R.O. (Graves registration office), often called by our troops, the "buzzard squad."

One of the last dead soldiers that I picked up that horrible night must have been hit directly, because I only found three pieces of him, each probably not weighing over ten or twelve pounds each. I didn't know how to pick him up and keep all of his remaining parts together, as I figured he would probably like to have it that way. I would also. I took my G.I. raincoat out of my backpack and laid it on the ground. Then I cut a small fork from the nearby brush and raked the three pieces together on into my raincoat and tied the four corners into a knot. I threw the entire parcel of his remains together over into the same ditch, but this time, I did not look over the edge.

I never did find his dog tags to go with the bloody remains, as it was dark and I was not able to search the ground very well. His company commander would just have to go by the process of elimination of those who didn't show up for a couple of days, and who was in that immediate area, as there were a few hundred boys killed in that Bloody Gulch battle that lasted two days and one night. I got in on the last day of it.

Anzio Beach was invaded January 22, 1944 and the fighting lasted there on the beach until the breakout with the First Amored Division on May 23, 1944. These two divisions spearheaded the entire forty-five days of war through Sicily a few months before.

There were twenty-two Congressional Medals of Honor issued to the Anzio beachhead soldiers alone. The most in American history for any one battle. The battle lasted three months with about fifty-five thousand soldiers involved. Five thousand American boys were KIA.

4

Bloody Gulch

The day after I had finished throwing the dead soldiers over into the ravine, we moved on to some very fierce fighting in another creek bed, later to be known as "Bloody Gulch." It was one of the fiercest and most inhumane fighting I was to be involved in for the next year and a half.

The line company boys had been fighting a very stubborn German resistance stand at Bloody Gulch for two and a half days, and both sides had run out of ammunition and both sides had resorted to hand-to-hand fighting. Hand-to-hand fighting is a very dangerous and life-threatening situation for both sides. It is only resorted to when all hope of survival has been exhausted and it is now do-or-die. You do not have any other chances. There are no options. The odds are that you will either be killed or badly wounded. "Mayday, Mayday."

Both sides were now fighting with fixed bayonets. I saw some bayonets that had been broken off in the enemy with only a few inches left at the end of the rifle of the broken bayonet. But those soldiers continued to go from one German to another, jabbing them, trying to cut their throats with what was left of the broken bayonet.

Other soldiers were throwing our C-ration cans at them. The C-ration cans resembled the German concussion grenade, and when they saw the C-ration cans, they would hit the ground, waiting for them to explode and go off, which they never did. While the enemy was lying on the ground, the American soldiers would rush up to them and smash their rifle butts just below their steel helmets. This would break their necks, and they would soon die. No human being should ever have to be in this inhumane situation or even witness it as a spectator. Your worst nightmares could never equal this scene. But it did happen, combat fighting at its worst.

An American soldier, Pvt. Charles Hoffman (upstate New York), and I were helping a line company soldier fire his 80-mm mortar at the Germans in Bloody Gulch. While we were all praying to not get killed at this moment, I looked up at the German lines and saw a young German soldier running straight toward us. He did not have a weapon, his helmet was off, and he was grinning at us as he came in under the overhanging cliff to get in out of danger as much as possible. He looked to be about eighteen years old. I had just turned twenty-one that month.

We were running in and out, firing the mortar between the incoming German mortars and artillery shells; there were three or four of them in the air and falling on us all the time.

All of a sudden, this young German left the safety of the cliff and went out to our American mortar and changed the direction of our firing to another direction, at his own countrymen. I guess he was trying to take the pressure off himself and us by firing back at the Germans. We appreciated it very much. This was the exact moment that I was reborn again as a Christian. I asked Jesus Christ for three more minutes to live, and he gave them to me. I am now eighty years old. So you see, giving your life to Christ does help you.

Axis Sally, Germany's lead WWII radio propagandist, had made an announcement on the radio that this was going to be a major counterattack by them. She said, "We will drive the entire American army back into the sea, and we shall take no prisoners." When they say that they will take no prisoners, that means that they will kill everyone instead of capturing them as prisoners of war. But after our two-and-one-half days of fierce fighting in Bloody Gulch, we Americans finally defeated the Germans with a terrible loss to both sides. Axis Sally never again made that statement after Germany's loss there; although we continued to fight for another year.

As the artillery and mortar shells were still coming in very heavily, I could hear all four of us American soldiers praying. I also could hear the German POWs praying. But I could not understand them, as I was praying in English, First Christian Church, one was saying a Catholic prayer, and the POW was praying in his own language. I would like to think that we were all praying to the same God, just in a different way.

30

This was the exact moment that I was reborn again, May 30, 1944.

While this fighting was going on, I did not think for a moment that I would survive it, so I first asked Jesus Christ for just five more minutes to live. Then I looked around me at all this merciless killing, and I knew then that that was a selfish wish because there was no way that I could live that long. So I said, "Please, Jesus, just give me three more minutes to live so that I can repent and prepare myself for death by telling my mother, father, brother, and sister good-bye. If you let me live just three more minutes, I will make you three promises that I will keep for life if I live." They were as follows:

1. I promise you that I will never curse or use the Lord's name in vain.
2. I promise you that I will never smoke a cigarette.
3. I promise you that I will never hurt a woman physically.

Jesus let me live those three minutes and another sixty years. I have kept my promise to Him exactly as I said I would, for sixty years. Many other soldiers owe their lives to Divine intervention. I am a great believer in that.

I also think that He expected me to do more with my life when he spared me that day in Bloody Gulch. I have tried in my own way to repay Him for that holy deed. I used the G.I. Bill to go to chiropractic college in Davenport, Iowa, and later on to become very successful in chiropractic in Lawrenceville, Illinois.

I asked Jesus for his blessing and life-saving intervention then, and I received it then, at that very moment. I knew then that I had received his blessing for this battle, but I did not know that I was to receive his blessings for the rest of my life. I called out, and He responded. I did not know until many years later, when I studied the Bible more, that if I remained a faithful Christian, He would always be there, supporting and guiding me whether I ask him or not. That he would never leave or desert me. But I should pray and thank Him for the past and present guidance. And I still do, sixty years after I made my three promises to Him and was reborn again in Bloody Gulch, May 30, 1944, about two o'clock in the afternoon. To me, death was very certain within minutes of that terrible, bloody battle in which many great and heroic American and German boys lost their lives. I cried out, and He, Jesus, answered and gave me salvation for the rest of my life.

Even though we were there to win a war for our freedoms, I always felt so very sorry for the dead young German soldiers lying so still and lifeless on the ground, never to breath again in the world that would be free and beautiful again someday. We didn't know when that would be, but we who lived would someday know it; the silent, dead ones would never know it. How sad for all mankind. I feel sorry for any soldier from any country that was killed in any battle fighting for what he believed in. There is always inner conflict going on in mind and body to kill and defend your country or to believe in "Thou shall not kill." That conflict in each Christian soldier will never leave him until the day that he dies. This is what separates the combat soldier from the support troops and the soldiers and civilians at home. They will never have to live with that mental conflict now or ever for the rest of their lives. Thank God for the brave soldiers who actually did the real combat fighting. We owe so much to them. God bless all of them, and may He find a place in Heaven for all of them. They have had their Hell here on earth.

At this time, I was standing under the dirt cliff with my German prisoner, I saw an American infantryman, a line-company boy go up to a German foxhole just a hundred yards in front of us and jab a bayonet into a German soldier standing in his foxhole not doing anything but looking and watching the battle. He had evidently run out of ammo and didn't have anything else to fight with.

Just then, another of our line-company soldiers ran up to this foxhole and jammed him twice in the chest, since our soldier was standing above him on the ground. He started to pierce him for the third time, as he was still alive, when an American medic came up to the foxhole and pushed our bayonet-welding soldier away. Our soldier came back and pushed our medic away and started to ram the bayonet in the German soldier's chest again. Then there were some words exchanged between our two men, but I was too far away to hear, with all the artillery and mortar shells still coming in like hail in a storm.

But the American medic won out and the American soldier took off, running toward the Germans with his bayonet fixed, ready for another encounter with the enemy. He had evidently run out of ammo, as most of us had. The Germans did also, as this battle in Bloody Gulch lasted about two days and a night without a let-up in intensity. There was a great loss of American and German boys there. Also a few prisoners were taken on each side as well as wounded.

The American medic went back to patching up the German soldier who had been stabbed twice, very severely, and I left soon with my prisoner to take him back for interrogation. I never heard another word about this stabbing, as very few soldiers saw the incident and it was just another day in the infantry of trying to stay alive. Cpl. Phillip Braun (Bloomfield Hills, Michigan–San Diego, California) helped me escort the prisoner back.

While we were firing our mortar and praying with our German prisoner, on the flat ground just ahead of us there were dozens of American and German soldiers fighting it out with rocks, bayonets, and fists, and kicking each other as in professional wrestling shown on television.

Soldiers on both sides had run out of ammo and were using the butts of their rifles to kill. It was a brutal and inhumane sight to see that no civilized nation should ever have to undergo. I still see it three or four times a day in my mind and at night before I go to sleep. I see it now as I write this. Combat is unbelievably inhumane, especially hand to hand.

Our division was all alone up front fighting the Germans as another division had run out of ammo at the same time as we did. Their general ordered them to retreat to the beach, as they didn't have any ammo to protect themselves with. That left our 34th Infantry Division up there outnumbered by the German three to our 1.

Our small battery-operated radio could not send messages out of the deep ravine, so our colonel carried the one-hundred-pound radio on his back and attempted to call Mayday to the Nisei 100th Battalion to come to our rescue. Their battalion was on reserve on the beach, playing volleyball when they got our "mayday" message. They dropped everything and came to our rescue, as they had some ammo left. They pushed through our boys and finished off the Germans. However, some of the Germans did escape and leave because the tide of the battle swung to our side. When the Nisei soldiers arrived to help us, they jumped off the back of their supply truck, some in underwear, with fixed bayonets and rifles blasting at

33

the enemy. They were the greatest soldiers that we ever knew. God bless these American-born Japanese, Nisei, soldiers.

Also, the artillery was rationed to three shells a day. This put us in a more dangerous situation because the artillery could now only fire three shells at large enemy concentrations, not small groups of the enemy to protect us and our supplies.

General Patton requested and was supplied most of the food, ammo, and all new replacement personnel. We were now the "forgotten front." Most of us now had to do extra duty, as there were no replacements for the dead and injured personnel, especially for the line companies. They were always the hardest hit, because they were the front line in any attack, the ones that had to drive the enemy out. The line companies were what caused American boys to enlist; he could get his choice of service and not end up a foot soldier, an infantryman. Infantry combat can be a fate worse than death.

At Bloody Gulch, Corporal Braun and I took the young German prisoner with us back down the ravine to our bombed-out building that was our headquarters.

We interrogated him there, and he was very cooperative. But like all German prisoners, he said he was not an infantryman fighter. He was either a cook or a mechanic. All German prisoners claimed this so we would not kill them, especially if we had just lost a buddy a few days before. It was not unusual to capture fifteen to twenty cooks and mechanics at a time. Of course, they were all lying, as their clothes were just as muddy and dirty as ours.

We didn't have time to take him with us, so after interrogation, we told him to keep going back toward our lines and let someone else recapture him. We had a German-speaking soldier in our platoon, who was born in Germany, came to the U.S.A., took out citizenship papers, then was drafted into our army. He did some German soldier interpretation for us when necessary.

The soldiers in my platoon who were up there fighting in Bloody Gulch that day was Pfc. John Buddy Despot (Homestead, Pennsylvania—Manhattan Beach, California), Charles Hoffman, Phillip Braun, me, Pfc. Harold C. Hammil, Pvt. James Vulanti (Philadelphia, Pennsylvania), Pvt. Max Rotopel (South Dakota), Cpl. Max Rush (Camden, South Carolina), Cpl. Joseph Buffalo (St. Louis, Missouri), S. Sgt. Barney Allickson (Montevideo, Minnesota), T.

Sgt. Kenneth Blake (Montevideo, Minnesota). There may have been others, but this was my first week in combat, and I did not really know their names. But it was a terrible, bloody battle, and all our American soldiers gave it more than they should have to in any situation. This was really a life-or-death battle and a "mayday" situation in all aspects. Our platoon did not lose a man in this battle.

Our 34th Division, Infantry was a National Guard division made up of men from three northern states, Iowa, Minnesota, and South Dakota. These are not heavily populated states, so it took three states to make up one National Guard division; it takes only one heavily populated state to make up a division.

In National Guard units, all the men from the same town make up the company of the regiment that comes from their state. This has its good points and its bad points. The good points are that the boys all know each other, went to school with each other, and in many cases, are even related. They can also exchange letters from home and local newspapers and keep them from getting lonely when they are in a foreign country. The bad part is that when there is a hard battle, and the boys that get killed are from the same town, it is devastating. In combat, there may be six or seven boys killed in one night and another few killed the next night also from the same town.

This is all right when the National Guard company is a noncombat or a support group that is behind the lines. They have almost a one hundred percent survival rate, while the combat infantry group have only about a fifteen percent rate. So which group would you want your boys to be in?

None of us were born killers. We were all born Christian human beings made in the likeness of God, our Creator. But eventually, there comes a time when we must defend our country, our loved ones, and ourselves. Wars can be won by many means, but sometimes we have to do battle, and on both sides, someone must do the killing. It is most regrettable that so many good and innocent people and God-fearing human beings are hurt in these conflicts.

Professor Albert Einstein said, "Time does not march on. Time is an infinity, no beginning, no ending; it is *we* who march on!"

It was against the Geneva Convention for a combat medic to carry a gun of any kind. His job was to save lives, not to destroy lives. However, on Anzio during the heavy fighting in Bloody

Gulch, our medics carried pistols stuck down the front of their pants. You could always tell which medic had a pistol, because the bottom button of his shirt would be unbuttoned so that he could get to the weapon quickly if necessary.

I was told that in Bloody Gulch, all the medics carried pistols and that some of the soldiers even saw them firing at the Germans. I, myself, did not see them fire any shots, but I was in the battle there for a few hours, and I am sure that it was possible that they did fire some shots at the enemy, perhaps even for their own protection. Both sides were fighting very fiercely, and there was a lot of smoke and dust flying from mortar shells landing and making a lot of dust and dirt fly when they exploded on the ground. I was told that the German medics also fired their pistols at us.

There was always a lot of smoke in and around an active battle. America and Germany both used black powder in their ammo, and after an hour or so, the battlefield would be covered with a blue haze of smoke from exploded black powder. When I first got into combat, I could not understand why my asthma always flared up in my throat. The black powder smoke would burn my mouth, throat, and lungs, because of my asthma and other allergies from childhood. I am sure that many other young soldiers had these same symptoms from black powder smoke. Today, I don't go to our local turkey shoots because I can still smell the black powder from the shotguns. Also, the sound of the guns brings back too many bad memories. I never go to large organized fireworks displays on July Fourth either.

Both sides of this battle had young boys from home that all looked alike. Possibly, they were just sleeping. Possibly, this was not a war, just a bad dream and it will eventually go away. You could see that some of them were dead because their legs and arms were in twisted, abnormal positions. However, most of them were just lying there in an almost normal sleeping position, except that their clothes were dirty and torn from shell fragments and many of them had dried blood all over them. However I was to soon learn that this was a normal condition for a dead soldier in combat.

The ground that we were standing on and where we had fought the day before was completely pitted with holes that the artillery and mortars had made while I was there with my first prisoner, who had come up to me and surrendered. One could not take a step without stepping in a shell hole. It was estimated that the Germans brought in extra troops to attack us and that we were outnumbered ten to one, but that was a battlefield estimate.

We watched where we stepped so as not to step on any soldiers from either side. That would be a military disgrace after what they had all gone through. And I was there for part of it. In a way, I am glad to have been in one of the fiercest battles in Italy, but I cannot be too proud because of the many deaths and great misery that was inflicted on both sides there. Some of those boys were suffering pain and fear and were seriously wounded, and I cannot help but think that to some of them, the final death blow was a welcomed mercy killing. Most of us do not fear death as much as we fear suffering. I know that I fear suffering more than I fear death. Since being in combat I have said, "If you have never had to seriously pray for your own life, you do not know the meaning of prayer!" And remember that all wounds do not show or heal.

Many a soldier who had been in combat for a while and had taken about all that he could take, mentally and physically, would wait until the Germans started their artillery shelling of our positions, then they would stick their left arm out of the foxhole, deliberately, in order to get in injured or cut off by shrapnel so that they could get to go home with a small pension. "At least I will be alive when this war is over. That's more than you guys can say for yourselves," they would always tell us. Eighty to eighty-seven percent of all deaths in all branches of service occur in the infantry, according to the American Veterans Association. A combat soldier in any branch of service has about a fifteen percent chance of survival when in combat. Most branches of service have a one-hundred percent chance of survival, such as all support troops and the ones back in the States.

Many of these same soldiers would also crawl down in their foxhole head first and leave their left leg sticking out of the foxhole so as to receive a shrapnel wound. If they got their leg or foot cut off, then they could go home. But if it was just a slight wound, they could be patched up at the tent city hospital and soon be sent back to the lines to fight again.

The doctors could usually tell if it was a deliberate wound, because a right-handed soldier would always get wounded in the left arm, or left leg if he was wounded in his foxhole during a German artillery attack. It would be the right arm and right leg on a left-handed soldier. However this is considered a self-inflicted wound (S.I.W.), which is a very serious offense in wartime.

Very few soldiers were lucky enough to get wounded this way, but they would always say, "Well, you can't have all the luck. I'll try again next time."

In this battle, as in many other battles that were to come in the next year, our boys would run out of ammunition with their MI .30-caliber rifles, which most of them carried. They would then try to find a dead American soldier and go through his pockets and bandoleer looking for extra rifle shells. If they could not find any extra shells this way, some of them tried to use the German .31-caliber rifle shells in our American .30-caliber rifles. But this would not work; it caused the rifle shell to explode back into their faces, or the rifle would just jam and not work at all.

I am sure that the German soldiers did this very same thing with our American shells when they ran out of their own ammunition. So our soldiers soon learned to use the German rifle and the Germans .31-caliber shells together and abandon their own rifle on the ground. They could always pick up another American rifle off one of the many dead American soldiers lying around.

Not many American combat soldiers cleaned their own rifle. When theirs got dirty and they found a dead American soldier with a clean rifle, they would just exchange them and reset the rifle sights and take the dead soldier's extra shells and food that he might have on him. Food and shells became very scarce after the second front opened up at Omaha and Normandy beachheads on June 6, 1944. They received priorities on everything, including new young soldiers to replace the ones killed in action under General Patton.

We were told by Washington, "The war will be won on the road to Berlin. You boys have held the entire German army off during North Africa, Sicily, and Italy, so stop at the French border and let the second front take over." We had to stay at the French border only one week before Berlin fell May 7, 1945. We awaited the news that the "War is over" with great anticipation. Then we began to think back about all our buddies that will never hear those beautiful words. The young soldier boys that are now silent, ones who we

38

used to talk about what we were all going to do after we got home from this terrible war.

The reader will notice that I do not use much dialogue between soldiers on these dangerous missions. It was because as soon as we discussed our individual job on this mission and we left our hiding place, we never spoke another word to each other, as we were always in no man's land, and any noise could be a give-away and possibly bring in enemy fire power or the enemy himself while they were on a search-and-kill patrol looking for us Americans.

Neither did we talk to each other while we were on a life-saving mission. We were there to save someone else's life besides our own. This was no time to visit. We did not talk from the time that we left our hiding place until the mission was completed and we returned back down the trail to our original hiding place, slightly behind the front lines, a few hundred feet.

Any sound made by talking, coughing, sneezing, or farting would surely bring the enemy down on us with mortar fire or a German patrol looking for us American soldiers. We learned in basic training how to prevent these sounds coming from our body.

Since it was too dangerous to talk, we used a few basic hand sign language signals, which we were also taught in basic training. But when we got back to our hiding place, we could talk and discuss the mission. We did not really talk much about the dangerous side of the mission until we got relief from the front and were in reserve at the rear, where some of the support troops were. Then we could really let down and relax enough to have a good time, play volleyball, drink wine, and look for girls. However, this seldom happened, as all of the Italian front was short of line company soldiers. We could not stage a major attack against the Germans if we wanted to. We never had enough line company combat soldiers to start a major attack against the Germans, anyway. We sure could have used a lot of those support troops back in the towns that we had already liberated.

It is very difficult for me to talk about our combat stories, because I must remember and relive many of these terrible incidents that I cannot talk about them without choking up and having to stop in the middle of many sentences. It is easier for me to write them down with this typewriter than it is to talk about them. Most of these stories have never been told to another human being, and only the young boys in combat who were there know about them, and they are not able to talk about them either. God bless them, as I knew too well the miserable thoughts that they have had to carry in their head, minds, and hearts for the last sixty years or more. I sincerely hope that they have had work and family interests to divert their mind from going back to those combat days in Italy or whatever country they were in fighting for America. There is no way that I or anyone else can put into words what any combat veteran has gone through, so I won't try. I will just tell you interesting war stories for your historical knowledge of WWII.

My dad once told me, before he died of cancer of the prostate gland in 1974, that when you are young, you always pray to live forever. But when you get about eighty years old and older, you will find yourself sometimes praying to die soon so that you will not suffer anymore. I believe this now, because I am the same age that he was when he died. His father, my grandfather, also died from prostate cancer in 1930. Now I also have prostate cancer, which was discovered by my doctor in 1990. I then took thirty-seven radiation treatments for it, which have prolonged my life pain-free. But I know that radiation does not cure cancer of the prostate. Radiation creates a stage of dormancy in the prostate, but it will eventually return and terminate the patient if he is not lucky enough for something else to take his life before the cancer does.

My dad, whom I loved very much, also told me that "You only live once, but once is enough if you live it right." I would not want to live my life over. I have kept my promise to Jesus of Nazareth that I made May 30, 1944, in Bloody Gulch near Rome, Italy, and he has kept his promise to me by letting me come home safely and pursue a very successful career in chiropractic healing, which has allowed me to help more people than ever hurt during the war.

I made three promises to Jesus if He would let me live just three more minutes in the Bloody Gulch fighting. He gave me those three minutes and more, and I have kept my three promises to Him. They are:

1. I would never curse,
2. I would never smoke a cigarette, and
3. I would never hurt a woman physically.

Because of these promises, I have achieved every goal that I ever set out to achieve and all with his help. I was never alone.

Freedom was not free for many people, but it was free for most Americans.

5

Rescuing the Truck

On the first day of the German counterattack in Bloody Gulch in the middle of May 1944, they overpowered us, and we had to retreat a short distance to get reorganized and possibly try to find more ammunition for the line companies. All of our front-line troops were low on ammo due to the fact that we were rationed because the second front was to open in a few weeks, and they were saving the ammo and food for the large invasion, having no idea what the consequences were going to be once they invaded the continent. Our line company soldiers were rationed to three shells a day.

Our supply truck was a three-quarter-ton, olive green Dodge personnel carrier with all of our P & A engineering and special demolition supplies for the entire Third Battalion, 135th Regiment. We used some of these supplies on a regular basis. Without them, our entire battalion would be jeopardized when serious situations would surely arise in combat. It also contained all our bedrolls and personal backpacks. We needed this supply truck back very badly.

T. Sgt. Kenneth "Kenny" Blake called four of us selected soldiers to a corner and explained to us the importance of someone retrieving this supply truck from behind German lines at night. For this suicide mission, I was one of the four boys selected to enter German lines and try to rescue this important truck with all of our supplies. This was my first week of combat in Italy and one of my busiest with the enemy.

T. Sgt. Blake said, "Take no identification with you except the military dog tags around your necks. No weapons no ammo on you at all, as you are going there to get the truck. Do not come back without a very good attempt at the rescue of it." He further said, "You are on your own; under no condition can we come to help you if something goes wrong. You are entirely on your own, as no help can be sent to you. No matter how much the Germans question and threaten you, if you are captured, you are to give them no information except your name, rank, and serial number. Under no condition are you to give them any information as to our position so that other soldiers here could get killed. You four guys are to leave tonight soon as it gets dark." We all four were very quiet the rest of the evening.

The four of us worked out a plan of how we were to approach the enemy lines to look for our truck before we could attempt to steal it back, quietly, in the dark of night.

"What do we do if they start firing at us?" one soldier said.

"We are on our own; every man for himself to escape any way possible. Do not worry about the others, but get the truck if possible," we all said.

I knew, while praying that this was suicide mission. The army needed this truck worse than they needed us. In the infantry, soldiers are as expendable as flies on the farm on a hot summer day. Supply trucks are not.

"Boys, here is your plan," said T. Sgt. Blake. "S. Sgt. Dorin is small, so he will get into the truck and turn on the ignition. You other three boys are larger and stronger, so you three will get behind the truck and push it as fast as you can. S. Sgt. French Dorin will release the clutch pedal and put it in second gear to get it started on compression. This way, there will not be any noise, and you will have a running start on them. If you try to start it by the battery, it might take longer and the enemy will hear the noise and bring down machine gun fire on all of you, and the rescue mission will have failed. We need this truck very badly for its supplies." This truck already had thirteen shrapnel and bullet holes in its tailgate alone. It was our home, supply depot, sanctuary, place of comfort, and security. And yes, it was our mother and father to us. Without this old Dodge truck, our platoon would fall apart. It was everything to us in this foreign world.

When nightfall came, we started out on our dangerous mission. Our jeep driver took us part way, and then we started walking, our hearts in our throats as we entered German territory, knowing that we could be mowed down by machine-gun fire any second now. I actually thought that I could feel the bullets penetrating my body as we split into two groups now, as we had planned it. Two of us would crawl on our bellies on each side of the dirt road, silently, until we sighted the truck or got killed. On each side of the road was a shallow ditch in which we crawled along. No one was to say a word to each other until the mission was accomplished or failed. We also knew that these ditches contained mines.

We could see each other in the bright moonlight and some light from the ever-present, large searchlights that the Fifth Army had on every night. And behold, luck was with us, because in front of us we saw our beautiful three-quarter-ton supply truck in the middle of the road just where we had left it a few days before. What a beautiful sight that was! If a person could love a truck, we loved this one. Things were looking better now. Some of the great fear and apprehension was leaving me, and I am sure that the other three boys felt better also. We silently followed our prearranged plan.

Just as we had planned, Cpl. Frenchy Dorin got in the truck and turned on the ignition. It was still in the truck, to our great amazement. The other three of us got behind and to the sides of the truck and pushed just as hard as we could, as if our lives depended on it, and, of course, it did. After we had pushed the truck about forty to fifty feet Cpl. Frenchy let out the clutch and the motor started right away; that was the most beautiful sound we had ever heard. This meant that we still had a fifty percent chance of getting out of here alive. The other two soldiers jumped on the sides of the truck, and since I was pushing from the rear I waited until the motor kept running and the other two boys were safely on. Then I crawled on from the rear with the help of one of the two other soldiers holding me by my jacket, making sure that I was completely on while the truck was going down the road.

With the old type cars and trucks that had the floor board stick shift you could start them this way. However, when they came out with automatic transmissions after the war, they would not start this way unless you could get it pushed by another car at least forty-five miles an hour. Some of them would start on compression, but not all.

S. Sgt. Kenny Blake had said to us before we left our camp for this mission, "Now, guys, once this truck is started, you had all better hop on immediately, as he is not going to slow down for anyone, and most assuredly, he is not going back for anyone. So when that truck motor starts, you are on your own to get on it as fast as you can or be left behind in German territory. As you know, our main objective of this trip is to get this supply truck back safely to our outfit."

So far, everything was working as planned, as the Germans had not fired a shot at us. Our hearts had stopped beating over half an hour ago, because we knew that the German soldiers could probably hear them beating in our chests very loudly and possibly give our position away.

As soon as we got in the truck, we all lay on the truck floor and pulled our bedrolls and other equipment over us to help shield us from the enemy bullets that were sure to start any second. I could feel bullets hitting me and going through me all the time as we were going down that dusty road to freedom. But there was not a shot fired at us at any time. This, we could not believe. We were in German territory, and everything had worked to perfection. But why would the enemy leave our supply truck where we had abandoned it, in the road, with the key still in the ignition ready for us to capture and drive again? They didn't even rummage through it for equipment or any souvenirs. We always went through their captured things.

They must have left in the night after our victory over them at Bloody Gulch, because we drove up there the next day, and there was not a German in sight. If not for the artillery and mortar shell holes pitting the ground as far as you could see, you would have never known that a week-long bloody battle had taken place here, as the Germans always left a clean battlefield. When they left an area, they never left any trash for evidence behind, as we did. I still think that there was divine intervention on that mission and a few others that were to follow for the next year in dangerous combat.

"Boy, am I glad to see you guys." T. Sgt. Blake said to us when we got the truck back to our camp. "I never thought that I would ever see any of you again."

"When we left on this suicide mission, we did not expect to ever see you guys again, either," I said. I never expected to come back alive or that any of us would make it back because of the nature of the dangerous mission. Our good luck would not have been possible to predict ahead of time. God must have intervened! I actually believed that He did because this was a just war, for Christianity and human rights. Those of us who were in actual combat and

had to do the killing in order to survive had to keep reminding ourselves that this was a just and necessary war or go crazy thinking
about what we were going through just to live and possibly go
home some day. It must be legal and necessary—otherwise, what
am I doing here, a Christian?

About a week and half later, while we were on the road to
Rome, S. Sgt. Allickson, who had sent us on that mission, called the
four of us in who had made that suicide trip to rescue our supply
truck and said, "I have written to Washington and recommended
each of you four boys for a Silver Star medal. The government and
secretary of the army have accepted my Silver Star recommenda-
tions for each of you, but they will not accept my account of the entire incident. We must leave out the paragraph about the other
infantry division withdrawing and leaving us up front all alone just
because they had run out of ammunition.

"As you know, our line-company soldiers had run out of
ammo also, but we stayed and, without ammo, fought and finally
turned the tide of the large German counterattack, and we sus-
tained a terrific loss of lives of many of our fine soldiers because we
were outnumbered, but we stuck and fought them with everything
that we could lay our hands on.

"Washington has sent back to me a watered-down version of
the incident because, they said, they would never put on record that
an American division retreated and withdraw in the face of fire,
leaving another American division on the battle lines alone and outnumbered to defend America's stand until the Second front opened
up."

S. Sergeant Allickson further stated, "You boys can accept this
watered-down version, or I can send it back to them and request
that our original version be accepted." So we all said no, send it
back. We want credit for all the dangers that we went through.

Sgt. Barney Allickson sent it back two more times. And each
time, it came back with the watered-down version. So he called us
four in again.

"Boys, I have sent it in three times now, and I have gotten it
back three times. So it is time for you to make up your minds. Either
accept the watered-down version or forget the whole matter, because Washington is not going to change its mind. Now let's take a

vote among you four boys. How many of you want to accept the watered-down version?"

We all said no.

"How many want me to tell them to forget the whole thing if you do not receive total recognition for your hazards?"

"Tell them it must be as it was, or forget it," we all said.

Then I went to Sergeant Allickson.

"I would like to have my Silver Star even if the other three boys don't want theirs."

"No. Since you all went together, you will all get it together, or no one gets it."

And he was correct.

Then he said, "I think that you boys made a mistake by not taking that medal and you will see the day that you wished that you had taken it. It's a great medal, only given out for exceptional heroism."

I regretted it that day and every day since then. If I had it to do over, I would have called the boys together, and we could have had more time to think it over and possibly take the medal. I wanted it so that my father at home could have been proud of me. I don't think that I ever did any one great thing to make him proud of me, and this would have been the perfect chance. Also, in the eyes of many people, it could have changed my life in many ways. The Silver Star is a very coveted medal, and it would impress many people throughout our lives. I miss it today more than I ever did.

Ten years later, in 1955, all of us had been awarded the Combat Infantry Badge. We were mailed the Bronze Star for our regular duty as a combat infantryman, for our heroism and dedication to duty. This made me and most combat men holders of eight medals. I did not receive the Purple Heart, as I was never wounded. If you were wounded, some soldiers would ask you, "How many horse shoes are you carrying in your butt?" How any times have you been wounded?

That beautiful old Dodge truck had a .50-caliber machine gun, air cooled, sitting on top of the driver's cab. It was mounted on a 360-degree swivel so that we could fire it at any angle and completely sweep an area if necessary. We never used this machine gun while I was with this battalion, because when we needed it, we were usually a mile or two into German territory and the truck was usually left behind forward lines. It did not have any battle scars on it except for the rear tailgates. The rear tailgate had thirteen shrapnel and bullet holes in it. No other bullet holes were evident on the entire truck. Just on the tailgate as if we were always retreating instead of attacking, which was just the opposite of the truth.

Praying, being scared and afraid is not the same as being a coward. All combat men are scared when on a bad mission, but they continue forward and complete their mission regardless. That is a real soldier not a coward, who runs away and disregards his duty. We never had a soldier in our platoon run away or leave his post in time of fierce battles. God bless all of them.

The four young soldiers who went on that truck rescue mission were Cpl. Max Rush (Camden, South Carolina), Pfc. John Despot (Homestead, Pennsylvania now Manhattan Beach, California), Cpl. French Dorin (Rhode Island), and Pfc. Harold C. Hammil (Lawrenceville, Illinois; Fairfield, Illinois). We four made many dangerous details together and formed a great bond. They were some of the bravest soldiers that I ever fought alongside of.

6

Russian Silver Tooth

In late June, just after we entered Rome on June 6, 1944, we were advancing very fast, trying to keep up with the line companies who were chasing the Germans back to their next stand-off position. When we were told to search this small village very well, especially the basements and tunnels under the stone houses, for any lingering spies that the Germans would often leave behind to fire at us, mainly to slow us down so that they could get dug into their new retreating position.

I had just finished looking through this large stone house, especially the basement, where I did not see anything suspicious. As I was looking around in the backyard, I heard a slight rustling above my head in a small tree. I looked up, and there I saw a small man, possibly a German soldier, sitting on a limb, looking down at me, grinning one of the largest grins that I had ever seen on a man. In the middle of his upper teeth, he had a silver tooth that really shone.

I motioned for him to come down out of the tree by pointing my rifle at him and motioning toward the ground in front of me. He came down very slowly, and all the time kept looking at me with this big smile and that silver tooth showing. As soon as he got to the ground, he handed me a white handkerchief filled with old, dirty potato peelings and some fresh cherries that he was in the process of picking to eat when I captured him. Of course, I refused to eat any of the food that he offered me and kept my rifle on him all the time. This was my second prisoner taken in this war.

I took him back to our platoon, where we had a soldier in our platoon who was born and lived in Germany until he was eighteen years old. He and his family came to America to get away from the war in Germany. When he came to America, he had to register for the draft here. He was drafted into our army infantry to fight

49

against his homeland, Germany. We used him a lot as an interpreter when we had prisoners who did not speak English or Italian. He was Pvt. Bill Zimmerman from New Jersey, a good soldier. Pvt. Bill Zimmerman got the full story from my prisoner. He was a Russian soldier who had been fighting for Russia against the Germans on the northern Siberian front in the battles of Stalingrad and Leningrad when he was captured by the Germans and brought to the Italian front to work as a slave laborer in the kitchen. That is where he got the dirty potato peelings that he had hidden, so as to have something to eat if he could escape the Germans in their hasty retreat from our infantry boys.

He was successful in his escape and was up in that cherry tree, getting some fresh cherries to eat, as he was hungry. We all believed this story and did not turn him in to the proper authorities as we were supposed to. Instead, we fed and clothed him and accepted him as one of us because he had had enough combat and war experiences already. He soon became a trusted friend and very valuable to our platoon as a scout and a very good soldier. We never knew his name. We just called him "Silver Tooth" or "the Russian soldier." We liked him very much and hated to say farewell to him when the war ended and he started back to Russia on foot to look for his family, if he had any left. We were all very quiet for two or three days after he left. We were better men for having known him and having been influenced by his actions of bravery and unselfishness. He was a very brave and great soldier. I am proud today to have been associated with him. I certainly hope that he made it all the way back to Russia safely and found life a little more pleasant for himself than in the past.

Silver Tooth stayed with us for a couple of weeks, and we gave him a rifle to carry. He was a sight to see in his mixed uniform. He wore high, black, German boots, gray Russian pants, American G.I. shirt, and a red scarf around his neck. Sometimes, he wore an Alpine green cap. But most of the time, he was bare-headed, showing his great head of premature gray hair, which always needed cutting. But we all always needed a haircut ourselves all during the war.

He soon became weary of our slower type of battle, so he joined a group of two or three independent partisans, and they continued to fight and harass the Germany Army. One day, he came to our camp and said that there were Germans floating back down the Adriatic Sea on our right flank (which was always open due to the seashore) in a large raft, quietly, without the motor running. After they got behind our lines, they would start up the boats motor then start spraying the shore on our side, trying to kill as many Americans as possible.

S. Sgt. Barney Allickson sent four or five of us back there at night to attempt to catch them while on this killing spree. We went back there and waited all night in the freezing snow, but they never attempted that maneuver again that night or any other night that we ever heard of. I don't remember who the soldiers were that went on this detail.

In all of Europe, I noticed that most European dentists used silver to cap their patient's teeth instead of gold, as they do in America.

Silver Tooth was very good about bringing us messages about German movements if they were too large for his small band to take care of and destroy. He was a great silent fighter, and he loved to kill Germans. He would always grin and laugh when coming back to our camp and telling us about killing them. We moved every few days in our advance toward northern Italy and France, but he would always find us somehow. We never knew how. He could not read a word or speak a word of the English language; neither could any of his partisans that he lived with. He always had that silver tooth showing with a permanent smile on his face. He helped our cause very much in those bitter days.

Another time he caught up with us, he told us about how he and a buddy partisan coming upon three German soldiers lying side by side, sleeping. So he and his buddy examined and checked the shoe laces of these three soldiers to make sure that they were Germans. Then they slit the throats of the two soldiers sleeping on the outside, then got behind a small bush and threw a rock at the soldier sleeping in the middle. He woke up and looked to his right and saw that soldier had his throat cut and bleeding to death. Then he looked to his left at the other soldier, his throat also cut and bleeding to death. He jumped up and started to run as fast as he could. Silver Tooth and his buddy let him get a short distance away, the shot him between the shoulders with their German automatic burp gun that they had collected along the way. Silver Tooth

51

thought that was a very clever joke to play on the Germans. He laughed all the time he was telling it to us. We were very glad that he was on our side.

Silver Tooth told us one thing to always remember that we did not know. "You Americans always tie your shoes by Xing the strings in the eyelets, but Germans, and most Europeans, run the shoestrings straight across, all the way up to the bow at the top of the shoe. So when we are out at night and happen upon a soldier, we always look at his shoelaces, or feel them in the dark if necessary, before we kill them. That way, we won't kill an American soldier."

We were very glad to get this small, seemingly unimportant, piece of information because it could save our own life if we did not tie our shoes as we always did in the crossover, X manner.

Thereafter, when we saw a stranger on the battlefield, we always looked at their shoelaces to see which way they were tied so we could determine if they were American or European. If their shoes were not tied like ours with the X pattern we would immediately suspect them of being a spy or someone we should watch very carefully. He further said that "The partisans always checked their shoestrings first, also before killing anyone." We American infantrymen had very great respect and admiration for all of the partisans and gorilla fighters. They were made up of men and women, but mostly men though.

They fought without any clothing, food, or supplies from their government. However, the Italian government gave each one of these individual freedom fighters a one-thousand dollar bonus after the war was over for their dangerous work in fighting for Italy's freedom. That is more than the American government gave us boys when we were discharged.

I received three-hundred dollars with my discharge and then an Illinois bonus a few years later about the time that I graduated from college in 1948 of another two-hundred. However all states did not give the veterans a bonus, as did Illinois.

7

Liberating Rome

After we left Bloody Gulch, we encountered very little resistance from the enemy as they were leaving Rome, and Germany had many American prisoners there that they had to evacuate quickly. We, the 34th Infantry One-thirty-fifth Regiment, Third Battalion, bivouacked just outside of Rome the night of June 5, 1944, along the famous Appian Way.

It was still daylight when we reached the outskirts of Rome, (Roma), and we could have very well entered the city that evening or night, but our Gen. Mark Clark had received a message from another general friend of his not to enter Rome until he got there with his troops in order to enter the great city with us.

Gen. Mark Clark agreed to wait for him, as his troops had helped back on Anzio; that is why our division had to stay outside the city that night of the fifth instead of entering the city when we arrived there. The Germans were still on the south side of Rome and leaving fast at the same time we were entering the city from the north. This was the first time in Roman history that it had ever been taken from the north, due to the Alps and the deep snow there in the winter. The Alps mountain terrain is rough in the summer, much worse when further hampered with three- to seven-foot snow drifts in the winter. Consequently, it was very seldom attacked from the north.

The next morning, when General Clark started to line up his trucks to make the triumphal entry into Rome, with the newsreels rolling, to his surprise, he found that he was now in the second place to enter the city, as his general friend had come in during the night and stationed all his vehicles and men at the head of the glorious victory parade. Rome was a city of about eight million people; I think that about half or more of them were there to welcome us into the city. All of us enjoyed and appreciated that glorious reception very much. I have seen it on the newsreels many times. We who were the real liberators of Rome were second in line. I heard that General Clark threw a fit when he saw the deceit that his buddy general had pulled on him.

General Clark was so mad at his former friend that I am sure that he had a few chosen words for him, and that their friendship deteriorated from then on. Gen. Mark Clark was supposed to have been heard saying, "I will never again trust another general."

However, the Italian government knew who were the real fighting "liberators," and they still give us the credit. As we rode through town, there were millions lining the streets to greet us. Many shook our hands, kissed us, and had us drink out of their bottle of red wine. This was reported many times in the future upon our liberation of many towns in the next year after dangerous combat with the enemy. We lost 25,000 boys in Italy, 5,000 of them killed on Anzio beachhead alone.

The June 6, 1944 invasion of Normandy and Omaha Beaches was not delayed, as we had originally thought, to coincide with the entering of Rome the same day. Their second-front invasion was supposed to have taken place three days earlier, but due to the high winds and rain, it was delayed three days. The Allied commanders said that had they gone ahead and had the invasion on the original day, three days earlier, that they could have experienced at least twenty to twenty percent loss of their soldiers because of the stormy weather and high seas while the troops were leaving their landing ship personnel troops (L.S.P.T.) boats.

Rome was a large city, about eight million people at that time. After we entered Rome, without any German resistance, we parked our trunks and equipment by a large fountain. It was customary to throw coins in the fountains in Italy and make a wish and it will come true. I did not have any coins with me, so I threw an empty C-ration can in there and made my wish: "Jesus, please me let come home alive." And I would find out a year and a half later that my wish did come true, as the Italians said it would. But a lot transpired between that wish and the boat trip home in December 1945. They also say that if you throw a coin in the fountain, you will return to Italy. That part has not come true as yet. I hope to.

For a few years after the war was over, I did not want to return to Italy because of the memories of so many young boys that were killed there. But now I would like to go back, because I don't feel like I really experienced all those horrible things in combat, that no one died or was injured, that it was just a bad dream that is about to all fade away. And I am sure that it will all fade away the day that I die, as General MacArthur said in his famous farewell speech, "The war is never over for the old combat soldier until the day he dies." I now believe that. I am still remembering the war at the age of eighty years old, and I was nineteen, twenty, twenty-one and twenty-two years old at that time of my horrible experiences. Cpl. Max L. Rush and I were standing by a fountain, and we decided to take a walk, as we were told that we would probably be here all day. So we left our rifles at the truck and started walking down one of the main streets of Rome. As we were walking, we saw a green shutter slowly open and a long-barreled rifle stick out of it. We just stood there in amazement. The city was declared an "open city" and the city had been liberated for two days now. He fired the rifle over our heads into the concrete wall about fifteen feet from me, then slowly closed the green shutter. Cpl. Max Rush and I looked at each other and said, "Let's go back to the truck." We did just that.

We thought that he missed us on purpose, as he was just across a narrow street. I think that anyone could have hit a target as big as we were and that close to him. We think that he might have been a German sympathizer or a German soldier trying to slow us down until the rest of the German Army got out of the other end of town. But we never knew or worried about it. However, a year later after the war was over and I was attending the University of Florence, I went to Rome for a day to visit St. Peter's church and a few other churches. I went to this very spot where we had been shot at and the chipped area of the cement was still there where his bullet had hit the concrete. I examined the bullet hole more slowly and carefully this time than the first time. I also looked across the street where the green shutter had opened and where the shot came from. It was all still as it was June 6.

While we were bivouacked, at the fountain there was a large convoy of army vehicles going down the road toward the front.

They had a green pine tree emblem on their vehicles and on the soldiers' shoulder patches. We had never seen this division emblem before. It turned out to be a new division coming in to help us fight.

It was the 91st Tennessee Volunteers Infantry Division, to fight beside us for the rest of the war. They were a very good fighting unit and had a very tough time of it all through Italy with us. They lost many good men, I knew some of them personally. I began my infantry training with some of them at Camp McCain a year earlier.

We later learned to respect this 91st Infantry Division very much.

When we were in the 5th Army under General Clark, we entered (Roma) Rome, Italy (Italia) on June 6, 1944; this was the first time in all of Roman history that an invading army had ever been successful in capturing Rome from the north side.

The high Alps mountains created a natural barrier in the winter as well as the summer months due to the high mountains covered with deep snow in all of the winter months and the steepness of the mountains and mountain passes that one would have to cover for hundred of miles on foot, as no large beast of burden could easily walk this rocky terrain with any kind of a load.

About 200 B.C., there was a very successful and brave army general from Carthage, by the name of General Hannibal, who had a daring plan in his head that he could attack Rome from the north in the winter with large, mature elephants from the African continent to maneuver the Alps in the winter, when the guard of the Roman Empire would not be expecting it. This winter attack would so surprise the Roman army that victory would be his very easily. Carthage was a small country on the southeast border of Spain.

So he got a few very wealthy shipping merchants to finance his plan to go to Africa, just across the Mediterranean Sea, and purchase a few hundred mature elephants and their trainers along with a few hundred African soldiers to come to northern Italy to make the attack through the Alps in the snow-covered mountains for a victorious entry into Rome in the early spring.

I, and a lot of the American 5th Army spent the winter of 1944 and 1945 in these same Alps mountains that General Hannibal did, and I couldn't think of a worse place to spend the winter, unless it would be the Arctic Circle, to which I have never been. Nor would I ever go even if they paid me a general's salary, much less a pfc.'s salary which I spent two years over there on.

General Hannibal did not have as much luck that winter in the

Alps as he had planned. The snow was deep, and due to the high altitude of these mountains, there was a lot of wind every day and night with snow drifts that a man can suffocate in and the wind chill factor will drop very low. The elephants and their trainers and the few hundred professional soldiers were from a tropical climate. They had never seen snow before or had ever been cold before.

They lost many of the elephants and their trainers because of sickness or freezing to death. Many of his African soldiers who did not die deserted him and tried to escape to warmer climates or back to Africa, back where they came from.

When spring finally did arrive and General Hannibal came down out of those miserable Alps mountains with his much-depleted fighting forces (those who were still with him) in bad shape, he was met by the great Roman army, who easily defeated him in their first battle. The Roman army had spies watching General Hannibal's movements all winter and were kept abreast of the enemy's progress all winter by the Italian natives. He and most of his troops were sent back to Africa on the merchant ships.

The Italian natives were so afraid of the large elephants that they got on their knees and prayed that the elephants would not stomp them to death and eat them. The elephants were capable of stomping them to death, but, they are complete vegetarians so they would not eat them.

So on June 6, 1944, our 34th Iowa National Guard Infantry Division made world history, as we were the first army to ever capture Rome from the north. And I was with them, with the first bunch of G.I.s. We have always been very proud of this accomplishment.

Just north of Rome, we were advancing very fast, as the Germans were headed to the foothills to take another stand of defense, and were attacked by a German airplane while we were in the large truck carrying about fifteen to twenty of us in our platoon. We were helpless in that truck with only a canvas hood over us, so the truck driver stopped so that we could unload and seek some kind of cover by diving in the ditches, culverts, or just behind a rock. If we would just scatter, the pilot could not get many of us.

We went in all directions, but I stayed by the truck, and every time the airplane would make a pass overhead at the truck, I would get behind the large rear dual wheels of the truck. Every time he came at us at a different angle, and I would have to get directly behind the wheels on line with the path that he was coming from. But I was not the only soldier doing this behind the large truck tires and rims. There were three of us behind each tire. At times we would be on top of each other, like cordwood stacked in a yard, as we wanted to be directly behind the heavy metal part of the tire rims. Each of us scrambled to get on bottom of the pile.

The German airplane pilot made about five passes at us, dive bombing directly at us each time, but he did not fire a shot from his airplane. We figured that he must be out of ammunition and that he kept buzzing us to stall the forward movement of our troops so that his German soldiers could get dug into their defensive positions better.

But as time went on, I think that, possibly, he took pity on us and did not fire on us deliberately because he was a young German boy caught up in the war that he didn't want any more than we did. Or possibly this could have been another divine intervention. I would like to think so. Many times the Germans refused to kill me when they had the drop on me. I also tried not to kill unless absolutely necessary to save my, or another American's life.

Our entire platoon was in that three-quarter-ton truck when the German airplane came at us the first time, but we all scattered as soon as T. Sgt. Kenneth Blake hollered, "Scatter and seek cover." I particularly remember the soldiers who were scrambling behind the iron truck tires to ward off any strafing that might come from that plane. They were Pfc. Charles Hoffman, Pvt. James Vulanti, Pvt. John DeHore, Pvt. Muso Rotopel, Pvt. James Keane, Pvt. Mike Lipp, and possibly a few others. The others sought protection in a ditch or a culvert nearby. None of us were injured, just scared again. I think that the German pilot had had his fun for the day as he watched us run and scramble for cover.

I remember the other soldiers from our platoon that were there, but where they went to seek cover, I do not know. They were Cpl. Joe Buffalo, Pfc. Max L. Rush, Pfc. John Despot, Sgt. Barney Allickson, S. Sgt. Kenny Blake, Cpl. Phillip Braun, Pfc. James Keane, Pfc. Freeman James, Pvt. Red Thompson, Pvt. Jake Jacoby, Pfc. George Loechner, Sgt. Frenchy Dorin, Pvt. Bill Zimmerman, and Pvt. Maab.

I think that he saved our lives on purpose. Before this war was to be over, I was to experience the fact that about four times that I really know of the German soldiers deliberately saving my life. And if I know of four times that they saved my life, there must have been a few more times that I was in their rifle sights that I did not know of. I am very sure of this. This is why I and most of the boys in our platoon tried to take a German soldier alive rather than shoot him. However, as we all know, not all soldiers can be captured that way, and the front line company boys did not always have a chance to take prisoners, as they were being shot at to be killed by the enemy and they had to kill to save their lives and the lives of their buddies. It is a dirty job but someone has to do it. This was a just war. I never had any doubts about that. We must keep reminding ourselves that this was a just war. No one is born a killer, not even the great and brave infantrymen and all other men who are called up by their country to serve in time of war. I would have enjoyed my three years in the service, in any branch of it, if I was not shot at, taught to kill, gone cold and hungry and lonely. I was single, and I loved the outdoors, the physical demands made on the body, and the fellowship of many boys from all walks of life. I even considered re-entering the service at one time after the war in peace times. But that would have been a mistake as we soon entered the conflict in Korea and I would have been at it all over again. *No, thanks. Once is enough or maybe one too many.*

I was given a 1A classification three more times after WWII, Korea, Vietnam, and the Bay of Pigs. But I talked them out of it. The officer on the telephone said, "We cannot make you go again, but we can sure make you wish that you had gone again. We will give you a second lieutenant's commission and let you stay in the States and just train new recruits as part of the career." And I said, "No, I don't trust you guys. Remember, you had me once for three years."

8

Butchering a Hog

One day I looked down in a small valley very near our bombed-out, dirty hut that we were lucky to find deserted, so we holed up there temporarily. The First Armored Tank Division had some tanks down there. They were a great Division and we owe them very much. They were usually not very far away from our Infantry Division.

What I saw down in that valley was a very beautiful white sow hog eating grass, and I guessed her weight at about 300 pounds. I was the only farm boy in our platoon who knew anything about killing and butchering a hog. On our farm back in Illinois, we kept about eight or nine brood sows to litter pigs, and we usually shipped about a hundred or more feeder hogs to St. Louis stockyards every six months. We always did our own butchering for our own meat, and my brother and I always helped. So I knew how to kill and butcher this beautiful white sow for our meat.

The boys said, "Shoot it now," And I said, "No, we have to wait until the Germans send some shells in and make a noise, otherwise my rifle shots will give away our position. We just have to hope that she doesn't wander away before I get a chance to shoot her." We didn't have to wait more than five minutes or so, as there were three German artillery shells coming in (incoming mail). I went down in the valley so that I could get a closer shot at the sow and I shot her just above the line between both eyes as we always did on the farm. My dad had taught me that many years ago while I was still in high school.

I always carried a long-bladed knife in a leather sheath fastened to my belt. I then took the knife out and slit the throat of this sow so that the blood would drain out quickly and not settle in the meat and spoil it. This I also learned on the farm, helping my dad butcher hogs every fall around Thanksgiving or on the day of the first light snow. That was our annual butchering time, and usually, we had an uncle who would come and help us also.

Next, I cut around her rectum and tied the rectum tight with a string so that no fecal matter could leak out of the colon and ruin the meat. Then I slit her from the rectum to the neck as soon as I had the carcass hanging from a rafter in our refuge house. This way I could take all the intestines out at one time and throw them away into a snow bank outside.

Now all we had to do was wait for the body heat to leave the carcass, which was no problem, as it was cold and there was plenty of snow on the ground. This was our "walk in cooler" since the cold temperature was on our side in preserving the meat, even though it was hanging outside in the open air. We were very lucky in that respect. The cold mountain air would keep the meat from spoiling.

I stuck my long knife in the side of this life-saving, beautiful hog and told the boys that "you can cut off the piece of meat that you want, anytime that you want." They were all city boys, and they did not know where to cut to get any certain piece of meat. I had to show them where to cut to get ham, shoulder, pork chops, or bacon. I was the only farm boy in our platoon and the only one who had also been a Boy Scout. I hate to think what that hog meat would have looked like if they alone killed and butchered it. I am sure that it would have all been tainted by the hog's intestines. You must tie off the rectum immediately as the bowels move soon after death. My father had that long knife made especially for me.

But we still did not have a frying pan to cook any meat in. I looked everywhere in our gear and in the deserted hut that we were staying in. The only thing that I could find was an old, dirty, white porcelain toilet potty that most of us had in our bedrooms at that time before running water and indoor plumbing came about right after the war was over.

I looked at it very sadly with the thought that I must make skillet out of this thing somehow or killing the hog will be useless and all this fine meat that we need will be lost.

So I decided to cut the bottom part of the potty off with my long knife and just keep the small bottom piece and about two inches of the top rim to keep the meat and grease in. I took a rock and my knife and punctured the pot and hammered the knife blade all around the pot until I had a low, shallow container.

But it was still dirty, and I knew we had a problem, as E-Coli is very dangerous and could make us very sick, or worse, it could kill us. So I wiped it out with snow and dirt as best that I could. Then I filled it with water and boiled it over our small G.I. issue Coleman gas stove that we usually had with us but very seldom used. After boiling it three times, I figured that it was now sterilized enough for safe usage. It was a terrible-looking skillet.

So I took my knife and cut me some ham and fried it with the Coleman stove for heat, and I enjoyed good ham again as I remembered it before the war. Soon, all of our boys were cutting their favorite piece of meat and really enjoying it. We left my knife sticking in the hog for any soldier that came along. We showed them how to cut themselves some fresh meat and eat it. We soon became very popular with the company runners, who came by, delivering messages to the other company commanders from regimental headquarters.

Soon, word drifted down to the kitchen crew in the rear that we had butchered a fat hog and we were enjoying it immensely. Our mess sergeants sent word that if we would send it back on a jeep, that they would have the kitchen crew make us some sandwiches and send them back up to us. Now there were about fifteen to twenty men back in that kitchen and the motor pool squad and I am sure that we would have been lucky to have gotten back about one sandwich apiece.

Now this was the same group that said it was too dangerous for them to send a jeep up there and bring us any cans of C rations.

So I took a vote and asked the other boys what they wanted to do. And they all said, "Hell, no. They have never worried about us before. All they want is our fresh meat. Tell them no." So we did and I understand that they got very mad about that back there in the safety zone.

When we left that area, I took my knife with me, which I still have today and I use it to cut flowers and vegetables in my garden. When I look at it, every day I can see a beautiful 300-pound, white sow in the valley near an army tank. There was still some good meat left on the hog when we left. On the Italian market, I am sure that his hog would have brought a lot of lire, as all food was scarce. How that hog managed to live that long near the German Army, I'll never know. Maybe God put it there. He works in many strange ways, you know. Anyway all of our boys there wish to thank someone. I think that God intervened again on my behalf.

My father, I love him so much, had this knife made in Fairfield, Illinois by a horse harness maker. He made the blade with a large hand file and ground the milled sides on smoothly and mounted a dull red plastic handle on it. Plastic was very new then, in 1943.

It still bothers me when I see an old white porcelain pot for sale at an antique or garage sale. I just look away and pretend that I never saw it. So many little insignificant things bring back terrible memories, but we must remember that this was a just war.

We were told a few days later that our mess sergeant was angry at us for not sharing the fresh hog meat with them. We worried about that for about five minutes, then something else came up, and it was never mentioned again.

When I got home and told my father that I was the only boy there who knew how to butcher a hog correctly, he smiled very big for then he knew that he had a small part in our war effort. This was about the only incident that I told my parents about regarding my army experiences. I knew that even though the war was over and I was safely home, the actual combat experiences would bother them.

There was another personal reason that I never told them or anyone else of my war experiences until now, fifty-seven years later because like all combat-experienced veterans, some of these incidents made me choke up and not able to finish the story. Most of us found it easier just to listen to the stories of military life from a noncombat veteran. People cannot understand the fear and tension of life-threatening situations hour after hour, day after day, and month after month, anyway, and there is no way that you can describe it, so it is better that you don't try to explain it. A lot of people will think that you are lying anyway, or possibly shell-shocked and are not in control of all of your actions.

We must always remember that this was a just war, to end all of the terrible injustices that many countries were perpetuating on their own people and the people of many smaller countries. We must keep telling ourselves that we were right and that God was on our side. Even though we were baptized a Christian and do not believe in killing another human being, we must do this to prevent further killing of more people, especially of our own families in our own country. None of us were born killers. We were brave enough to save your lives, possibly at the expense of losing ours. Maybe we were modern day crusaders fighting for God, Jesus Christ, and all that is just and right.

Our great Mess Sergeant's name was Bruno. He was an original member of the Montevideo National Guard that made up all of our original platoon. And what a great bunch of young soldiers they were. The finest boys that I have ever met in my life.

9

Partisans

When Italian guards, also prisoners, walked away from the P.O.W. camp of captured Americans, the Americans also walked away free soldiers.

The free American soldier later on found his original unit and joined in again as an on-line combat infantryman. However, he was already showing signs of combat fatigue.

To reiterate the point that I have made many times here, *he should not have been sent back to the front lines to fight again.* He had already done more than his part and should have been sent back to the States and given a medical discharge. He should have been replaced by one of our American U.S.O. warriors who were making all the noise about having done their part, but never left the States, or a warm bed.

When WWII ended, May 7 1945, he was still with us on the combat lines. But his nerves were so bad that we who were new replacements left him and others back when we went out on dangerous missions. We were afraid that their nerves would crack and our position given away to the enemy. He was a fine person, and we thought a lot of him. He never asked for any favors, kept to himself, and was never in the way of any of our activities. He had been a great soldier. But the human mind can take just so much trauma, and in the front line infantry, you see this in most boys who have been there a little too long. But they kept us there with no replacements.

If Italy had remained a declared enemy of war, he could not have been sent back into combat against the same enemy that had listed him as a prisoner of war. So the army sent those previous P.O.W.s that had been captured in Europe to the South Pacific to fight again. *What a national disgrace.*

Do not be misled or misunderstand. I am not bitter because of the misfortune of being left on the front lines along with my good buddies. There is no one in this world prouder of his country than one who has risked his life so many times that he has no knowledge of how many. It can be two times an hour then go a week or so and not actually see the enemy, but the artillery shells and the machine guns are coming in most of the time, or you may be walking through a minefield and not know it.

Many times on patrol or a surprise encounter, a German soldier would turn his burp gun to the side away from us and fire in the other direction. We would usually return the life-saving favor by doing the same, it means that we will not kill you if you won't kill us. Then we would move out very rapidly, because, sometimes, they would call in the mortars or artillery on us.

General MacArthur once said, "If you want to know how much combat time a soldier has had, just look into his eyes." His eyes are never looking directly at you; they are looking past your ears, head, or shoulders, into the distance. He hears you, but at the same time, his eyes and thoughts are in combat, reliving an incident that he has seen thousands of times every day, and at night when he can't sleep for a few hours. They are terrible scenes that you would not understand. Just like some of those that I have written about here.

Never have so many nations owed so much to so few people. From fifty-two dollars a month before take out, I got thirty-five dollars a month take home. We received ten dollars a month of this while overseas so that we would not cause inflation in a particular country. Many times, we would be in combat for three months at a time. Then we got three months' pay at a time, or thirty dollars, and two needle shots in the arm for something, probably malaria and the flu. Don't ever make the mistake of questioning the loyalty of any combat veteran from any branch of the services, army, navy, air force, or marines. You have never walked in his boots, and since you were not in combat, you could not expect to know what it is like to go for years within reach of the enemy's mortar, machine gun, rifle, and artillery fire.

Some days, you will be pinned down by enemy artillery fire for one to two hours at a time, while some of your buddies are being hit, killed, or yelling for the medic to come and give first aid to the wounded, dress his wounds, and possibly get him to a first aid station that is miles back.

I am not belittling the other branches of service who have been in combat, but the navy and the air force always go back to their quarters after a battle with the enemy, and they get a shower, drink maybe, change of clothes, a warm cot, and a warm meal.

Not so for the combat army infantryman or the marines, because the battle is never over until the peace treaty is signed. He is left at the front to do it all over again in less than an hour, possibly in another five minutes and may last for another year or so.

We very seldom got a hot meal, and usually we went three to four months without a shower or a change of underwear, shirt, or pants. Our private parts would bleed for a month or two from the salt and other ingredients from our perspiration. We would pour bottles of iodine on our scrotum. But if you haven't been there in battle for one to two years, you won't believe this is possible. Lucky for you and all your dear friends and family that you never experienced this discomfort and don't want to know about it. But a few of us went through it.

We were one of the few branches of service that were taught to kill from the first day of our service. In combat, we were sent to Europe and the South Pacific as replacements for other combat boys who had been killed. We were to soon find out that combat is the lowest form of human existence known to civilized man. We lived like rats in a sewer as we wallowed in the snow and mud and slept without taking our shoes or any clothes off for three to four months at a time.

People at home still laugh at me when I tell them that a shower every three to four months was all that we got. They think that I am lying. Even other veterans in noncombat service do not believe this or how the line company boys suffered. We didn't live. We just survived a terrible dream for two, three, and four years to save America and you.

The main line companies all have a letter preceding their names, such as A-Able; B-Baker; C-Charlie; D-Dog; E-Easy; and M-Machine and Mortar. That is the last line company, M, heavy weapons. That was my first company in Camp McCain. The 87th Division, 347th Regiment, 3rd Battalion.

These line-company boys are the ground troops that all

branches of service depend on to invade, assault, liberate, and occupy any country in any war. This is the most dangerous detail of all services and the proudest of our American heritage. Because we have to risk it all two or three times a day for many months and years.

Many times we have had to run through minefields, dodge machine gun bullets, hit the ground, as artillery shells from the enemy were coming in like popcorn in a skillet, then lay there and wait and do it all over again the next day or night without food or sleep. Yes, it was a terrible life. But someone has to do it, so that the rest of America could enjoy their usual luxurious life.

Another great inconvenience to combat men was the inability to be able to brush their teeth. At the P.O.E. (Point of embarkment for overseas duty) the Red Cross gave each one of us a small cloth sack containing a deck of cards, cake of soap, comb, razor blades, toothbrush, and a small vial about the size of a large fountain pen. This small vial contained a mixture of salt and baking soda that was to be used as our tooth powder. I was one of the only boys in my platoon that used their toothbrush at all. I could brush my teeth only when in the rest area off the front lines.

When I did get to brush my teeth with the salt and baking soda mixture, some of the soldiers would laugh and say, "There goes Hammil, brushing his teeth again, ha, ha." But today, I still have thirty of my thirty-two original permanent teeth. I had my first tooth pulled when I was seventy-four years old and my second tooth pulled the following year. I wonder how many of the soldiers who laughed at me for brushing my teeth in combat have at least thirty good teeth left.

During the Great Depression at home, my mother always made us three children brush our teeth with Arm & Hammer baking soda when we had it. If we children did not have a toothbrush, we had to put the baking soda on our forefinger and rub our teeth and gums with that.

I also missed wearing pajamas at night as we three children had to wear at night at home. Mom would make each of us a pair of flannel pajamas for the winter and a pair of cotton ones for the summer. As soon as the war was over, I sent home for Mom to buy me a new pair of cotton pajamas and mail them to Florence, where I was attending the university during my seven months of occupation duty. I got laughed at again by another bunch of soldiers for wearing pajamas in the army at night.

There was one group of very important fighters that were made up primarily of Italian soldiers who were dismissed from their divisions when they surrendered to the Allies in North Africa in 1943 and deserted Adolf Hitler's German pact.

As they made their way back across the Mediterranean somehow, they banded together in small groups of about twenty to twenty-five men to continue their fight, guerilla style, against Germany.

They were also joined by American and British soldiers who had been captured in North Africa and escaped when Italy surrendered. Many young Italian men and women joined their ranks as partisan fighters in Italy. They were the mainstay of the Italian underground resistance group throughout all Italy and southern France. We American combat men respected them very much.

They usually wore a red scarf around their neck to identify themselves.

The partisans would try to tie a red scarf around a statue in town where they were active to let the civilians know that they would do their best to protect them from the Germans, that they were active there. The partisans' favorite trick to kill German soldiers was to go along the highways or mountain roads that the Germans traveled and get at the end of a curve in the road, which would give them ample time to aim and fire their .30-caliber rifle into the windshield of a German vehicle and kill as many of them as possible. This was very successful, especially on the road where the Grand Prix was held. We fought along some of that winding road.

However, there was one very sad drawback to this type of vigilante ambush. For every German soldier that the partisans would kill, German officers would take then of the most influential citizens from that town and murder them and drag their bodies into the town square for all to see. They always shot them just once in the head.

This was very sad and risky for the partisans to put their townspeople in such jeopardy.

For two years during the war, they lived in the mountains, in caves, by themselves. They welcomed any newspaper or any information that we could give them, even if it was a year old. One of them asked me who won the World Series last year and who was now the heavyweight boxing champion of the world. Joe Louis was. He was traveling Europe and Italy, giving exhibition boxing matches with the local division heavyweight champ boxers. I never got to see him, because entertainers were not allowed near the front battle lines. They got to entertain the rear echelon support troops. On the front lines, we didn't even know when the entertainers were in our country. We were making sacrifices in the mountains, fighting to stay alive and win the war.

Many times, as we passed through a small town or village, we saw ten highly decorated coffins all laid out in a neat row in front of a church or a courthouse square and knew that the partisans had killed a German and the Germans had retaliated by killing ten of their prominent citizens in cold blood. We saw this many times as we advanced toward the enemy.

The bodies of these slain people were usually buried side by side in the town square or some prominent place in the town as an everlasting memorial to the resistance movement.

These partisans had a hard time getting any food to eat while hiding in the mountains all alone, so about once a week, they sent one of them down into the town to leave word that he would be back the next night for some food and wine and information that they could give him about the war: where the main forces of the Germans were, and how far away the Americans were with our forces.

This lone soldier partisan was probably from that town, so the villagers trusted him. The civilians had a special name for the partisans, "bandits of the mountains."

In combat, we ran into these partisans many times, and we always had a very good relationship with them. Often they would come to us and tell us where some Germans were and what they were doing. We trusted them completely and found them to be a very reliable source of information during the war.

When the war was over, one of them cut his shoulder patch off and gave it to me. I still have it in my WWII souvenir box. It says, "liberty and justice for all," in Italian. Not all partisans wore the patch, because it would mean sudden death if a German caught him with it on or in his possession. God bless the partisans and their supporters because theirs was an important part of this war.

When Benito Mussolini was caught by the partisans with his girlfriend, they were just thirty miles from the Switzerland border, trying to make their escape to freedom. However, had they not been caught, but escaped to Switzerland, I am not sure that he would not have been brought back as a major war criminal and tried at Nuremberg trials same as the high officials of the Nazi Regime were.

The women of Italy hated Mussolini's girlfriend because he was married and his wife was still alive. In their eyes, he was living in sin with this woman. Mussolini and his wife had a son who served in the Italian Air Force as a fighter pilot and was killed in Ethiopia while flying and strafing native Ethiopians.

The last few days of the war, they gave orders for us infantry men to stop at the French border as the boys from the second front were nearing Berlin and the war would be ended there very soon.

While in this town we were ordered not to unpack, as we would not be there very long, which we weren't, so most of us enlisted men stayed on the truck. Laid out in a white row in coffins set on the ground were ten local citizens that had been assassinated by German soldiers because one of the local people had killed a German soldier. Our truck was parked about fifteen feet from this terrible sight. All the caskets were draped in white with a lot of flowers on and around them. It was a beautiful but a useless tragic sight. We were not allowed cameras or radios in WWII near the front lines, so we have very few pictures of this war. However, in Korea and Vietnam, front-line soldiers must have been allowed cameras, as we see so many pictures of their wars.

A few of us in our platoon talked about trying to hitchhike a ride with the army trucks to go and see Mussolini and his girlfriend, Carla. But just then, an officer came along and said that "anyone going north to try and see the body of Benito Mussolini would be court-martialed." So we looked at each other, and I said "Hey, it's not worth a court-martial. We have waited three years for the war to end, and it looks like it finally is going to end, so let's not take any risks. Let's just wait here." We did, and we never got to see Mussolini and Carla hanging upside down in their now-famous picture which I have a copy of.

If you will look very closely at Carla's chest, you will see two dark spots where the local Italian women cut off both her breasts for spite because she was living in sin with her lover, a married man, Benito Mussolini. This is all still very clear to me almost sixty years later. Or were those three years just a terrible nightmare that I cannot forget along with the three million other young soldier boys who were in combat? Of all the deaths that occurred to American boys eighty-seven percent of them were in the infantry. This was about the same percentage of mortality that was in WWI. So an infantryman only has about a fifteen percent chance of not being killed. That is a small chance. I do not blame any young boys for enlisting to get his choice of a better branch of service. Those of us who did combat infantry duty and became part of the *great survivor generation* are all so very proud of our war and the sacrifices that we made to accomplish the final victory. We feel like we fought a hard battle for all the world to now enjoy. Most of us are gone now, but the hearts and minds of the people who are alive still honor and remember these gallant and brave souls.

There was a standing joke in the infantry that you cannot really tell if an infantryman is dead or not by just smelling him. Infantry men do not get to take a bath any oftener than every three or four months at a time. Infantrymen stink all the time, even when they are alive in a combat zone.

In the summer, he cannot bathe in the streams or rivers because he is in the front lines and the Germans would have picked him off before he removed his pants. Possibly the support troops in the rear could swim or bathe in the summer in the local river, where there would be no danger of being shot by the enemy, but not up front. The support troops also had regular shower trucks at stations.

In wintertime, a soldier would not dare swim in the creek, as the Germans would see him then also, and he would die of pneumonia if they didn't kill him first. So there was no way that any combat soldier on any front could take a bath regularly and he soon became used to it and accepted it, glad that he was still alive. We never knew what day it was. We didn't worry what day of the week it was, but I always wanted to know what month it was. Sometimes, it would be the third or fourth of the new month before we knew when the old month went out. Those everyday things became so unimportant when they were shooting at you. In 1944, the army sent a shower truck around to all the regiments to let us boys have a shower. They had a very strict routine that you had to go through to take the shower. First, everyone had to take all of their clothes off and put pants in one pile, the shirts in another pile, the underwear in another pile, and so on, because we were going to be issued all new clothing as soon as we finished our shower. They sent the shower trucks around for us twice that year. So you see how difficult it was to tell if a combat soldier was dead or not. You simply could not judge by the smell alone if he was dead or alive.

A lieutenant gave us all strict instructions as to how we were to take the shower. The complete shower would last three minutes from the time the water was turned on until the water was turned off. You were supposed to wash for two minutes and then take one minute to rinse off. They gave each one of a cake of soap and a G.I. towel.

The entire shower unit was mounted on the longbed of a G.I. olive drab flatbed truck with the water heaters, hot storage tanks, and shower stalls. When the officer said, "Get ready and shower," we all ran to the nearest showerhead that was not being used and started to lather with the cake of soap. After two minutes, the officer said, "Now rinse," and we all started to rinse. After one minute of rinsing, the water valve was turned off whether everyone was through or not. I was not through rinsing and think some of the soldiers were still washing when three minutes were up.

We stepped down off the flatbed truck and went through the quartermaster line for all new clothes. We would call out our pants size and they would throw them along with the two-piece winter underwear that matched the size that you hollered out. I hollered out "34–31," which meant 34-inch waist and a 31-inch inseam. Everything fit pretty well. We also got new socks and new boots if we needed the boots.

We didn't have to take the underwear off. We just gave them a pull, and they were so rotten, they just tore and fell off; it had been over three months in the mountains, of fighting since we had a bath. We all smelled the same, so no one knew the difference.

I have told this story to a few civilians and stateside soldiers, but I don't think they believed me. Some of them said, "I would not go through not getting a bath for three to four months for anyone." And I said, "You would if you were trying to stay alive and get back home, like we were. I thought that you folks back in America would appreciate what we went through for you so that all of America would not have to go through this in the future with another country, as your conqueror." But I never reached their appreciation level for them to understand what a few boys went through for many people in this world. They would just walk away and think that you were lying. We were young and could take it then. I think that is why they called it the infant-ry. Only the young mind and body could or would take that kind of merciless and brutal treatment for fifty-two dollars a month.

That winter on Montibelmonti was so long and cold without a bath that we would take our shirts off and scrape the hair and grease off the collar of our wool shirts with our bayonet, and then clean the bayonet by wiping it on the snow. Then we would scrape the rest of our shirts and pants with the bayonet to make them look as clean as possible. But the collar and shirt cuffs were always the worst. And I don't remember that we could smell each other, because we all smelled the same. You must remember that we did not have a warm house, heat, or electricity that terrible winter. We could not build any fires.

Before the shower truck got there, the salt and other poisons in a person's perspiration can cause irritation to the skin. I have sensitive skin anyway; I have had four skin cancers removed in the last few years.

The three to four months'-long bathless period had caused my inseam in my crotch to break out, bleed, hurt, and itch. I went to a medic, and he gave me a bottle of iodine, which I would pour on my inseam to help any infection that could easily occur as filthy dirty as I and the others were. This helped quite a bit with the pain, but it still hurt to take long steps when walking in the deep snow. But the shower truck finally came, and we all got new, clean clothes.

Since then, I have found out that I am allergic to wool, and if I wear wool slacks in the winter, even now, I will start to get that same rash again. So I have to alternate and wear polyester pants with some cotton in them as much as possible. The scars from that rash that winter stayed with me for a number of years. I could see the tendons going to my hips when the rash was at its worst.

Perspiration and urine are both nature's way of eliminating

poisons from the body. There is very little difference in their chemical content and odor.

In the infantry, in combat, you never get to take your shoes off at night. You just loosen the top strings with the bow tied and put your helmet over the front of your face so that you will have some facial protection if the German artillery comes in during the night.

In case of an attack, you will not have time to put your boots on, so you had better keep them on all the time. Your legs, feet, and knees will be so stiff, that you will not be able to walk on them during the winter months as soon as you get up. You will have to walk on all fours until the circulation warms them up again. And don't look for breakfast, because that is not a word that is used or understood in combat infantry or marines. We didn't have breakfast in over two years.

You will soon discover that during the night, if you sleep in the same spot all night, in the winter, you will warm up the mud and snow on the ground, and it will feed back some heat to the body after a few hours. So don't roll around in different spots on the cold ground, or you will never make a warm spot for yourself in the mud.

When we would take our shoes off to change a pair of socks every few weeks, we were always surprised to find that we did not have any foot in the socks; all we had was an ankle band around the top of the socks. We had completely worn out the sole of each sock. We could never find a single thread of it. We would often speculate where it went, because there never was any evidence that we had a full sock in that shoe. It would just vanish without a thread of evidence.

Most of us went almost two years without a bed, mattress, sheets, or a pillow underneath us. We entered one town, Montecatini, and were in rest, not in combat, and were billeted in very fine house with marble floors. And I said to one of my buddies, "I have always wanted to sleep on marble floors, and now is my chance." So we all lay down on our one G.I. olive drab blanket and went to sleep. About three hours later, I woke up with the worst backache and sore muscles, so I got my blanket and went outside on the ground, and out there was most of my platoon already on the soft dirt, sleeping instead of on that beautiful solid marble floor. It was hard!

My favorite place to sleep was in the feed stall of a cattle or horse barn or stable, down between the slats on the sides. I felt safe and alone there, deep in my thoughts of home and what it would be like to be a human being again with all the comforts of home. Will this ever end so that we all can go back to eating three meals a day, bathing, and taking our clothes off at night and putting pajamas on? We knew that most of the noncombat troops and the soldiers at home were not going through these hardships.

There was a story going around about that time that there was an infantry soldier who wore out his combat boots without ever taking them off. This was entirely possible with someone that was hard on their shoes. But personally, I had my doubts about this actually happening that year in Italy. But we all would wear the foot of our socks off.

All the time that we were in Italy and so far from our home and our family and other friends, we were constantly thinking about the other soldier troops at home and the supply and support troops in the European theater that were not in dangerous combat, fighting for their lives and the future safety of America. They had no way of knowing what we were going through, didn't really want to know what we were going through for America and the rest of the free world.

We were told not to write home any bad news about our personal hardships and most certainly not to mention about any of your buddies getting killed. They told us, "We must keep up the morale of the home front. Do not mention your hardships even to our parents, because that will just worry them, and you don't want that, do you?"

Many of you received letters from overseas with some of the words and sentences cut out with a single-edge razor blade. That is because the chaplain reads all of the outgoing mail. This is why we couldn't seal our free postage letters; they were going to be censored by the chaplain and his assistant. I wrote a very sad letter home one day on Montibelmonti. The chaplain called me in and said, "Hammil, you know better than this. Now throw this letter away and write a decent letter home to keep up the home morale as you should." So I went back and wrote a nice letter home. If anyone needed their morale booster, it was the poor, starved combat infantry boys doing all of the suicidal fighting not the home front. Most of the time our morale was very low because of fear and the lack of any appreciation for the hardships we were going through every day for months on end without any relief in sight for us to hope for.

10

Getting a Bath

For hundreds of years the Pope, in the Vatican City, always held public audience every afternoon at two o'clock except on Sunday. During the German occupation from 1939 to 1944, when we Americans arrived in Rome, the Pope had discontinued these public audiences for that five-year period in history in open defiance from himself and the entire Catholic Church to the unwanted occupied and the unfriendly treatment that the Italian civilians were receiving from the entire German Army.

About six weeks after we liberated Rome and were fighting toward Pisa, T. Sgt. Kenneth Blake came up to me.

"Hammil, we have just received word from Gen. Mark Clark that the Pope in Vatican City wants to commence having his two o'clock daily audience with the public again after a five-year absence of them. Now he wants to commence them again since we have liberated them and all the German troops are gone. He wants a few members of each company that was the first in Rome to be his first audience to start these audiences all over again, and I want you to represent our platoon."

"Yes, sir, I would be glad to," I said.

Besides the honor, we were in combat, and I would get a short rest from combat conditions.

The officers said that "All you boys will have to take a bath and get new, clean army clothes." To which we all agreed. I don't think that even Pope Pius XII could stand to be in the Sistine Chapel with about one hundred of us combat infantrymen if we did not get a bath for this occasion.

So we all went to the shower truck and got our three-minute shower and rinse job, then issued all new underwear, socks, shirts, and pants. Boy, did I feel good and clean, because I had not had a bath of any kind for the last two months. My other buddies back at the front didn't get that bath; they had to wait another two months or so. I had one on them.

After we were all cleaned up and shaved, we were trucked to Rome and Vatican City. First we were taken on a tour through St. Peter's Cathedral with an English-speaking guide. He pointed out to us all of the famous statues and paintings of Michelangelo and all of the other famous works of many other artists. This was very interesting, and I made the most of it. I knew that in all probability, I would never get here again. Even though I was brought up in the First Christian Church at Fairfield, Illinois, I was awed at these magnificent churches with these great sculptures and paintings that I had read and heard about most of my young life. And here I was now, amidst all that history even before Jesus Christ our savior was born. I tried to take it all in, as my mother had been a rural one-room school teacher and educated me.

Then our cardinal tour guide said that now we would be led into the Sistine Chapel, where we would be greeted by the Pope, and he would like to thank us and all the American troops for coming to Europe and liberating Italy and many other countries from the Nazi occupation and brutality.

We were all standing in the Sistine Chapel, about one hundred of us combat infantrymen who had been part of the original soldiers who fought up from Anzio-Nettuno to Rome in some very terrible battles. In front of us was a large stage platform with a door to the south of that. Pope Pius XII entered through that door and, immediately, all the young Catholic soldiers went up to him and kissed the ring on his extended hand. He was beautiful in his white robe.

I was a Protestant, so I did not kiss his ring. Soon as these boys were through kissing the ring, the Pope walked up the short steps to the elevated platform and began to speak in perfect English, thanking us for braving the dangers of war and coming to the aid of his country and all religions.

We all liked the pope immediately, as he was a very down-to-earth person, and smiled at us all the time that he talked. I think that he was the Pope for about forty years. I remember when he died. I felt sad, because he had treated us soldiers very well and recognized my division as the "Liberators of Italy," as we were often called after that by many civilians in Italy.

After the audience was over, I went out into St. Peter's Square and walked all around, looking at the many statues, at the Swiss Guards that guard the Vatican, the art galleries and the library. They wear a very gaudy, funny uniform that is yellow and purple. While on duty, they must stand perfectly still and not move their head, talk to anyone, or smile at anyone.

All around St. Peter's Square, there are many Italians selling religious mementos. They hawk and sell their wares out loud, much as they do just across the border into old Mexico. I bought a few religious items to bring back, which I still have in my WWII collection box. I could buy only small pocket items because I had to carry them the rest of the war, and at that time, we did not know when, if ever, that would be. We could also roll them up in our blanket roll or put them in our backpack that we were to get later on.

American soldiers were not issued backpacks until the winter of 1944–45. The officers had them all the time, but this was the first time that enlisted men in the army ground forces were issued them. This was about the same time as the WEASEL and the new sleeping bags came out.

One of our platoon boys had taken about as much combat as his nerves would stand. He had fought very bravely on Anzio beachhead for months, and he had also fought in North Africa and Sicily. He had been in front-line German fire too long and should have been rotated home, same as the entire Thirty-Fourth Division of the original National Guard boys. There were too many soldiers back in the States doing menial tasks, which some of our women soldiers could have been doing, and should have been sent to the front to replace the already battle-weary troops. I was a replacement into this division and many others could have been also.

During a heavy battle with the Germans, this soldier took his dog tags off and exchanged them with a dead American soldier that was lying still on the ground never to fight again. His dog tags were now on the dead soldier's neck, so now he would legally be declared dead, and his parents would receive a ten-thousand dollar insurance check, which we pay for out of our own meager salary. We had to pay our own premiums.

He was now free to try and make it back to the rear lines and live as an Italian civilian in one of our large, liberated cities. He could possibly find an Italian girl and get married and live there the

80

rest of his life, or he could eventually get back to America if he wished to later on, when the world became normal again. He was seen by one of our boys back in Rome with a young Italian girl. But no one squealed on him. He was a good soldier, but he had already done more for America than most soldiers and civilians. This was an isolated incident, not a regular occurrence in the infantry.

We had only one more young soldier to go AWOL, but he waited until a couple of weeks after the war was over. He also had fought bravely in North Africa and Sicily and very hard at the Abbey at Casino, where, I think, his nerves began to get the best of him. But no human should have to go through that much combat every day for about three years. I didn't go through North Africa, Sicily, or the early part of Anzio, but I had enough. Those original boys had over five hundred actual combat days under rifle, machine gun, mortar and artillery fire. There were sixteen million boys and girls in service in WWII, and over nine million of them never fired a shot, saw the enemy, or had one combat day to their credit. There should have been a better system of rotation with all service personnel.

He came to us one day after the war was over and said, "I am leaving. I have had enough. I am leaving today. Will any of you boys loan me some money that I can go back with?"

We all said, "The war is over. Surely you can put up with this until you get to go home."

"No, I have had it. I am leaving now. Can you guys loan me some money?"

So we all gave him all the money that we could afford, and he took off. We felt so sorry for him, as we all knew that he was not his regular self anymore. We stood and watched him walk through the gates and front yard of the nice house we were getting to stay in for awhile. We never heard of him again. We hoped for his safe return home some day, some way. God bless him. I hope he made it without any prison time. But I imagine that he would have to do prison time in Fort Leavenworth, Kansas, military prison. You just cannot do that in the army. Possibly he should have gone on sick call and got some help. But the army didn't worry about us much. As long as America was winning the war, we were just a number on a sheet of paper. We were called "Desert Rats" in North Africa, and that pretty well described our way of living and thinking during the entire Italian campaign. Like a rat, we lived in dirt holes, never bathed, and sometimes had to eat just what we could steal or scrounge from the countryside. This now sounds unbelievable that we went through all this. It was a good thing that we were infants in the infantry, because a sane adult would not have gone through all this. He would not have been able to. Now I know why the government puts young, innocent, and inexperienced boys in the infantry. They will not question a suicidal order to attack. They are too young to be afraid or analyze the dangerous situation that they are going to be exposed to time after time. I was one of those proud, young, innocent boys then. I was one of the fifteen to twenty percent of infantrymen that made it back home safely without a wound.

Some readers may find some of these stories offensive, but war is war, and we boys were over there, fighting to save our lives so that we could possibly come home. It was a fifty-fifty chance that we might make it home. We didn't ask to be put in combat. We had nothing to gain over here any more than you did. But you sent us, hoping that your boys and friends would not have to go. And we served you very bravely and proudly as we remain today, very proud of America and all of the freedoms that it stands for, and we know exactly how America got it. Freedom is free for a lot of people but not for all people; some gave too much. I am glad that you were not one of them.

We were not born killers. We hated killing worse than you do. But in our position in the armed services, we were forced to kill against our wishes. You have never been in that situation as yet, so you do not know what you would do in our situation. And I sincerely hope and pray that you or anyone else doesn't experience what you are now reading in the comfort of your home, which we made possible by our sacrifices. No words or gifts would be great enough to repay any combat soldier for what he did for his country. No one is prouder of his country or his red, white, and blue flag than someone that has fought and bled for it. How many Veteran's Day services have you attended?

You say that you do not believe in war. Neither do we combat soldiers. We have been there. We hate war more than you do. "You cannot be an expert at something that you have never done." We have been there and back, as a survivor, not a hero. I do not make any apologies to anyone for anything written here, as we were there risking our lives for you at home. We thought that one day we would be appreciated. So how do you feel about these combat experiences that some of our younger boys went through?

History tells us that in early Roman times, people who practiced Christianity in the Roman Empire were killed and sacrificed in their coliseum, battling with lions, other prisoners, and professional gladiators. This was for the entertainment of the royal families and their guests mostly. They also used court jesters as entertainment.

This preceded the traveling entertaining groups that were mostly made up of tumblers and storytellers. Later on, we had vaudeville, the traveling circus, radio, and now television. These are steps in family entertainment that has taken over two thousand years or more to accomplish.

History says that the last Christians to fight in the Roman Coliseum was in about 1400 A.D. But we American infantrymen surely made modern history when the first front-line boys there were shot at and exchanged fire in that Coliseum with German front-line soldiers. However, no American Christian soldier was killed in the Coliseum, and I do not think that any German soldier was killed there by our American forces. I do think that they made Coliseum history.

Usually the line-company boys could take a town from the enemy in a couple of days. If they couldn't, then we would often catch up with them and they would request assistance from our P.A. platoon. We usually just did land-mine sweeping on the roads and ditches so that the infantry could walk them and the jeeps and larger trucks that would follow could drive down the roads without driving over a mine and setting it off and doing a lot of damage.

A land mine of any kind would usually blow the legs off the vehicle driver and passengers that were riding with them. It could possibly kill everyone in that vehicle. To offset some of the mine's explosive force, there were small sandbags put on the floor of all vehicles. This would stop enough of the force to maybe just blow off the feet, maybe just one leg. So when you went home, you would be just slightly crippled.

This would also protect the driver or anyone riding in the jeep.

We never liked to fight and have to stay in a town for a week or so in the summer, as the stink of our dead American boys, dead German soldiers and dead Italian civilians that somehow got killed by the Germans for some reason was more than the human sensory organ, the nose, could stand. Once that odor of death gets in your nose, it will stay there for a while. We had this problem in Rosignano, where we had to stay and fight for a long time. We also were called back to furnish a buzzard squad to carry the dead American boys back to the rear so that the Graves Registration office support troops could pick them up and load them in the back of a truck to take to the rear for identification and burial. How the dead American soldiers were cared for after this point I never found out, even though I asked some of the G.R.O. personnel soldiers.

I was on this buzzard detail one night, and the stink was so terrible that when we would bend over to pick up our own boys, we would vomit all over them, as there is no odor like the protein petrification of a human body. If you ever smell it, it will come back to you years later if you smell it again.

The next night, we got the same job of picking up bodies. But I got the bright idea that if we wore our gas masks while on this duty, the carbon filter would absorb the odor and we would not smell it. So I told the other boys in this detail of my plan, and they all agreed to try it with me.

So we put our gas masks on and went out looking for bodies. As soon as we found some, we started to pick them up and carry them back to the edge of town for the trucks to pick up. But the gas masks kept the death odor out for only a few minutes, then it came right through as if there was no gas mask.

It was worse than ever, as we now were vomiting back on ourselves and in our own faces. The gas mask just kept the vomit from going away from us. So we all threw our gas masks away right then and never tried that trick again.

The Italians were told to remove all their dead bodies also, as there was an unbelievable stink in the entire town. So they went out and put them all in one pile, poured gasoline over them, and lit a match to them. This pile of dead flesh did not burn very well, only the outside edges of the bodies where the gasoline was, and they smelled worse than before. They were ordered to bury them this time, which they did right away. That sure helped the entire town.

The worst smell ever was of a soldier who got just halfway out his tank, then burned. In the summer, it takes only about four hours for the odor of rotten flesh to be detected nearby. It is a horrible, heartbreaking odor of young bodies.

We were chasing the enemy in central Italy, when we had to stop and sweep some mines for the infantry-line company boys. We were out of food as usual, and I saw a good-looking vegetable garden across the field that was in the minefield that we were supposed to clear a path through. Now, the Germans are a very methodical race of people. When they laid a minefield, they always laid the entire minefield in a predetermined pattern and never varied from that pattern in that certain minefield—never. After we swept the first few feet of that minefield, we knew the pattern, therefore, where the next mines would be in that field. This helped us a lot. Thank you, Germans.

However, the next minefield would have a different pattern. We would have to figure out the pattern each time. It would not vary an inch. We admired their consistency in pattern because it made it much easier for us to find the mine and we usually did not have to worry about missing a mine or stepping on one as we were always sure of where the next one would be.

We were stopped at one place where a vegetable garden was, and I could see that there was a minefield there that the Germans had not had time to finish correctly, and it ran right through the potato patch.

So I told some of the boys that I believed that I could go over there with some German communication wire and attach it to a mine in that potato patch and blow up some fresh potatoes for us, as there was a foxhole that I could get into before I pulled the commo wire to set off the mine. So I went over and attached the wire to the mine and then I slowly strung the wire to the foxhole and gave the wire a pull after I was safely in the foxhole. It blew up beautifully, and all I had to do was to pick up the new, fresh potatoes off the ground.

S. Sgt. Barney Allickson said, "How silly to try that dangerous trick." But I could see where the mine was. We all ate raw potatoes, and then we boiled the rest in a gallon can without any salt and pepper. That was all we needed or got for that day or two to eat. But we were used to that.

Gen. Mark Clark did not believe in feeding his troops hot meals in the field because it would bring many soldiers together at one time in the same spot and the enemy could kill too many at a time. He believed in great disbursement of troops. (Keep them apart or in small groups or individually separated.)

General Patton, in the second-front invasion, was just the opposite. He believed in feeding most of the front-line companies a hot meal every day. This caused him a heavy loss of men. When they were congregated in large chow lines, one artillery or mortar shell could land among them and kill many with that one shell. They should be kept disbursed at least fifteen feet apart from any other soldier as much as possible. This was the way I was taught in basic training at Camp McCain. I still think that it is a good rule to go by when in a combat zone.

In my original platoon from which I was transferred before Italy, they were all sitting together around a jeep in the Battle of the Bulge under General Patton when a German artillery shell came in on them and killed five young soldiers that I had taken basic training with the first year in service. It also killed the jeep driver, which was my job with them in the States. I knew all five of them very well. At one time, I was going to have a double wedding with the sergeant while we were stationed at Fort Jackson, Columbia, South Carolina. But I got a "Dear John" letter while in combat, and I never married. The sergeant was one of those five soldiers killed by that one enemy shell under General Patton in the Battle of the Bulge.

11

Battle of Rosignano

We had a lot of close man-to-man fighting in Rosignano. You could usually see the enemy at just the next house in front of you, or see him running for cover only to eventually stop and fire back at you. In this type of fighting, neither side has time to remove their dead or wounded. The dead lay very still, but the wounded usually called out "Medic, medic, over here," and were usually taken care of very well for the battle conditions that we were in at that time. The medics were some of the bravest soldiers that any country ever had in combat. They were the greatest and bravest soldiers when the chips were down.

It was just getting dark one night in Rosignano, when we found out that all of the town's people that were left were huddled together in the lower floor and basement of one house at the edge of town.

They had moved away from our battles with the Germans until there was no place to go, as this was the last big house in town. There must have been sixty or seventy men, women, and children huddled in that house without water, food, or any guns to protect themselves with. We asked them, "Where are the Germans?" "Just outside at the edge of town," they said. And they were right, because just then, we saw a great big German soldier coming at us and hollering something in German that none of us understood. He was waving and brandishing his rifle, but he was not firing it at us. We expected him to start firing it at any moment, as he was screaming and hollering like a madman.

We all of us started firing our rifles at him, hitting him most of the time. We could tell when we hit him as he would flinch and his body would jerk as if he had been hit. But he never went down. He just kept on coming and screaming at us. Sometimes it looked like he did not even see us, as he just kept looking ahead and walking briskly, briskly forward toward the house where all of the local people were huddled in the basement.

Everyone kept shooting and hitting this large German soldier until he finally fell down on the front porch of the house, face down, never to move again. We all felt relief when he went down, but we also felt a sense of sadness for him. The way he acted, he must have lost his mind after too much combat, was drunk, or was seeking revenge for a buddy that was just killed.

We left him alone that night. The next morning, most of us went over to his body, still lying there as when he fell mortally wounded in battle. We turned his body over and counted the bullet holes in him. There were sixty-four bullet holes in his body. We all admired him. What a great soldier he must have been for his country. One soldier from any country always recognizes and admires a great deed done by another soldier from another country. Just as one athlete admires another athlete for his athletic ability and performance.

This German soldier was about six feet four inches tall and could have weighed about two hundred and fifty pounds, in great shape and very muscular. He would have been a great soldier for any country to have. We all regretted his death very much. But we had no other choice than to bring him down. We all remember him and speak about him with respect and admiration to this day.

I was a land mine sweeper, so I was issued .30-caliber carbine rifle that weighed only six pounds, the regular M.I. Garand rifle weighs nine pounds. The M.I. rifle was not issued to us mine sweepers because they were too cumbersome to carry with the mine-sweeping equipment that we also had to carry. That carbine was a mighty fine gun, and I liked it very much. I wanted to bring it home, but they would not let me. So I bought one similar to it about thirty years ago, but it is a .22 caliber and my army carbine was a thirty-caliber, a larger shell.

There are times in combat when it is easy to kill the enemy, and there are times when you feel that you cannot kill the enemy or anything else. Many days, you feel like you want to go looking for the enemy and kill them all right away, without any misgivings whatsoever. This is the feeling that you get after you have lost a very close buddy who was a typical American boy as all the young draftees were.

Other times, you realize that the enemy probably had a draft system the same as yours and he is in the same predicament that all of you are, and if you leave him alone, maybe he will leave you alone and all of you on both sides can eventually go home. Sometimes you can kill and be proud of it, and other times, you have a sad feeling that will make you vomit on an empty stomach every time you shoot.

Even at home in Fairfield, Illinois, before the war, when I was in grade school and high school, I would often hunt rabbits on our farm with my brother Hayward and my two cousins Howard and Walter Palmer, also from Fairfield, but I could not shoot and kill a rabbit or any other animal or bird. One time when I was with them, I shot a rabbit with my twenty-two rifle. I went over to pick it up, and it was still warm and kicking its legs some and I apologized to this rabbit. I said, "I am sorry, Mr. Rabbit, that I killed you. If I had been by here two minutes earlier or later, you might still be alive and could go back to your loved ones." I dressed and skinned this rabbit to eat, but I never shot another rabbit or animal except a snake. I went hunting with my older brother and my two cousins, but I never again shot at anything. I never told anyone this story until now, because I liked to walk in the fields and woods with or without my brother and my cousins.

I just cannot take a life except to save my own, and that is just exactly what war is, it's them or us, him or me, and I want it to be him, not me, and so did my parents and friends.

But I can kill a snake anytime. I will hunt it down if it takes hours. I have an uncontrollable desire to kill snakes. I lived the first twelve years of my life in Oklahoma and Texas, and to me, all snakes are rattlers and should be killed. They killed many young children in the West, years ago when I was young, in the 1920s and 1930s.

It was ironic that the front porch on which this fine German soldier fell fatally wounded was of the same house that we had stopped at and asked where the Germans are. The rest of the Germans fighting in that area left the same night that we had to shoot this fine soldier of theirs.

We took off that day, trying to find out where they were going to hole up and defend again and again and again, usually on high ground on a mountain so that we would again be at a disadvantage in having to cross an open valley and fight uphill every time that we encountered them. We did this ever since Anzio beachhead, January 22, 1944, to May 8, 1945.

In Rosignano, as in many towns that we fought in, there were many three-story apartment buildings. These were Italian government housing projects that the dictator, Benito Mussolini had built during the early part of his dictatorship. This was done to clear out the many slum areas of Italy. He also built many canals leading from the large rivers for free water irrigation to many of the remote and unproductive areas. He did much for Italy before he ruined the country by joining military forces with Adolf Hitler, dreaming of conquering the world. Mussolini's dream bubble burst very fast. He first invaded Ethiopia and didn't even conquer it. Ethiopia under President Haile Selassie fought back with blowguns and spears and defeated Italy. Benito Mussolini himself lost a son who was an airplane pilot brought down by an Ethiopian spear because he was flying too low and strafing the African natives with machine gun fire.

These stone apartment buildings were very well built and arranged. Each covered a full block. The front faced the front sidewalk and on the inside of each block apartment building, there was a small playground and open air space. There was one opening in the middle of each block for entrance and exit. The entire building was solid wall to wall with a concrete wall between each of the many apartments of this one-block complex hold. They did not have elevators but plenty of stairways to each floor.

The open air playground kept the children off the streets, and the adults had a place to watch the children and also visit with others living in the same complex. I admired these complexes and often wished that there were some here in America like them, but keeping them one or two floors high.

The only bad thing that we soldiers found about these apartment complexes was that when the German soldiers were fighting a retreating battle as they did throughout the entire campaign, they would fight in the front room of the first-floor apartment. Then we would go into that room and drive them to the second floor and then onto the third floor, fighting with hand grenades on each floor. Their slave labor had knocked a hole in the concrete wall before to the next apartment, and they would slowly fight back down through the second floor to the first and then, through a hole in that wall, start all over again to the second and third floors.

This was a very dangerous way to fight and cost lives very heavily on both sides. The first thing that we would do was to throw our "calling card" in first (hand grenade), and as soon as it exploded, in five seconds, you could probably enter and shoot the remaining Germans if they had not already made it to the next room or to the entire next floor. Sometimes you would get the grenade back at you as a German soldier would pick it up and throw it back quickly. So the American soldiers soon learned to pull the pin, count one-two, and then throw the grenade. Five seconds was too long a time to throw at close range. The German hand grenades had only a three-second timer on them, so we did not have time to throw them back.

House-to-house fighting and street fighting was very costly for both sides. In this type of fighting, you had always to look out for your buddies across the street because they could not see above themselves or around a corner as well as you could and he did this for you. We would much rather have fought in the open countryside than in towns or villages.

While we were on a clean-up search-and-destroy patrol in Rosignano, I captured a young German soldier. While I was holding him at gun point, he kept pointing to his left ear and talking to me in his German language which I knew very few words, certainly not enough to understand what he was saying, but I could tell by his motioning that something was wrong about his left ear. I kept my carbine on him all this time because we were still cleaning out a few lingering Germans that always stayed behind to slow up our advance so that their main defensive infantrymen would have plenty of time to dig in and get the best strategic positions and usually leave us the low ground with little cover positions.

While I was there, trying to figure out what he was talking about, he pulled out his penis and started urinating on the ground between us. I still kept my carbine on him, when he was stirring his voided urine with a small stick, then made a mudball out of this mess. He finally had a mudball made and he put it in his left ear.

91

Then I knew that he had a burst left eardrum from a concussion of some kind, probably a grenade or an artillery shell landing nearby. He smiled at me, and I smiled back, because now I understood the burst eardrum. I was born without any eardrums. I failed the army examination three times at the Chicago Dearborn examination building, but the captain said, "Hammil, you have failed our exam here three times today, but you are just too healthy-looking to be walking the streets when everyone else is going. You were born without eardrums, have third-degree flat feet, varicose veins in both legs, one ruptured testicle, and wear glasses. I am going to put you in restricted ground services in the army. Next man. Let's keep this line moving."

We were still cleaning out Rosignano, and the other soldiers were moving out at the end of town, and I did not have any way to take him with me and look for other Germans at the same time. Besides, if we were to get into heavy fighting again, he might even turn on me and kill me. So I looked around, and right behind me was a large stone house that had a rabbit pen built under the stairway that led to the main entrance to the house. So I motioned for him to get in that rabbit pen and squat down and stay there and let another American soldier capture him again. I put him in the pen and found a small stick to put in the door latch and then I took off, following the rest of my platoon. He could get out any time he wished to, but I didn't think that he would, as he was glad that combat was over and he was now an American P.O.W. He waved at me as I left, but I did not wave back at him. We were on a search-and-destroy mission when I captured him, but I and most of my platoon tried to capture and save the enemy's life when it was possible. I never saw him again. I hope he made it home after the war ended and was not shot by some trigger-happy American infantryman. He was probably a couple of years younger than I was at that time. He seemed to be a very nice, pleasant boy. We must at all times keep reminding ourselves that this is a *just* war and that God is on our side.

Another night in Rosignano, we Americans were taking a beating, so the line companies called back to our platoon and asked if we could spare some men to come up to the west side of town and give them some extra fire power.

As soon as we got to the edge of town, walking uphill near a small stream of water coming from a drainage ditch, a mortar shell came and landed near me. I jumped into the small drainage ditch nearby to escape the shrapnel that was sure to fly in my direction. The shrapnel missed me, but to my surprise, that small ditch of running water was the city's sewage system. And the stink! You have no idea how badly I smelled after lying there for two or three minutes waiting for all the shrapnel to dissipate.

I could see and hear the rifles from both sides firing, and it was anyone's guess as to who would conquer this town, them or us.

As I made it to the second house in town, a soldier asked me to help him carry a wounded U.S. soldier who was already on a wooden ladder lying on the ground. There are no litter bearers and stretchers at the real front. They are just behind us a little. I helped carry the soldier out on the wooden ladder to just about where I had jumped into the sewage stream. I think the soldier was dead that we carried out. He never moved, and we went in town to fight again.

We did eventually conquer the town, as the Germans left before sunrise the next day. Both sides lost very heavily there. Nobody won.

Most of the soldiers in our platoon were on that clean-up "search and capture or kill the enemy." They were T. Sgt. Kenneth Blake, S. Sgt. Barney Allickson, Cpl. Joseph Buffalo, Pvt. John Red DeHore, Pfc. Charles Hoffman, Pfc. John Despot, Cpl. Max Rush, Cpl. Phillip Braun, Pvt. James Keane, Pvt. Maab, Pvt. Bill Zimmerman, Pvt. Max Rotopel, Pvt. Mike Lipp, Pfc. Freeman James, Pvt. James Vulanti, Sgt. Frenchy Dorin (awarded the Silver Star and Legion of Merit medals), Pfc. George Loechner, Pfc. Robert Seyl, Pvt. Red Thompson, Pvt. Jake Jacoby, and myself.

When I was very young, about ten or eleven years of age, I lived in Optima, Oklahoma, and both of my parents were very good Christians, and both of them were raised in very Christian homes. They instilled Christianity in all three of us children. My older brother, Arlie Hayward, and my younger sister, Juanita, were raised in very strict Christian ways. There were no playing cards allowed in the house, no sexy literature allowed in the house, and no dancing or cussing allowed. Also, we were not allowed in a pool

93

hall or to use alcohol or tobacco in any way nor were we to know-ingly associate with any one who did any of these forbidding things.

We three children were supposed to be in Sunday school and church every time there was a service there. I had a very fine Sunday school teacher, by the name of Merline Serface. She was one of the many people that had a lasting influence on my Christian life. She gave away a small Christian booklet, quarterly, to the student who had learned and repeated the most Bible verses that quarter. I think that I usually won nine out of ten times. And my mother let me know about it in no uncertain terms when I did not win it.

Merline had a son by the name of J. B. Angely. He went to min-isterial college and became a minister. He preached his first sermon, after graduating, in our church at the age of nineteen. I was there. The entire town of about 110 people were so very proud of him. This would have been about 1933 or 1934.

After I was nineteen years old, I was drafted into the infantry, and I saw that he was then Captain Chaplain J. B. Angely, chaplain of my division in Italy, the Thirty-Fourth Infantry Division. I wrote his mother, Mrs. Merline Serface, and one day while our division was in rest at Rosignano, he came and surprised me with a personal visit. I appreciated that so very much.

12

Black Market

We had another serious incident in a town that the line-company boys were having a hard time taking. A German tank had become disabled because one of its tracks were blown off by a bazooka by our line-company boys and this tank was sitting in the middle of the town square. It could spin around on one track and machine gun our line-company soldiers at will. They evidently didn't have any more bazooka shells to fire at the tank and finish it off. Our boys were pinned down that day for a few hours and could not advance.

So our P and A platoon got the call to take care of the German tank some way so that the line-company boys could advance and completely capture the small town. We could look down on it from the third story. So Sgt. Buffalo got the brilliant idea of borrowing a .75-mm cannon from cannon company, which was part of our battalion, and put it in a room on the third floor of a house very near the disabled tank and shoot it from there.

So we took the wheels off the cannon, tied a rope around it, and pulled, with block and tackle, the heavy cannon up to the third floor of this concrete and stone apartment house. It was very heavy and awkward to handle, but we finally got it up there after a few fruitless tries.

After we finally got it up there, we sandbagged it down very well on the tile floor so that it would not slip and get off target line. This took us at least two hours of heavy and hard work. All the time, we could look down on the German tank and watch him swing around looking for American soldiers to shoot at and kill.

We finally got the .75-mm cannon lined up to shoot the tank and finish it off so that our boys could advance.

After we were set and the 75-mm was lined up to shoot the tank directly in the middle and destroy it Sgt. Joe Buffalo pulled the lanyard and fired the cannon at the German tank. But low and behold we did not hit the tank. The recoil of the exploding shell sent the entire small cannon and sandbags in reverse, completely backwards across the room, sliding on the slick tile floor. It was a good thing that none of us boys were standing behind this cannon as the recoil back against the wall would have broken our legs or cut them off at the knees. We were all standing near the open window so that we could witness the shell hitting the tank and see what the German soldiers would do when it was hit.

But this idea didn't work, and it was still our duty to destroy that tank so Sgt. Buffalo got the idea of our getting a bazooka and firing at it, as this was always a good way to disable a tank. We finally found a bazooka and a shell, and Sgt. Buffalo came back up to the third floor and fired the bazooka at the tank. This made a direct hit on the turret and hull of the tank and set it on fire.

Soon the young German soldiers came out of the turret hatch opening at the top where they must enter and exit at all times. When an iron tank catches on fire, the iron get so hot inside, that one must get out immediately or suffocate due to the iron heating from the fire and the gasoline or diesel fuel burning. The best time to shoot the enemy is as he is coming through the hatch of the turret. The turret opening is so small that he cannot look for the enemy or handle his weapons very well. So it was easy to shoot them when they were just climbing out of the tank. This was what our boys did this time. Even though this was our objective, we still felt sorry for the German boys getting out of the burning tank. They were all killed. Sometimes we would say that this was a mercy killing, as they will not have to suffer any more combat. For them the war was over. We must continue to go through this hell and dehumanizing experiences for another year. So who are the unlucky ones, and who are the lucky ones? I have never figured that one out yet. One day, they are the ones that got killed, and the next day, they are the ones who came home. I think the worst scenario would be of the ones who fought on the lines in combat for two to three years then got killed toward the end of the war. Most of you who have never been in combat will not understand the above paragraph. If you have been in combat no explanation is necessary.

There is not any way that an article, a movie, a book, a story, or a poem can give the sensation of death-facing fear, hunger, loneliness, and cold all at the same time, as it would be experienced in actual combat against an enemy who is hunting you down like you were a mad dog about to do someone great harm.

"Please, God, have mercy on those that have gone through it. Every soldier who was ever killed or injured in any war in any country has gone through this terrible anguish just before he is killed or crippled. Many soldiers have gone through this experience many times before being killed or possibly making it home in bad condition."

That is my prayer for all combat men and women sixty years later. The platoon boys who worked hard on this dangerous detail were: Cpl. Joe Buffalo (in charge), Cpl. Phillip Braun, Cpl. Max L. Rush, Pfc. John Despot, Pvt. John "Red" DeHore, Pvt. James Keane, Pfc. James Freeman, Sgt. Frenchy Dorin, Pfc. Robert Seyl, Pvt. Mike Lipp, Pvt. Charles Hoffman, Pfc. George Loechner, and Pfc. Harold C. Hammil. These were all great and brave soldiers, who had been with the division in combat for one, two, and some for three years overseas. Many of these soldiers fought in North Africa, Sicily, the Abby at Cassino and Anzio Beach and remained with the outfit until the end, May 7, 1945. God bless all of them.

After the battle of Gettysburg in 1863 a newspaper reporter asked Gen. Ulysses S. Grant what it was like to be in combat and he thought for a few moments then he looked directly at the reporter and said, "If you have never been a battle, no explanation is possible. If you have been in a battle no explanation is necessary.

And General MacArthur in his famous farewell speech in the 1950's said, "The war is never over for a combat soldier until the day that he dies." This is a very true statement.

I was with our platoon for almost two years and there is a big difference in the boys who were trained to kill and those who just put on a uniform for Uncle Sam. No explanation is possible.

God bless any soldier who ever fought in combat in any country in any war. All of the other people will never know what his life was like. Maybe this is the way it should be. After all, sixty percent of the people living in the world today were not even born until after WWII was over in 1945, May 7. There is no way that we should expect them to be interested in ancient American history. But to many of us, it was very real or possibly a very bad dream that we all had from 1942 to 1945. I hope that this that I am writing about was just a bad dream that we all had for three years duration and some day it will go away forever.

At all times, our young soldiers who believe in the Bible must keep reminding themselves that this was a just war and that God is on our side. It is with God's will that we are here to make the world safe for democracy.

I never could understand why the Italians did not like our salted peanuts that we got every month in our government rations when the war was over. Sometimes we would get these rations during combat duty but not often, as there was no way to keep up with us, and it would have been too dangerous for the rear support troops to look for us anyway. When we would offer the civilians some of our salted peanuts, they would take some and then wash the salt off them with running water. I never could understand that. Salt was a luxury condiment that they very seldom had during the German occupation. I am not sure that peanuts were introduced to many European countries until after this war. Their favorite to ask for was chocolates and anything that contained sugar.

We were notified that our infantry division would probably be sent to the South Pacific to help end the war there, since our front ended May 7, 1945, and their battles were still continuing against Japan. We were winning terrible battles, but with great loss of lives. So our officers told all of our division soldiers that if they had one hundred combat days or more, they could apply to transfer to a noncombat job in the infantry. I had about two hundred sixty combat days in the front, so I was entitled to transfer to a less hazardous job. If I stayed at my present job when I would be sent to the South Pacific, I would be a flame thrower at the caves that were in most of the islands that the Japanese were defending. But I had enough dangerous, life-threatening combat for a lifetime, so I asked to be transferred to the kitchen as a cook to replace one of the cooks that was being transferred back to the States on the point system.

I enjoyed my short time in the kitchen. I had always been fascinated by cooking all of my life, but I had done very little of it except at home on the farm, Mom would often have me stir the milk gravy or turn the fried potatoes. However, Mom was a very good cook and was always experimenting with condiments and inventing different dishes for us to eat. My father had worked as a cowboy cook on the Anchor D ranch in Guyman, Oklahoma, and liked to cook also. We later owned sixty acres of homestead ground that my grandfather's sister had homesteaded in the Oklahoma land rush of eighteen ninety eight. It adjoined the Anchor D ranch, which now owns our sixty-acre homestead. A very good ranch.

One day while I was in the kitchen in San Remo, Italy, someone told us where we could get a jeep trailer-load of fresh dug potatoes from a rural Italian farmer. So our mess sergeant went out to the country and talked to the farmer about buying a jeep trailer-load of his fresh dug potatoes. They struck a deal. The farmer wanted five five-quart cans of our American orange marmalade for the load of potatoes. They made a deal and shook hands on it. The only thing wrong with this deal was that we did not have five five-quart cans of orange marmalade in the entire kitchen. But we did have one five-quart can of orange marmalade and four five-quart cans of peanut butter. Now the Italians did not care for salted peanuts or our peanut butter either. So our mess sergeant had a small problem. He did not want to lose all of those beautiful potatoes that he knew our boys would like, since they had not had any fresh potatoes for years. He wasn't about to lose those potatoes because, surely, some other mess sergeant would hear about them and buy them.

So the next day, he took me and two other cooks with him to get the potatoes. He took one five-quart can of orange marmalade and four five-quart cans of peanut butter and hoped for the best.

The Italian farmer helped us load all the new potatoes in our jeep trailer, then he asked to see the orange marmalade cans. We gave him the five five-gallon cans as he asked for them. He asked us to open one so that he could see that he was not getting cheated. Our mess sergeant opened the can of orange marmalade that we had with us. He looked at it and tasted it. It was just what he wanted, so we gave him the other four five-gallon cans of peanut butter. All of the G.I. food containers were the same olive drab color they all looked alike. The only difference was the printed labeling on the outside, which he could not read or spell English. All the cans looked alike to him. That was what our mess sergeant was depending on, and it worked so far.

However, the Italian farmer was not to be outsmarted. He asked our mess sergeant to sign his name and address on a piece of paper, which our sergeant did. Our sergeant signed his name on the paper as all American soldiers signed their names for anything that they purchased or did not want their real identity known—he signed his name "Sgt. Joe Blow, Chicago, Illinois." This name and address was about as common as "Kilroy was here."

We then got in the jeep and drove away so that we would not be there when he opened the cans of peanut butter. However we never went back there to get any more potatoes as we would be moving before we ran out of potatoes. We did expect to see him come to our company commander and raise heck, but he didn't, and those soldiers sure did enjoy those fresh fried potatoes.

I was there almost two years and that was the only time that I personally knew of us soldiers taking advantage of the local people. We always treated them more than fairly, and they treated us with great respect. I love and admire the Italian people very much. I really enjoyed my seven-month stay in Italy after the war was over. It was beautiful. I stayed, there after the was over awaiting my point system return.

All of us young soldiers liked to make a little extra money when we were not in actual combat at that time and trying to save our lives. So we would sell to the Italian civilians what few items that were available for us to get hold of and sell, such as hand grenades for seventy-five cents to the local fishermen who would then take them out into the ocean, which is always right at hand, and pull the pin out and that gave them five seconds before the grenade would explode and kill the fish nearby. They would then dip them up in the nets and take them back to shore and sell them as fresh fish. They had good fresh fish, as the grenades did not harm the fish flesh unless it blew away the flesh from the fish. When we knew that we were going into reserve off the immediate lines, we would start saving grenades as well as many cans of C rations as we could do without. They also sold for seventy-five cents a can to any Italian civilian that we met on the street.

We also sold our cigarettes for $2.50 a package, and they were free to us during the war. After the war, they cost us a nickel a package, but we could still sell them for $2.50 each.

Condoms or birth control prophylactics were also a good item on the black market even in this predominantly Catholic country. Many large black marketeers would buy these up from the local civilians and drive a truck to Switzerland and sell these black market items for an even greater profit.

I said then that we soldiers would never see cigarettes sold in America for the outlandish price of $2.50 a pack as they were .15 and .20 cents a pack here then. But due to the lung cancer scare in the 1990s the price soon rose to over $4.00 a pack. I didn't smoke then nor have I ever been a smoker, nor has anyone in our family ever been a cigarette smoker.

On the Italian black market, the most expensive item that we could sell was an American all-silk parachute. Rich Italian families would buy them for about $500 if they had a daughter getting married soon. Of course, only the paratroopers had them. One silk parachute would make a beautiful trailing gown, underwear, and possibly a dress or suit. This would make for one of the more expensive and beautiful weddings.

The young, poor-to-middle–class girls would beg us for a pair of our G.I. cotton socks. They would unravel them into a ball of cotton, then knit themselves a pair of thick underpants.

For a brassiere they would take two pieces of string and tie each one in a four- to five-inch circle, then tie these two circles together with a six- to seven-inch string in the middle. Then they would tie a long string on each side of the circles to go around the back while the circles went over the nipples to pull them up.

Their shoes were made from wood for the soles cut to fit the foot and a piece of cloth or string across the top of the foot, like our modern sandals. They were called "*scarpe di guerra*," or shoes of the war.

This kind of black marketing was small to what some of the rear echelon support troops were involved in, especially the quartermaster groups that supplied all the troops with uniforms, shirts, pants, blankets, beer, canned food, coffee, and all other items too numerous to mention that all of the troops men and women would use while over there during the war.

The G.I. supply truck drivers would have a prearranged place to park a G.I. truck full of supplies. They would leave it in this designated spot always near a U.S.O. canteen, so that they could use the excuse of just getting a cup of coffee and a donut on their break on the way to delivering it to where it was needed, like for the front-line combat soldiers.

When they finished their cup of coffee and doughnut, about twenty to thirty minutes later and went outside to drive their truck load to its destination, it was always gone, and no one knew where it was.

A full truck loaded with American supplies would usually bring the American driver at least twenty thousand dollars each time it was stolen.

They could not send more than one-hundred-dollars-a month home without an officer signing for it, and that was risky, because there was no way a service man could earn that much money except black marketing or having a good night playing poker. Some was sent back home from poker games. This was done a few times with an officer's signature of approval. Each officer could sign for the other one and get by with it. This was a very big business overseas in most foreign countries that we were fighting in. The troops up front that were supposed to get the supplies never saw most of what they were supposed to get. We were hungry and cold most of the time that we were in combat, but in the rear, we were well taken care of.

In April of 1945, just before the end of the war, we were told not to go into France or Yugoslavia to chase the Germans, but to stop at the French border and wait, because the end of the war was imminent in our favor. We had held off the enemy for over two years. There were no visible lines of a country's border. Three of us went on into some of the Yugoslavia territory and met up with three members of the Yugoslavian guerrilla patrol fighters. We thought how lucky that they were, two young boys and one young girl. Cpl. Max L. Rush, Pfc. John Despot, and I made that patrol. We could not speak Yugoslavian, and they could not speak English or Italian. We were all fairly fluent in Italian by now, and we had all done interpreting when we captured a German soldier. The Germans had been in Italy for five years, and we had been there two and three years, so we used Italian language as a common denominator to converse. We were all used to that and we American soldiers often conversed in Italian among ourselves to improve our ability with the language. I liked the Italian people very much. They cooperated with us in every way, and I was never mistreated by an Italian civilian. I would like to visit there and possibly live there for a few months every year. Of course that is just a wish and a dream.

102

The infantryman has been known by and called many different names since its founding: minutemen, foot soldiers, ground troops, dogface infantry, fox hole rat, desert rat, mountain fighter, gorilla fighter, cannon fodder, grunts, and others.

But there was never a more patriotic group than these young boys who gave their all for America. How much did you give?

By sending the bulk of the lower I.Q. test scorers to the infantry, each soldier lost in battle would mean less loss of technical knowledge to America and the world. Adolf Hitler used the same plan to build a super race in the late 1930s and early 1940s. And he failed.

If we left our higher I.Q.s in college or put them in a support troop where there would be no danger of them being killed, we would not drain America's brain power that we might need to re-build our country if the war lasted a long time and we had a great many casualties. I am sure that Congress would very strongly deny these statements, but in my opinion most countries in this world use this system of self-preservation.

All county law enforcement agencies in America were told to try and send the able-bodied young boy to the marines or the army ground forces, which meant being sent to the infantry combat troops where the mortality rate is very high. In WWI 87% of all service deaths occurred in the infantry. In WWII, 80% of all deaths occurred in the infantry. These percentages are about the same for the Korea and Vietnam conflicts of war. What percentage of all branches of service were in the infantry, I do not know, but I would guess about ten to fifteen percent. Being in this branch of service could be interpreted as a death sentence in a year or two for your country.

It does seem that this is discrimination to send one group of Americans, or of any country, to possible death or disabling injuries to protect another group. This could be eliminated by having all ser-vicemen take the same combat basic training, then have an indiscriminatory form of rotation into and out of combat without personal preferences and political pull and maneuvering, as we now have. Senator Strom Thurman said as soon as you put the word "except," in a draft, you have destroyed it.

On the day that our E.T.O. European theater of operations was ended we were in Biella, Italy, up near the French border. The German 34th Combat Infantry had just surrendered to our American

34th Combat Infantry. The German sergeant who drove the German officer to our building and let out the German officer who was to surrender to our colonel was driving a black 1936 Ford touring car. I had a nineteen thirty-six, four-door sedan Ford very similar to it at home jacked up in our barn at home in Fairfield, Illinois.

I got a little homesick when I saw his car, so similar to mine that I went over to the German sergeant driving the car after their German officer had gone into our building to officially surrender as is required by the Geneva convention. I tried to strike up a conversation with the German chauffeur of the Ford, but he would have nothing to do with me. I asked him three or four questions about this Ford, but he just looked straight ahead, with both hands on the steering wheel. He did not look at me or respond in any way whatsoever.

But I did not blame him in any way. I might have acted the same way or even worse than that if America had lost the war and this incident was totally reversed. The next day was when they all had to line up in military formation and surrender all their weapons to us America infantrymen, which we got to keep all of the weapons that we received from them. We were allowed to bring one ordinance piece home with us for a souvenir. I sold all mine for twenty-five dollars each to the local Italians, as I had already gotten my piece to take home while I was up on Montibelmonti from that drunken German officer in the previous winter: a German holster and a P 27 pistol, which I still have here at home, never fired by me.

So many times a wounded combat infantryman was sent back to the front lines to fight again too soon after he has been wounded and discharged from the hospital. Instead of keeping him until he is well, or better yet all wounded soldiers in any branch should be sent back to the States and possibly discharged after they have been wounded once and possibly given a small percentage pension.

I have personally seen our own infantrymen released from the hospital after a combat wound and they were sent back up to our company and platoon still having to walk with a cane. I have heard of them being sent back to the front on crutches, but I didn't personally see it in our platoon. And don't tell me that there wasn't a stateside U.S.O. warrior who could not replace a combat soldier who had been wounded several times and is still in combat. I think that this is a military disgrace.

Some turnip patch experts might want to say that so many of the stateside boys were not trained for combat. I'll tell you what it takes to train an American boy for combat. Put him up front in full gear and let the enemy shoot at him just once and he will learn how to fight and survive in less than one minute. That's how we mostly learned most of our knowledge, in the actual combat. They will use the same methods that we used as kids playing cops and robbers or cowboys and Indians. It is all the same game, to seek cover and fire when you have the advantage. In combat, you either get wounded, killed, or live to fight another day and go all through that again and again.

Some front-line soldiers were wounded so badly that they were sent back to America and doctored until about well then sent back to Italy to fight again with their old platoon. That was a disgrace! They should have been replaced by an American Stateside soldier. They had done too much already and so many soldiers did so little.

When we arrived on Montibelmonti in December of 1944, the 91st Tennessee Volunteer Infantry Division had already taken part of this terrible mountain range and they were due a rest. They had just previously taken *third base,* a very dangerous pass in this mountain range that left them under observation of the German artillery every time that any of them would pass by it. And all of us had to pass by it to make any advances toward the enemy, as this was the only road on that mountainside. The 91st was a very good and great division of fighting men. I had served with some of them earlier in my service at Camp McCain. My hat is off to that division. They suffered a lot and lost many young soldiers in heavy dangerous combat. So did the 88th Division.

When we arrived, there, we were told by some of the other soldiers that we wouldn't be there long, as the last division that fought there lasted only seventeen days, so we could look for relief after that many days also. Seventy-five days later, on April 1, 1944, we left that mountain to enter Bologna. And we and all of our regiment had been on that same mountain all that time without relief. That was probably the worst winter that we ever spent in combat. We could not go on the attack. But we had patrols day and night and so did the German's harassing us and artillery shells never ceased to reach us daily from the Germans.

It was also here that we went for over three months without a shower or bath and very little food. We could not attack because of the heavy snow. Neither could the Germans.

That winter we often saw young German soldiers running through the woods in the snow going to our lines to defect or surrender. We just let them go back toward our lines for someone else to capture. I always hoped that some trigger-happy G.I. would not shoot them, because I could have captured some of them and possibly saved their lives as prisoners of war. But after a few months here of looking at dead, stinking bodies, life becomes very cheap. Sometimes you don't even care if the enemy shoots you.

When the line-company boys arrived on Montibelmonti, it was December and the ground was frozen hard, as we were in the high altitude atmosphere that causes it to snow all winter long. There are many large and beautiful ski lodges and ski runs there now. I understand, by watching the winter Olympics on television, this whole area in Italy, France, Germany, and Austria are all full of ski lifts and ski runs around Innsbruk, Austria, where we ended up some of our worst fighting near Brenner Pass and Innsbruk, home of the 1986 Winter Olympics.

Innsbruk was the home of the German S.S. panzer divisions, Adolf Hitler's prize troops. Also all German personnel replacements and supplies had to come through that Innsbruk/Brenner Pass to Italy, as that was the only negotiable pass to the south from Germany and Austria. They put up a terrible last stand there and we only took it just before the war ended.

They had one railroad that left Innsbruk through Brenner Pass over the gorge to the south. Our air force bombed it out early in the war, but they kept building it back after each time. Finally the Germans quit rebuilding it, but we could tell that they were still bringing soldier replacements and supplies through there, as there was no other pass that they could travel through.

After we captured Innsbruk/Brenner Pass, we discovered how they got their supplies and men through there. Both sides of that mountain were hollowed out to contain many hundreds of their troops in bunk beds and vehicles. They had a machine workshop on each side of the mountain to make most anything that they might need.

We discovered that the Germans had built a portable suspen-

106

sion bridge in each side of the pass, or gorge, as it is sometimes called. They built one-half of the suspension bridge on each side, and at night, when the air force could not see the bridge, they would roll it out on railroad tracks and connect it in the middle. They would suspend it from the top and brace it from the bottom so as to strengthen it to support light loads. It was a great, ingenious piece of work that was enough to keep their supply lines open during the final days of the war.

They would put the bridge to work at night, then reel it back in before daylight. The air force photographed it during the daylight hours and could not see any bridge because it was detached in half and moved back into the respective sides of the mountain.

We knew that they were getting new replacements, because our line-company boys were killing so many, but the German foxholes would be full of new German soldiers the next morning, and wasn't any way that the new troops could get there without our boys seeing them. We posted guards on these foxholes twenty-four hours, day and night.

After we took Bologna, we found out how the new German replacements were getting into their foxholes. Our boys in one week shot sixteen Germans out of a two-man foxhole, and others were still coming in the next day. The Americans would leave good combat soldiers to guard these foxholes to make sure that no new Germans would come in at night. But they could never catch them.

Some of our boys almost got court-martialed because their officer said that they must have gone to sleep while on this important guard duty that could risk a lot of lives. But the boys on guard denied ever sleeping on that guard or leaving their post.

After we moved out of our static winter position for the winter and started our spring offensive to head toward the northern Italian border and France, we discovered how the Germans could get so many boys in one foxhole without our catching them doing it.

The back north side of Montibelmonti was a straight up-and-down dirt cliff many feet high, too steep to climb without a ladder. The Germans had made a very tall ladder out of long, narrow tree saplings about thirty to forty feet high. Then they dug out a long tunnel about a mile long into the mountainside that connected to this two-man fox hole. Just before the foxhole entrance, there was

107

a large room dug out where about a dozen soldiers could stay and wait their turn at the sniper position, which was almost certain death for about three months all of that winter.

We examined this foxhole tunnel and were amazed and stunned at the ingenuity. Most of this work for their soldiers was done ahead of time by slave labor of captured prisoners from various countries. Their army general could anticipate where the next defensive positions should be and have the slave laborers dig the foxholes and build the cement machine-gun bunkers ahead of time. This way, they could utilize the soldiers to their best advantage in combat and killing the ever-advancing American troops.

We occasionally captured a slave laborer, or he would come to us and surrender, and we would turn him over to the Italian underground, civilians who were active in every town. The underground would feed him and give him Italian clothes, and he could stay with them and help their war effort any way that he could. It was too early to try to go back to their native country, so they would help there until the war would end—if ever—then they could try to make it home to Russia, Poland, Yugoslavia, Denmark, France, or any other place in Europe that they came from.

When you are in combat, under heavy fire or in a very tense situation that may last for two or three days, food is one of the last things that you think about. Getting killed or one of your platoon boys getting killed is foremost in your mind. Combat soldiers pray silently, to themselves every minute they are awake, even if their physical body is doing something else.

You must always keep a low silhouette against the sky line, crawl or roll over on your belly when going over a hilltop or mountain so as not to make silhouette or shadow. When a German airplane flies over, soldiers on the front lines know to stand perfectly still even if he is in open ground, because the pilot can see a moving shadow on the ground very easily, but a person standing still looks from the air like a tree, a rock, or a break in the terrain. So he doesn't move at all.

When there is a lull in battle or tension is less, you will become hungry, very hungry. But usually, there is no food or your buddies may have only one can of C rations to share with you until word can be gotten to your platoon for food.

It is very dangerous for the cooks to get a jeep or a cook's helper to bring any food up near the line company's position. I find fault with the cooks here because we have been on the lines for months, and some of them were never on the line for one hour. Yet *they* eat three times a day, usually not very good food though: such as dried eggs, hot C rations, pancakes, spam, coffee. Most line-company boys never ate that good for two or three years at a time.

They say an army travels on its stomach. Not so for the combat infantrymen. They travel on prayers, hunger, guts, fear, and loneliness. Who is going to bring food and mail to the front lines—nobody?

Sometimes the cooks would send a jeep up to our position, which was very dangerous, so the jeep driver would drive by, slow down, and throw out a case of C rations that would land in a ditch or in the snow where Germans had laid their minefields. We were land mine sweepers, so we would send one man out to sweep the path to the case of C rations and carry them back the same way that he went so as not to set off a mine and blow off both legs or lose his life. Getting any food this way was very common and most of us would lose thirty to forty pounds while under fire for months at a time. I lost forty pounds in 1944.

The army C ration menu never changed during the entire four years of WWII. It was mostly potato and beef hash and pork and beans, but very few cans of the pork and beans were in a case. We all liked them. But if you were on patrol that day and night when the rations arrived, all that would be left were a few cans of the hash. I blame the government's menu director for not furnishing us with a better variety of food. Three million of us overseas soldiers in Europe and the South Pacific complained about this all during the war. This is just another example of the home front warriors just watching the clock on the wall for quitting time and saying, "Boy, I'm sure doing my part." Heck, if he didn't read the papers every day, he wouldn't know that a war was going on. If we could have put some of those soldiers in the front lines with us, they would have changed things. Of course, that could be said for all the boys who never saw combat. I am a little bitter about the unfair rotation, but, mostly, just disappointed.

I had an army buddy in Panama City guarding the canal, and he had to write home to Mom and Dad to get enough money to keep him going to his favorite red lite brothel. His cigarettes and beer took all of his regular pay monthly. He never saw the enemy or fired a rifle. What a way to fight a war!

Sometimes we were sent on a three-day, search-and-find mission to capture Germans in the winter, when we were in a static position because of the heavy snow, and neither side could advance well enough to make a strong attack. We would put C-ration cans one for each day that we would be gone, inside our shirt next to our belly so as to keep the cans from freezing.

But this didn't always work, depending on how cold it got in the mountains where we were fighting. Sometimes the C ration would be thawed throughout the can and we could eat all of it, and sometimes the food would be thawed just around the outside perimeter of the can and the middle would be frozen.

If we were out there in no man's land for more than two days and we hadn't captured a German and brought him back to camp for interrogation, we could come in, and another bunch of boys would go out there in the waist-deep snow.

We didn't usually look very hard for a prisoner to bring in. We just usually went out in the deep snow, disbursed a few feet apart and settled down in the snow and hoped that the Germans hadn't seen us and would come on their search and capture party and capture us. They never did in our platoon, but I can't say that for all of the other platoons because I know that the Germans got some of our boys that winter, and we got some of theirs.

The jeep drivers and truck drivers would wire their C ration cans to their motors to keep them warm in the wintertime. They offered to let me do it to my cans, but it took too long to heat the cans up and we had to keep moving on other details, so I never had the luxury of a motor-heated C ration meal. Didn't miss much, I don't think. The vehicle drivers put their cans on in the morning and left them there all day long, that way they would be warm.

That winter the young soldiers that went on most of these search-and-find patrols were Sgt. Joe Buffalo, Cpl. Phillip Braun, Cpl. Max L. Rush, Pfc. John Despot, Pfc. Charles Hoffman, Sgt. Frenchy Dorin, Pfc. James Keane, and Pfc. George Loechner, and I. All were great and brave soldiers who you could count on to stay and hold their ground until the mission was completed. They were the greatest. They were put to the test and all passed with flying colors. They never left any soldier stranded in combat.

110

To you who are offended by any facts or opinions written here, I make no apologies to you or anyone. As you know, this is not a romance novel written to entertain you. This is a true actual story of one man's experiences in front-line infantry combat in the Italian campaign during WWII as an ordinary draftee from the farms of Illinois.

I wish to repeat what General U. S. Grant told a newspaper reporter when he was asked "General, what is it like being in combat?" General Grant hesitated for a few moments trying to think of the proper words that this non-combat man would understand what surviving hell would be like, then he said "if you have never been in combat, no explanation is possible, if you have been in combat no explanation is necessary." This is so true, I very seldom go a day without repeating these exact words to myself a few times.

I have never seen a movie or a television program yet that can depict to its audience the fear of hunting down to kill a human being such as you are, and know that they are hunting you to kill you also as a man would hunt to kill a rabid infected dog and protect his loved ones. This is one of the worst inhumanities from man to man. There are many smaller inhumanities in the world today, but none as inhumane as man against man in actual infantry combat. It is very fortunate that eight out of ten soldiers never see combat. Many soldiers came back home and lied a little and said that they were in combat but they are lying. What a beautiful way to fight a war!

I wish that every young soldier that was killed in action (K.I.A.) could come back to America and write a book about his personal battle experiences, it would make most of you get on your hands and knees and cry like a baby. There is no way that you could even imagine the acts of heroism and suffering that they went through before and while they were dying. Wouldn't it be wonderful to know their last thoughts? You write about your WWII experiences, and I will write about mine.

There were no counselors or psychiatrists appointed to work with the boys who had been over there in combat too long or who had experienced too much killing or just the everyday experiences of infantry combat.

When we were leaving Italy, months after the war was over, an officer came to us and said, "Many of you will experience combat neurosis, shell shock, flash backs, and combat stress syndromes, but there is nothing that the government can do for you. There are too many of you that will be affected this way, and it would cost the government too much money. As of now, we have to spend billions of dollars rebuilding the countries that we have just torn up, like Japan, Germany, Italy, Yugoslavia, Poland, and other smaller countries. You should experience a gradual withdrawal of these combat nerves for about seventeen years, then they will level off at that time and remain at that level for the rest of your lives."

13

Senator Clare Boothe Luce

After June 6, 1944, when we took Rome and the "longest day" began as the second front opened up at Omaha and Normandy beaches, the Italian campaign was known as the "forgotten front." We carried the war to the Germans all by ourselves except for the Russians on their front. When the second front opened, they knew that Germany would be captured from that invasion and our front was no longer the most important one.

Gen. George Patton, who had previously been our fifth corps general, was now on the new front. He got about everything that he asked for because he was a personal friend of President Franklin Delano Roosevelt.

Because the Allied command was afraid that the second front would not be amply supplied with everything, we were short on injured personnel replacement. We were limited to three rifle shells a day per man, and the artillery divisions were rationed to three rounds a day per gun. They were now unable to give us adequate support as they could fire only at large concentrations of enemy trucks or personnel, which made it much harder on the front-line boys, who had it hard enough the way it was.

Those of us who were left and able to go out on patrols or special details were now making two a day. I remember in the winter of 1944–45 that we did one-hundred-and-twenty-one-days straight on details on the front lines without any break or relief. These were all in German territory.

Our Thirty-Fourth Infantry Division was made up originally of National Guard boys from Iowa, Minnesota, and North Dakota. My platoon were all from Montevideo, Minnesota originally, but due to so many deaths and wounded, there were now replacements like myself from many states. It was the first infantry division sent overseas in WWII. They originally went to Ireland, then on to Oran, North Africa, to support the Thirty Sixth Infantry Division from Texas, which made the invasions.

In the winter of 1944–45, while we were still in Montibelmonti, we had a distinguished visitor from the States, Senator Clare Boothe Luce. She visited the division and regimental headquarters of our Red Bull Division and found out how long we had been overseas, that the original 34th boys had too many combat days, 520 at the end of the war. She said that she would see if she could get another infantry division from the States to replace and get us home.

We were all elated that now we would be going home and another division taking our place. But this morale lifter was short-lived, as Washington soon told her that the war effort needed our combat mountain experience with the Germans and we would have to stay until the war was over plus a few months of occupation to maintain peace in this country. We stayed seven months after the war as occupation peace keepers. We went home in December 1945; the war was over the previous seven months, May 7, 1945.

This was another example of unfair rotation. The older and married men who were drafted later in this war could have replaced us. They were very seldom sent overseas except as a support of some kind. Never were the older draftees or married men with children sent into combat infantry. These combat boys were mostly poor, young country and big city boys seventeen, eighteen, nineteen years of age. But, boy, did they make good dead soldiers. A small percentage of these boys made it back. Eighty percent of all of the deaths in all of the armed services occurred in the infantry. (That leaves about 20% to return of those sent over ever made it back and there are about 30% more wounded than killed.) I don't think that there is an accurate account of them or of the posttraumatic stress syndrome boys who returned and will not admit it, as it is not a badge of honor but a stigma which they do not deserve.

Our 34th Division was the first division to go overseas and one of the last to come home. Army history tells us that this division had accumulated the most combat days in any war that the United States had ever been in, and that some of their soldiers had the most combat days of any American soldier in any American war. The original National Guard boys that made up the division had over five hundred and twenty combat days from and including part of

1942, all of 1943 and 1944, and to May 8, 1945. I was not with them all this time. I came in as an infantry replacement the later part of April 1944, just on the Anzio beachhead breakout. I had a little less than 300 combat days.

The American soldiers that made up the second-front invasion, on June 6, 1944, accumulated one hundred and sixty combat days, including the Battle of the Bulge. These were the soldiers that invaded Europe at Normandy and Omaha Beach. They saw some terrible action, and we lost many fine American boys. Five boys in my original squad were killed by one German artillery shell December 3, 1944. I had entered service with them at Camp McCain. They were my original mortar squad, and I would have been killed with them if I had not been sent to my present division when I was. I still miss these boys and not being able to visit them after the war.

14

Daily Combat Experiences

One day in combat, I was walking past an American soldier stockade's woven wire enclosure where they keep American soldiers who have been court-martialed or were going to be court-martialed soon. I heard someone holler, "Hammil," and I turned to see who it was. It was an old barracks buddy from back in the States while we were stationed at Camp McCain in 1943.

He had refused to go up to the front lines and fight the Germans. Most of the boys in that enclosure were there for the same reason. They had either refused to go or had run and got caught after being up there for a short time.

These American boys were treated horribly, not as well as German soldiers whom we had captured, who were housed in barracks and fed three times a day, or had been shipped back to America and were living a life of luxury in our old army barracks and had very little work to do. The German P.O.W.s at Oran that I had helped guard before coming to Italy had it much better than our own American soldier prisons did. The Germans in Oran had nice wooden barracks with double bunk beds with pillows and blankets. Our American boys lived outside with no building to protect them from snow and rain and cold weather that winter on Montibelmonti. It was usually ten to thirty degrees above zero. Very seldom did it get below zero degrees in that high altitude.

At the American stockade, each prisoner was given a long, wide, flat board and two buckets for his personal use. The six-foot flat board was for him to lay on the ground in the snow and mud to sleep on, with one army blanket to keep him warm for the whole winter. Of the two buckets that he received, one was for his drinking water and food container and the other was his toilet. Both buckets were kept side by side with his sleeping board in his private corner of the enclosed stockade. They received very few cigarettes or army rations. It was a disgusting situation. Their fear of combat and getting killed was no greater than the support troops who were afraid to come to the front and bring us supplies or the soldiers in the States who never went overseas and did not volunteer to.

These soldiers did not have any building to go into to get out of the weather. This was December of 1944 and January and February and March of 1945, a very cold winter with a lot of snow and rain. All of us combat men felt sorry for them, even though we were doing their fighting for them, because we could usually find a cave, a railroad tunnel, or a peasant farmhouse to get in during the worst weather. We also had companionship with our fellow combat soldiers.

These prisoners were thrown one can of C rations a day. That was just barely enough to maintain life. It was possible that these court-martialed soldiers were kept in our plain view to set an example to the rest of us as what to expect if we decided to refuse an order or leave the combat lines to escape to safety. Most court-martialed soldiers automatically received a seventeen-year sentence at the military penitentiary in Fort Leavenworth Kansas, where most of these boys would be headed eventually.

There was a mess hall tent not far from this stockade, as this was the rear command post. There was also a motor pool, chaplain, first aid station, and mail delivery. This was a much better place to be than at the front lines in the snow and foxholes. We envied the soldiers who were stationed there, even though they could be caught in a major German breakthrough, which never happened; the line companies were always in front of them, ever vigilant, watching for any enemy movement. They would give their lives to prevent any breakthrough, and many of our American soldiers did just that on all war fronts during WWII. But the P.O.W.s were not fed in regular chow lines with the other soldiers there, they received their one can of C rations daily.

They would stick out their one gallon can through the wire and beg everybody for food and cigarettes. The last time I was there and saw my friend, the guards were letting them stand at the end of the garbage-can line where the rear command post soldiers dumped the remains of their meals in the garbage cans. These prisoners would stand at the end of the garbage cans and say, "Don't throw that away," "Give that to me." But many of the other regular soldiers would not give them anything because they had refused to go to the front and fight. I thought it quite ironic, because most of these rear echelon soldiers were not and had never been line-company boys, either. No one knows how any soldier will react under fire. He doesn't even know himself. Even though a good experienced combat soldier made a right decision under fire, in the same situation, thirty minutes earlier or later, he might not have made the same decision, even though it might still have been a life-saving incident with another decision.

I still do not think these boys should have been treated that badly. Of the boys back home that joined other branches of service, some went to factories to get military deferment, and others because of their age and family responsibilities, are just as morally guilty as a soldier who went to service and trained for a year for a low salary and away from home, then ended up in a P.O.W. camp at combat; he is still braver than those that I just mentioned.

Before the draft, Dr. Harold Hammil and his brother, Haymond, pose in front of their 1935 and 1936 Fords in Fairfield, Illinois, 1942.

118

Private First Class Harold Hammil at Camp McCain, Mississippi, in 1943.

Private First Class Harold Hammil was stationed in Florence, Italy, in 1944.

PFC. Harold Hammil
Florence, Italy   WWII
135 Reg. 34th Infan
1944   age 21
6 ft. 1 inch , 190 #

```
                The 34th Combat Infantry Division (Red Bull)
                    135 Regiment   3rd Batallion Hq. Co.
                        A.P. Platoon
         WW 11        North Africa and Italy ,  1943, 1944, 1945.

Standing in back row:
Cpl. Joseph Buffalo                              ST. Louis, Mo.
Pfc. Harold C. Hammil        1516 S. 12th St. Lawrenceville, Ill. 62439
Pvt. John (Red) DeHore        541 Laurel St. Ludlow, Ky. 41016
Pfc. Charles Hoffman              upper New York State
Pfc. John Despot           1535 Nelson Ave. Manhattan Beach, Calif. 90266
Pfc. Max L. Rush          City Auto Supply, P.O. Box 187, Camden, S. Carolina
                                                                    29020
Pfc. Phillip Braun       Braun Investments, Inc. Detroit, Michigan
Pvt. James Keane                             Chicago, Ill.
Pvt. Maaß  ——                                North Carolina
Pvt. Bill Zimmerman                          New Jersey

Squatting in front row:
Pvt. Max Rotopel                             Penna.
Pvt. Mike Lipp                               South Dakota
Pfc. Freeman James                           Akron. Ohio
Pvt. James Vulant                            Philladelphia, Pa.
Sgt. Frenchy Dorin                           Rhode Island
Bruno the dog
S/Sgt. Barney Allicson                       Montivedio, Minn.
Pfc. George Loechner                         Elgin, Ill.
Not in picture.
Pfc. Robert Seyl                             Chicago, Ill
Pvt. Red Thompson                            Kentucky
Pvt. Jake Jacoby                             New Jersey
```

Honorable Discharge

This is to certify that

HAROLD C HAMMIL

36640672 PFC HQ CO 3RD BN 135 INF 34TH DIV

Army of the United States

is hereby Honorably Discharged from the military service of the United States of America.

This certificate is awarded as a testimonial of Honest and Faithful Service to this country.

480

Given at   SEPARATION CENTER
CAMP GRANT ILLINOIS

Soldiers & Sailors Discharge Record

Date   ILLINOIS { s.s.11 DECEMBER 1945

Dec. 4th A.D. 1946

Wayne ... nty.

Page 480

This re ... d

on the 28   Dec ...

Recorder   Benj. Goeckler

Scott County Iowa

45 4:00   P ...

4 ... Soldiers & Sailors
Discharge Record.

PAUL J RITCHIE
LT COL INF

37 ...

Recorder

Certificate of Honorable Discharge

ENLISTED RECORD AND REPORT OF SEPARATION
HONORABLE DISCHARGE

1. LAST NAME - FIRST NAME - MIDDLE INITIAL	2. ARMY SERIAL NO.	3. GRADE	4. ARM OR SERVICE	5. COMP
HAMMEL HAROLD C	36 919 672	PFC	INF	AUS

6. ORGANIZATION	7. DATE OF SEPARATION	8. PLACE OF SEPARATION
HQ CO 3RD BN 135 INF 34TH DIV	11 DEC 45	SEPARATION CENTER CAMP GRANT ILLINOIS

9. PERMANENT ADDRESS FOR MAILING PURPOSES	10. DATE OF BIRTH	11. PLACE OF BIRTH
RR 1 GEFF ILL	12 MAY 23	FAIRFIELD ILL

12. ADDRESS FROM WHICH EMPLOYMENT WILL BE SOUGHT	13. COLOR EYES	14. COLOR HAIR	15. HEIGHT	16. WEIGHT	17. NO. DEPEND.
SEE 9	BROWN	BROWN	5 11	180 LBS.	0

18. RACE				19. MARITAL STATUS			20. U.S. CITIZEN	21. CIVILIAN OCCUPATION AND NO.
WHITE	NEGRO	OTHER (specify)	SINGLE	MARRIED	OTHER (specify)	YES	NO	STUDENT HIGH SCHOOL X-02
X			X			X		

MILITARY HISTORY

22. DATE OF INDUCTION	23. DATE OF ENLISTMENT	24. DATE OF ENTRY INTO ACTIVE SERVICE	25. PLACE OF ENTRY INTO SERVICE
10 FEB 43		17 FEB 43	CAMP GRANT ILL

SELECTIVE SERVICE DATA	26. REGISTERED	27. LOCAL S.S. BOARD NO.	28. COUNTY AND STATE	29. HOME ADDRESS AT TIME OF ENTRY INTO SERVICE
	YES	NO			
	X		1	WAYNE CO ILL	RT 4 FAIRFIELD ILL

30. MILITARY OCCUPATIONAL SPECIALTY AND NO.	31. MILITARY QUALIFICATION AND DATE (i.e., Infantry, aviation and marksmanship badges, etc.)
AMMUNITION HANDLER 504	COMBAT INFANTRYMAN BADGE MM W/CARBINE M1

32. BATTLES AND CAMPAIGNS

ROME ARNO NO APENNINES PO VALLEY

33. DECORATIONS AND CITATIONS

3 OVERSEAS SERVICE BARS AMERICAN CAMPAIGN MEDAL EUROPEAN AFRICAN MIDDLE EASTERN RIBBON W/3 BRONZE BATTLE STARS GOOD CONDUCT MEDAL W/CLASP WORLD WAR II VICTORY MEDAL BRONZE STAR MEDAL

34. WOUNDS RECEIVED IN ACTION

NONE

35. LATEST IMMUNIZATION DATES				36.	SERVICE OUTSIDE CONTINENTAL U. S. AND RETURN		
SMALLPOX	TYPHOID	TETANUS	OTHER (specify)	DATE OF DEPARTURE	DESTINATION	DATE OF ARRIVAL
	ST NOV 44	ST FEB 44		25 APR 44	ETO	4 MAY 44

37. TOTAL LENGTH OF SERVICE				38. HIGHEST GRADE HELD			
CONTINENTAL SERVICE		FOREIGN SERVICE			29 NOV 45	USA	4 DEC 45
YEARS	MONTHS	DAYS	YEARS	MONTHS	DAYS		
1	2	15	1	7	10	PFC	

39. PRIOR SERVICE

NONE

40. REASON AND AUTHORITY FOR SEPARATION

CONV OF GOVT RR 1-1 (DEMOBILIZATION) AR 615-365 DTD 15 DEC 44

41. SERVICE SCHOOLS ATTENDED	42.		
AMERICAN LITERATURE 20 HRS INTRO TO PSYCH 20 HRS	EDUCATION (Years)		
BEEF CATTLE 40 HRS PSY OF MARRIAGE 20 HRS (UTC)	8	4	0

PAY DATA VOU 17386

43. LONGEVITY FOR PAY PURPOSES	44. MUSTERING OUT PAY			45. SOLDIER DEPOSITS	46. TRAVEL PAY	47. TOTAL AMOUNT, NAME OF DISBURSING OFFICER
YEARS	MONTHS	DAYS	TOTAL	THIS PAYMENT			
2	10	2	300	100	NONE	17.20	$152.91 G F DOLBEAR CAPT FD

INSURANCE NOTICE

IMPORTANT IF PREMIUM IS NOT PAID WHEN DUE OR WITHIN THIRTY-ONE DAYS THEREAFTER POLICY WILL LAPSE. MAKE CHECKS OR MONEY ORDERS PAYABLE TO THE TREASURER OF THE U. S. AND FORWARD TO COLLECTIONS SUBDIVISION, VETERANS' ADMINISTRATION, WASHINGTON, D. C.

48. KIND OF INSURANCE	49. HOW PAID	50. Effective Date of Allotment of Payments Stops	51. Date of Next Premium Due (One month after 50)	52. PREMIUM DUE EACH MONTH	53. INTENTIONS OF VETERAN TO			
Nat. Serv.	V.S. Govt.	None	Allotment	Direct to V.A.	31 DEC 45	31 JAN 46	.6.50	Continue	Discontinue	Semiannual
X			X					X		

54.	55. REMARKS (This space for completion of above items of entry of other items specified in W. D. Directions)
RIGHT THUMB PRINT	LAPEL BUTTON ISSUED ASR SCORE (2 SEP 45) 63
	INACTIVE STATUS ERC FROM 10 FEB 43 TO 16 FEB 43

56. SIGNATURE OF PERSON BEING SEPARATED	57. PERSONNEL OFFICER (Type name, grade and organization - signature)
Harold C. Hammel	ROBERT O. BURTON CAPT FA

This form supersedes all previous editions of WD AGO Forms 53 and 55 for enlisted persons entitled to an Honorable Discharge, which will not be used after receipt of this revision.

WD AGO FORM 53-55
1 November 1944

Enlisted Record and Report of Separation, Honorable Discharge

WAR DEPARTMENT
THE ADJUTANT GENERAL'S OFFICE
RECORDS ADMINISTRATION CENTER
4300 GOODFELLOW BOULEVARD
ST. LOUIS 20, MISSOURI

IN REPLY REFER TO
AGRS-DA 201 Hammil, Harold C.
36 640 672 (6 Sept 50)

2 October 1950

SUBJECT: Letter Order - Bronze Star Medal

TO: Mr. Harold C. Hammil

         Lawrenceville, Illinois

1. By direction of the President, under the provisions of Executive Order 9419, 4 February 1944 (Sec. II, WD Bul. 3, 1944), you have been awarded the Bronze Star Medal for exemplary conduct in ground combat against the armed enemy on 30 May 1944 in the Mediterranean Theater of Operations, while assigned as Private First Class, 135th Infantry Regiment.

2. Authority for this award is contained in paragraph 15.1e, AR 600-45, as amended, and is based upon General Orders 32, Headquarters 135th Infantry, dated 30 June 1944.

BY ORDER OF THE SECRETARY OF THE ARMY:

W. A. Leary
Adjutant General

Copies Furnished
  D & A Rec Unit Files
  Statistical and Accounting
  201 File

Letter to Dr. Hammil awarding him the Bronze Star Medal for exemplary conduct.

WAR DEPARTMENT
THE ADJUTANT GENERAL'S OFFICE
WASHINGTON 25, D. C.

AGRO-O 201
AGRS-DA 201 Bardil, Harold C.
36 640 672 (6 Sept 50)

*Ammic Revised 17.
5-30-44.*

AUTHORIZATION FOR ISSUANCE OF AWARDS

TO:

COMMANDING GENERAL
PHILADELPHIA QUARTERMASTER DEPOT   Shipping Date: 13 Nov 50
PHILADELPHIA, PENNSYLVANIA

DATE

2 October 1950

CODE NUMBERS FOR AWARDS

1	MEDAL OF HONOR	(11) GOOD CONDUCT MEDAL	(21) EXPERT INFANTRYMAN BADGE	31	MEDAL OF FREEDOM
2	DISTINGUISHED SERVICE CROSS	(12) AMERICAN THEATER RIBBON	22 MEDICAL BADGE	32	ARMY OF OCCUPATION MEDAL W/GERMANY CLASP
3	DISTINGUISHED SERVICE MEDAL	13 ASIATIC-PACIFIC THEATER RIBBON	23 SERVICE STAR	33	ARMY OF OCCUPATION MEDAL W/JAPAN CLASP
4	LEGION OF MERIT	(14) EUROPEAN-AFRICAN-MIDDLE EASTERN THEATER RIBBON	24 OAK LEAF CLUSTER	34	
5	SILVER STAR	15 AMERICAN DEFENSE	25 BRONZE ARROWHEAD	35	
6	DISTINGUISHED FLYING CROSS	(16) WORLD WAR II VICTORY MEDAL	(26) GOOD CONDUCT MEDAL CLASP	36	
7	SOLDIER'S MEDAL	17 WOMAN'S ARMY CORPS	27 FRENCH FOURRAGERE	37	
8	BRONZE STAR MEDAL	18 ARMY OF OCCUPATION OF GERMANY WORLD WAR I	28 BELGIUM FOURRAGERE	38	
9	AIR MEDAL	19 DISTINGUISHED UNIT BADGE	29 BRONZE V AWARD	39	
10	PURPLE HEART	(20) COMBAT INFANTRYMAN BADGE	30 ARMY COMMENDATION RIBBON		

the Army
The Secretary of War directs that the following awards be engraved according to current regulations and issued to address shown below. (*Engraving to be as indicated in classification.*)

AWARD CODE NUMBER	STARS		OAK LEAF CLUSTER		ARROW-HEAD	CLASP
	BRONZE	SILVER	BRONZE	SILVER		
8						
12*						
14*	3					
16						
20						
21						
26						
11						

REMARKS
BSM - DA LO dtd 2 Oct 50

Three (3) Bronze Service Stars for the Rome-Arno, North Apennines and Po Valley Campaigns.

The Bronze Star Medal is based on the Combat Infantryman Badge. A citation in orders for the Combat Infantryman Badge awarded for actual combat against the armed enemy is considered as a citation for exemplary conduct in ground combat and entitles the recipient to the Bronze Star Medal.

3 Incls
1. DA LO dtd 2 Oct 50
2. BSM Certificate
3. Photo Cy Disch Cert

W. A. Leary
ADJUTANT GENERAL

MC

Mr. Harold C. Bardil
1103 CEDAR St.
Lawrenceville, Illinois
62439

War Department's Authorization for Issuance of Awards

Dr. Hammil at age 79 in 2003.

In America, we understand that we were all born equal. Try telling that to a draftee who has been in combat. I say that the only time that you are equal is as soon as you die, then you are equal before the eyes of God and He will be the judge. He is much fairer than the local draft board.

The Army and Navy say, "Older men, past the age of twenty-five, will not obey an order as quickly as a younger boy will. The older soldier will question an order in combat if it is dangerous or some soldier might get killed. A young soldier will obey a suicide order immediately and go after it 'gung ho.' " That is what we have to have during a war. We know that some are going to get killed, and every order that a soldier's superior gives to him is not always the best order under all circumstances, but it must be obeyed anyway. This is why we have to have the young boys up front and the older, married men in a support position. A combat soldier has about an 85% chance to return from each patrol.

General Patton was probably the one general that risked his infantry soldiers with the least respect for their life than any general that we had in WWII. He believed in victory at any cost to his line-company infantry soldiers. The Battle of the Bulge is referred to as "Patton's folly." History will never rate him as a great general. He did everything in military history to make himself a great general, but he made too many strategic military mistakes. He was the only general in WWII who had two photographers follow him all day and photograph everything important that he did. He also had two newspaper reporters follow him around all day and write down everything intelligent that he said that day. That evening, they would all get together and select which picture and which quotes they wanted sent to the presses.

He was over our division and the Fifth Army in North Africa, Sicily, and up into the battle for Naples, Italy, when he was relieved of his command by other generals who were also in that campaign. He was sent back to the U.S. to take training as an armored tank commander at Fort Campbell, Kentucky.

Gen. George S. Patton graduated from West Point during WWI and served as a second lieutenant under Gen. John "Black Jack" Pershing, our commanding general in France during WWI. He sent word back to the States, in 1917 and 1918 that this young, brash lieutenant was giving him some problems. He was a personal friend of Franklin Delano Roosevelt, who bailed him out of many army and political mistakes that he made. Roosevelt kept Patton from being kicked out of West Point because of having the lowest grades in his class and being a prankster at school. Franklin Roosevelt was supposed to have said, "George, you have messed up every job that I have given you. You have failed as a cavalry officer, you have failed as an infantry officer, and now this is your last chance as armored tank commander. Please don't mess this up, because it is your last chance."

During the battle of Naples, while the Germans were shooting at the American troops in street fighting, General Patton made the American infantrymen march three abreast as if on parade. He said, "I will court-martial or shoot any soldier who breaks ranks to fight the enemy. March, and at least look like soldiers." That was when the other generals relieved him of his command and threatened to kill him if he did not resign as their Allied commander. He was replaced by Gen. Mark Clark, whom we all liked. He was more conservative with his orders, so consequently, we did not lose as many men. His orders were not as risky. He had the lives of his men at heart. There was never any criticism or publicity about General Clark. He had a son by the same name later on in the army as general. They are all deceased now: Generals George S. Patton, Mark Clark, and Mark Clark II.

In a field near where I blew the potatoes out by detonating a mine, we came across a lone German soldier lying on his back in an open field with no one near him. He was a large and tall well-built soldier, but the peculiar thing about him was the fact that he made no effort to move when he came near me. He just lay there on his back in the sun, picking flies off one of his eyeballs, which was out of its normal socket and hanging a couple of inches down on his left cheek. He could see all right because as soon as a fly would light on the watery eyeball, he would take his finger and flick it off. I never could tell whether he could see the flies with his other good eye or with the damaged eyeball out of its socket.

He would not take food or water from us. Neither would he even recognize that we were there. He never spoke or moved, just flicked flies off his bad eye. We left him there after about half an hour of trying to help him but to no avail, he was too proud to accept help.

Two or three days later, we saw some soldiers coming from that direction. We asked the if they saw a German soldier lying on the ground with one eyeball out, picking flies off it. They said yes, but he would not let them help him. He just kept picking flies off his eyeball. "We left him some water, but he would not drink it. I think that the medic will pick him up and take him to the hospital and take care of him." That was the last we heard of him. But I am sure that the medics took care of him and that he was taken prisoner and eventually made it home. I hope so. I think that he was partly in shock and very disillusioned with the German empire at this time in his life, as they were retreating very fast back toward Germany, instead of advancing toward us to indicate victory for them.

One morning while we were in rest in the early part of the summer of 1944, I got up one morning, and I was very sick from something but never found out what it was: possibly nerves, homesickness, and combat brought together at one time. Anyway, I told my sergeant, "I'm sick, possibly the flu, and I need to go to the hospital."

"Hammil," my sergeant replied, "go and report to the local aid station," which I did. In a couple of hours, I was put in a small ambulance with a row of seats on each side.

As I got into the ambulance, I saw a young German soldier sitting on one side of the ambulance, so I immediately sat on the other side, on a long, narrow bench built onto it. As I sat down, this young German soldier boy kept looking at me and grinning. He was younger than I by about two years. He was possibly seventeen or eighteen years old. I had just turned twenty-one a few months before, on May 12, 1944.

I could see by his dirty uniform that he was a line-company soldier and had been wounded in combat against the American and Allied Forces. I would not look at him. He was the bitter enemy that we were here to kill to prevent the forming of the Third Reich in our world.

However, I did look at him long enough to see him pointing to his throat, which had a large white bandage wrapped around it. He kept looking at me and pointing to his bandage then to his mouth and shaking his head no. It was then that I realized that he was trying to tell me that he had been shot through the throat, and it had damaged his larynx and vocal cords, and he was unable to talk, probably would never speak again for the rest of his life. But in some ways, he was lucky because now he had a free ticket home with a small pension for the rest of his life, with his doctor bills paid also if related to this condition.

It looked to me as though an American rifle bullet had entered his throat from the side and just went through his Adams apple. A bullet through there usually causes enough damage to the throat muscles that it destroys the throat muscles and vocal cords forever.

I did not smile at him, as I had just been in combat a few months and was still full of the American gung-ho attitude that is supposed to be instilled in us young American boys so we will go all out to "go get them, kill them."

I sat there, wondering why a German prisoner would be allowed alone in an ambulance "for a couple of hours ride," like this trip back to the hospital, without having an M.P. here with him or at least have him handcuffed; after all, he was a prisoner of war. But there was just the two of us alone in the back of the ambulance. I could not speak his language, and because of his throat injury, he could not speak a word and in all probability never would speak again.

But as we both unloaded at the tent-city hospital in the rear zone, he looked at me and smiled, but I never looked at him nor did I ever smile at him. We were just two strangers, two similar boys caught up in a war that we didn't like, both wishing that it was over and we could safely go home where we belonged in our own country to our own family and loved ones. I'm sure that he made it home as a P.O.W. I surely hope so. I would speak and wave to him now if I saw him again. I was in the hospital for two days, then back to the front.

Another time, we got a call that a lone German in a town that we had liberated a few weeks before was coming up out of a deep cellar and shooting one Italian civilian each night. He would go back down into this cave and wait until the next night and come up and shoot another civilian.

We had fought into that town a few weeks before and had

stayed there in a cellar in town for a few days, so we knew that town pretty well.

Some unknown officer told us to "post a guard there and shoot him when he came out at night to shoot another civilian."

Our Sergeant Blake said, "We don't have enough time to wait here for just one soldier. I'll fix him for good." So he put about two pounds of dynamite on the end of a long, wide board with about a five-second fuse on it, lit it, and shoved the board and dynamite down into the hole in the cave. Very soon, the ground under us shook with a tremendous boom.

The explosion had caved in the ground above the hole, and it totally collapsed. That German sniper was buried with full military honors because he went as he wished, dying for his country. He could have come out of hiding and surrendered anytime that he wanted to. We then proceeded, in our truck, to another destination nearby. Some of the soldiers in our platoon saluted the caved-in grave and said, "Another good German. The only German that is good is a dead German."

15

Entering Florence

Many of the tricks that we have seen in our Western movies worked in actual combat during the heavy fighting. The old trick of putting your helmet on the end of your rifle barrel, then sticking it out from your cover behind a building to draw the enemy rifle fire usually worked. This way, we could find out where the enemy was hiding.

Throwing rocks against a building across the street or some distant point would often get the enemy to fire at that position and also reveal their position.

Another dangerous thing that we often had to do was go from one hiding place to another hiding place as we would have to advance or to improve our position when we were under machine gun fire and there was no way that we could change our protective cover without being seen by the enemy.

So one of us would quickly expose himself then duck back to safety before a machine gun could swing into position and possibly hit us. Then the other soldier across the way would expose himself the same way, then jump back quickly before he could be hit. All the while, another soldier would be counting the seconds on his wristwatch to see how many seconds it took for the enemy machine-gunner to swing from one of our positions to another. The soldier with the watch would usually say, "It took that gunner seven seconds to swing from one position to the other. If we expose ourselves here, do you think that you can make it in less than seven seconds?" If he says yes, we proceed with our plan. If he says no, we have to wait until someone else knocks out the German machine gun nest or wait until dark to make our move. Often he would say, "I can make it if I run fast and then dive into that safe place." We may or may not discourage him from trying this.

A brave scared fighting soldier is not a coward. A coward refuses to obey an order in the heat of battle or runs away to avoid it.

One time, in the foothills, we walked into an old barn and saw an American soldier sitting on a pile of hay. He was all bent over, tying his bootstrings, but he did not move when we entered the barn. I went over to see what was wrong with him and saw there a large wooden beam lying across the back of his head and neck. His face and hands were completely black and blue. The large wooden beam had evidently been knocked loose from the ceiling and had broken his neck, killing him instantly. Black-and-blue skin is usually indicative of suffocation or lack of oxygen. I am not sure that he was tying his boots, but both hands were dangling beside them. He had not been dead long, as the saliva from his mouth was still running down his leg, his head resting on his right knee.

I did not know him, but I am sure that he was just another great young American boy that gave his life for us. God bless him and every person who was killed or injured in any war for America. I was never injured in WWII. I later on received the Bronze Star and had previously refused to accept the Silver Star just off Anzio on Bloody Gulch. I sure wish that we had accepted that Silver Star. It would have made our parents at home so very proud of us. I regret the refusal very much.

War is hell for a few people and their immediate family. It is very fortunate for most people in America that they do not know what real war is like. That is why we prefer to go overseas to fight and kill, so that America and all its citizens will never know the real ravages of war. If we had a real war here in America, maybe everyone would appreciate a combat veteran more. We have done the American people a great favor, but they don't acknowledge it to our face.

During basic training, we were told that the only way we could get out of the infantry was to volunteer for the paratroops at Ft. Benning, Georgia. We had one boy in my company who volunteered for it. He took all the tests and passed. I never saw him again.

I thought about it, but since I had never flown in an airplane and I was deathly afraid of heights, I had better stay where I was and take my chances of coming back some day, alive, in the infantry.

135

To the personnel in the army that say, "I just took the job they gave me, I would have liked to have been in combat." I always tell them that "due to the heavy losses in the infantry, all branches of service asked for and took volunteers to go into combat. All they had to do was sign up." Most infantry and other combat units fought at one-half to two-thirds strength most of the time and would have welcomed any new replacements. But they were few and far between, especially after the second front opened on June 6, 1944. Personnel, ammunition, and food was directed to General Patton's army. Our forgotten front was put on short rations, yet we had to continue the Italian campaign, fighting the Germans without any other military help for over a year. Yes, our campaign was called "the forgotten front." But try to tell that to the families of 25,000 boys who were killed in Italy, or of the many times that many young boys who were wounded, crippled, shot up, and have nervous problems for the rest of their lives.

Yes, it is the forgotten front to everyone except the poor, unfortunate boys who were there and their families. God bless every boy who has ever been in combat. You will never know what he had gone through and is still remembering and reliving most of these horrible experiences that only actual combat will stay with him for the rest of his life.

I hate the war for what it did to so many combat men. It did not affect the support troops very badly and the boys who got to stay in the States, they did not know the hazards of the war, just the few inconveniences. They could have joined our company and platoon anytime, as we were always short of good men to go to the front with a rifle.

It gave me the chance to meet the finest boys under pressure that I will ever know. They thought nothing of risking their lives two or three times a day for two or three years at a time. And the boys that died—people of America knew very few of their names, except for the ones related to them or a few in their hometown. What a pity! I often wonder if the boys who were killed on the battlefields of any war would be as proud of America now as they were the instant that they were killed? I often wonder about this.

I have had people tell me, "How could you do those things in battle? We do not believe in killing. We are Christians." Nothing makes me any madder than to hear that statement. I and all who were in battle hate war more than they do. But we have the guts to do something about it. No one is any more of a Christian than I was or any other boy that had the fortitude to save his country, family and loved ones from foreign tyranny, slavery, hardship, and death camps than we who do not believe in war but will defend it with our lives. Don't ever tell a combat survivor that you do not believe in war!

When I was drafted, I had two career choices that I wanted to accomplish when I grew up. I wanted to be either an agriculture teacher in high school or go to St. Louis Christian Bible School and be a minister of the First Christian Church. I did not do either.

No one can be an expert at something that they haven't done.

The draft changed all my life's plans, as it did the millions of other young people who served their country. I am not sorry or bitter about that.

They say that "all is fair in love and war." I should know, as I have over two hundred combat days in WWII, and my fiancée sent me a Dear John letter while I was over there on Montibelmonti in the winter of 1944. So I think that I qualify as an expert on both.

I feel sorry for the jilted boys. I also feel sorry for the girls, as I don't think that it is possible to ever get over a wartime romance. There is always something different and mysterious about it that you will never know or forget. You are young only once, and if you get to live it right, once is enough. Unfortunately, my generation did not have a teenage fling; neither did the WWI or Vietnam veterans. It was out of high school, into a uniform, and overseas. If you made it back home, it was a new commercial America that you did not know.

We saved the world from tyranny from two different sources, but nobody remembers that now, fifty to sixty years later. But why should they? Over sixty percent of the world was not even born in 1945 when WWII was over.

Khrushchev, the Russian Premier said in late 1955, that when we stopped their land and country acquisition in North and South Korea, Russia knew that Communism would have a hard time spreading to other countries, and "when you stopped us in Vietnam, we knew that Communism was defeated." Khrushchev, made those statements in Washington, D.C. while he was winding up his career in Russia. I wish all Korean and Vietnam veterans knew this

137

so that they would feel much better about their time over there. They should be able to feel as proud of their war and proud of themselves as we WWII veterans do. Their war was a just war also. Their combat troops went through the same life and death hazards as we did, without much sleep and food and with the terrible jungle heat and insects.

Our line companies, along with the British 8th Army accompanied by their New Zealand soldiers, called Kiwis (named after their local flightless, roadrunner bird), were the first and probably the largest element of soldiers to enter Florence the first day or two. Our American boys, the 5th Army, were clearing the rural countryside of Germans. We reached Rome first, but I think that some agreement was made to let the English 8th Army enter Florence first. That was all right with us, as that meant they would have some of the heavier fighting to enter the city.

The very deep, cold, and swift Arno River runs directly through Florence. It was a natural barrier for troops to cross. The Germans had bulldozed many famous old buildings and put the piles of rubble across the only few roads and bridges crossing the Arno River. So the original infantrymen had to cross on a water control dam, about two hundred feet below one of the famous old bridges built around 1400 A.D. The bridge, the Ponte Vecchio, was suspected of being booby trapped, and was a perfect spot for an ambush, so they did not attempt to cross it. The combat troops walked across the moss-covered, concrete dam.

This dam was a few hundred years old, so there was a deep layer of green moss growing on it. As some of the first boys tried to walk across it, their feet slipped on the moss, and they fell into the deep, cold Arno River and drowned. They soon learned to put one foot on the concrete and scrape the moss off at each step before taking the next step. Very slow and dangerous work, but at least they would stay alive for a short while longer. About 4,000 boys were killed either entering or around Florence. Their graves are still there to see.

The site of the 4,000 graves of these brave combat soldiers is probably the least visited by American tourists when they visit Florence.

Florence, Rome, Pisa, Milan, and a few other cities were declared "open city" (cittá aperta) which meant that both sides in WWII, America and Germany, had agreed not to bomb certain cities because of their historical importance. This was adhered to pretty well except for some bombing and combat around the edges of these cities so as not to destroy the main architectural structures that were mostly in their centers. However some destruction of some famous buildings did occur by bombing and shelling from both sides.

While they were fighting and trying to enter the main part of the city, the Germans pulled on us one of their smartest tricks of all. I still admire it. As our boys were trying to cross the Arno River to enter the main part of town, all hell would break loose from the German side of the river bank. Machine gun and rifle power would come down on our boys like we seldom heard except on a major attack or counterattack. The sounds were fierce, coming from all the buildings, their windows and doors.

The sounds were so intense that our boys and the 8th Army boys had to retreat and seek cover and wait until the firing would lessen before attempting another crossing over the moss-covered concrete dam. This took a few hours. This was before the American bulldozers could get to the city and clear out the debris that the Germans had put there to slow up the Allies' advance. And it worked for them very well. Our boys were just trying to stay alive without letting the Germans get too far ahead and get to dug in for another static position that would require our boys to be in great danger during our entrance to Florence.

A few of our soldiers finally made it across the Arno River and to their surprise, there were only two or three German soldiers over there, and they had loud speakers set up at all of the doors and windows of most of the Italian houses, and when our boys would start an attack, they would open up with one burp gun in front of a microphone so as to make it sound like there was a whole company of one hundred or more German soldiers there firing at them. And it worked, our boys all felt very sheepish about the incident, that they had been fooled by, but at the same time, they all admired the ingenuity of it all. It was very smart and it worked for a while.

This allowed the enemy to leave Florence and head to the foothills of the Alps for another strong defensive position. We then moved most of the Allied forces offices into Florence. It was again the bustling city that it had been for hundreds of years. When the war was over, we had seven months of occupation duty before our points system came to our number. I was then transferred to Florence. I attended the university there for one semester and played on the all-Fifth Army football team there that won the Spaghetti Bowl in 1945 in Florence.

My stay in Florence after the war was about the only time that I got to really enjoy Italy. And I did enjoy it to the best of my ability, as I knew that I would probably never return, and I haven't. But I would like to. I ended up loving Italy and their friendly people, who helped us so much during the combat days.

I would love to return to Italy with one of my buddies who was with me during that terrible war. I would love that.

I was in Florence (Firenze, flowers) twice during the war, for two days each time. There was a large railroad station there, Station Central. I lived there four months while attending the university. The U.S. Army had set up a kitchen there and sleeping room with bare army cots for servicemen.

Since Florence was founded about 1000 or 1100 A.D. and many of those buildings were still standing, there wasn't any place to run a new railroad through the town without destroying these ancient, historic and religious buildings. They had to run the railroad tracks into the edge of town, then back them up a few miles, and go around the town so as to preserve all of this great city.

I would personally love to live in Florence during the three winter months each year then come back to America for the remaining nine months. I like the people of Italy, and none of us G.I.s were ever mistreated by the Italian people the two years that we were there. We tried not to mistreat them. We always shared our food, cigarettes, and whatever else we had. And we loved their young Italian signorinas, and they liked us. I have many fond memories of a few young signorinas.

There was a Hollywood movie made in 1965, *Von Ryan's Express*. Many of their scenes were shot directly in front of my room at the General Station. I recognized a few of the railroad tunnels and countryside that I had fought through during the war. It was sad for me to relive some incidents as I viewed the movie. I have seen it three times. It is fairly typical of WWII.

During the war years, the military needed gold for many of

their precision parts, but Italy had very little gold reserve. So their dictator, Benito Mussolini, ordered all civilians, male and female, to turn in all their gold wedding rings in exchange for steel ones. This was to show their patriotism and for the war cause. If they did not turn all their gold rings in, they would be imprisoned and fined.

After the war, the well-to-do civilians wished to buy gold rings any way possible. I had my mother buy me four wide-band gold rings in the States and mail them to me. In America, each ring cost about eight dollars. When I received them in Italy, I sold them for thirty-five dollars each. If I was going to stay over there longer, I would have bought and sold more rings. But it was getting close to my time to return home and I did not have my mother send me any more rings. However, there was a good market for them.

When Gen. Mark Clark took over command of the 5th Army, after General Patton was relieved of the duty, he changed the way our infantry troops fought on the line. General Patton was always seeking glory for himself. He was reckless with his decisions and did not consider the lives of the men under him. He believed in taking a town or a mountain regardless of how many men he would lose. Once, in Germany, he made this statement: "I just lost eight armored tanks. Send me twenty thousand more men."

Gen. Mark Clark was just the opposite. He moved a little slower, but he had the safety of his men at heart at all times. He never advanced at one weak spot of the enemy's. He always moved the complete lines at one time, along a straight borderline front. In the Battle of the Bulge, General Patton advanced his men at a weak spot that the Germans left open on purpose for him to penetrate deep into their territory. Then they closed in on him with their elite panzer divisions numbering about three hundred thousand soldiers, with their artillery, armored tanks, mortars, and burp guns. The battle lasted about forty-five days with a terrific loss to both sides.

From my original infantry division at Camp McCain, I lost five who I went into service with. I was the jeep driver for the squad then, and the soldier that took my place was killed with these five young boys. I had trained with them for about a year. My original sergeant that was killed with these boys and I were going to have a double wedding while we were both stationed at Fort Jackson, Columbia, South Carolina. However, I was sent overseas before I could make the wedding arrangements. This turned out okay though. My fiancée could not wait to get married. She married a younger boy from my hometown, and I got the traditional *Dear John* letter while I was going into combat on Montibelmonti. She is deceased now, I never saw her again, even though she lived in my hometown. Her young husband had to eventually go into service. He went overseas about the time that I was discharged at Camp Grant, Illinois, near Rockford, December, 11, 1945.

The reason that General Patton was fooled into making that point advance in the German army in January 1945 was that for weeks, the German Army had been sending young soldiers to be near General Patton's soldiers so that they would get caught and give out the wrong information as to the condition of the Germans: low morale, false troop movements, poor food conditions, lack of gasoline, troops about to mutiny and surrender, among many other lies that General Patton took in as truth. He said, "Now is the time that I have been waiting for. Let's attack now." And he did attack now, only to be met by the finest divisions in WWII. It was a sucker's bait, and General Patton took it all in.

Instead of advancing all his troops together in one line, he sent a few divisions ahead without any backup combat troops to supply them. The Germans circled his troops and slaughtered them. We Americans eventually won, but I have never heard how many American troops were killed and wounded. This is why today, in history, the Battle of the Bulge is called "Patton's Folly." History will never rate General Patton as a great general. He is now regarded to have been a risky and publicity-seeking general. In 1916–17–18, during WWI, Gen. Johnny "Black Jack" Pershing, who was the head of the American forces in France, once said, "I have a brash young lieutenant just out of West Point that is giving me some problems."

Gen. George S. Patton was also known as "Old Blood and Guts." It was your blood and his guts. He died of a broken neck from a severe automobile accident in December 1945. He was still overseas in Europe at the time.

Just a few days after Florence was liberated by the English Eighth Army and the American Fifth Army under Gen. Mark Clark, the Italian civilians seemed to have returned to normal living very quickly. They had been under Nazi domination for five years, and the new-found freedom under the Allies was very easy for them to take.

As I was walking around the streets of Florence looking at the famous statues and churches, I noticed a crowd of Italian civilians standing and watching the M.P. who was directing traffic at a busy intersection. So I went over to this crowd. I asked, in Italian, "What's happening?"

"That American M.P.," a woman said to me, "put something in his mouth about one hour ago, and he has been chewing on it ever since. What in the world could he be chewing that long and not swallowing?"

So I told her it was chewing gum. I took a few pieces out of my pocket and gave her one and showed her how to chew it without swallowing it.

Now everyone in the crowd wanted a piece of *goma* (gum). I gave them all I had, which was not enough to go around for everyone to get a piece. Chewing gum was unknown in Italy and other foreign countries under German rule at this time, because America had ceased all trade agreements with them. These countries also did not have sugar, chocolate, perfumed soap, first aid equipment, white flour, candy, and many other common items that they considered luxuries. But to us Americans, it was just routine living items. There was also a great shortage of meat and milk.

The next day, another woman who was watching the M.P. chew gum came up and spoke to me. "My little six-year-old boy was chewing goma, and he swallowed it. Will his insides stick together, and should I take him to the hospital?"

"No, this is normal and safe," I said. "The goma will be digested like all other food. There's no reason to take him to the hospital. Just give him another piece of goma if you have it. I have swallowed my goma many times with no bad results."

With this explanation, she left a very happy mother. I never saw her again.

In a few weeks in Florence, chewing gum was one of the major items that they would beg you for along with cigarettes and chocolate.

Every G.I. on leave in Italy was required to carry three American condoms with him at all times. If he did not find a *signorina della strada* (girl of the street), he could always sell them to almost any Italian man for seventy-five cents so that he could get some extra vino money. There was a very big black market for condoms, even in this Catholic country. Italy is ninety-eight percent Catholic and two percent Protestant.

The street price for a brief romantic encounter was two dollars cash up front or a package of cigarettes. If you went with the same girl for awhile and promised to take her to America, and gave her your real name, "Sgt. Joe Blow, Chicago, Illinois," he could get plenty of free love. I am sure this was done many times during our occupation.

After we captured Florence and Barbarinno we were starting to get into the foothills of the Alps. Still on flat plains, but we were beginning to find a large hill or small mountain in front of us. The Germans always took the hills and mountaintops for their advantage to stand and stop retreating and put up a strong resistance. That left us the low ground. They were always looking down at us, which gave them a distinct advantage, as they could see us very easily. It is much easier to shoot down at your enemy than it is to shoot up at them, as was at Anzio.

In any attack that we Americans made to advance on the enemy, they could see us come down a mountainside that we had just captured, then we would have to walk across the valley between the two mountains, then fight our way up the next mountain to get to them. One time in the foothills, the Germans burned off the grass in the valley between two mountains so that they could see where our footprints were that we made the night before in our attempt to sneak up on them in the early morning hours. Our boot prints were very visible from walking on the black-charred grass as it was a dead giveaway—sorry for the pun.

No matter how many mountains we captured, there was always another mountain to climb and capture. Italy never ran out of mountains with the Germans shooting down at us, every day since the Anzio beachhead January 22, 1944. The morale of the boys who had been there a long time was very low, as we did not have any entertainment, newspapers, or radios, and mail was not dependable. I did not get my first six-month's mail until after being over there for about two years. Most boys would get a large stack of mail after six months of being settled. Maybe I didn't get any mail. Surely someone must have written me.

Some of the more hardened soldiers who had a great distaste for the Germans for causing this war became very bitter toward the enemy and were very tough combat men. I heard stories from some of them about seeing a German soldier trying to escape up a mountainside by scrambling among the rocks and shrubbery. The American soldier would fire his rifle to the right of the German, which would make him crawl to the left. Then he would shoot to the left, always missing him on purpose, and the German would go to the right. This continued until the German soldier would just about make it to the top of the mountain, encouraged that he was going to make it back to his outfit alive. The American soldier would take dead aim with his M-1 rifle and plug the German between the shoulder blades. The dead German would then roll all the way back down the mountain that he had just climbed in such a hurry to save his life. Some of the American soldiers were entertained by this, in North Africa and Sicily also. Personally, I did not like to hear those stories. But war is war, and somebody has to do it.

Those dead Germans were always good for a lot of souvenirs to mail home if you could get your package past the quartermaster boys in the rear, who checked your mail and usually repackaged your combat souvenirs and sent them home to their families. We had a lot of problems getting good, valuable souvenirs home through the quartermaster units. We had to disguise the article in the package to try and slip past them. They sent home more combat articles than did the combat troops that risked their lives when getting them. There was no way that we could trust them.

To lose an American soldier on these mountainsides or at the top of these mountains often meant having to carry him back down the mountainside with just two soldiers to a stretcher. Carrying a dead soldier down a steep mountainside among the rocks and shrubbery was a very dangerous and difficult task.

Their arms felt like they were being pulled out of their shoulder sockets. It was very painful because it took about an hour and a half or two hours to get to the bottom of that mountain.

Often, while they were carrying the dead soldier, a German airplane would fly over and, with a machine gun, strafe us, so the best thing was to lie on the ground and pull the dead G.I. and stretcher on top of them to shield themselves as much as possible. That's very little protection, but at least they did what they could under the circumstances. Many times, the dead American soldier had been in the hot Italian summer sun a few days, and the flies had already blown him full of eggs that were hatched into maggots and were crawling out of his mouth, ears, and eyes and traveling up and down through his arteries and veins, eating the rotten coagulated blood of a once young, handsome, brave boy who might have lived next door to you. Maggots will eat only dead flesh.

Meanwhile, when you were lying under the dead body, the maggots have now crawled on you, and you have to stand up as soon as the airplane passed and shake those disgusting maggots off yourself. Then they would probably vomit at least twice and then carry the dead soldier down to the bottom of the mountain so that the graves registration office soldiers could pick him up and put the body in a truck to be taken back somewhere, I don't know where.

After a few days of carrying the dead, gallant soldiers back down the mountains, we decided to work out a change. One soldier would ask, "Is he dead?" One of the other soldiers would say "He's dead and cannot get any deader."

We would then carry the body to the edge of the cliff, where we had clear view of the ground below, and we would let him drop all the way down. We were able then to walk back down that mountain empty-handed. Of course, we had to be always on the lookout for German stragglers or deserters, and so, had to have our rifles ready to fire even when we were carrying the bodies down all the way.

In the front lines, we never knew one minute to the next who will be the next dead, stinking, soldier left on the mountain. It could very easily be us or the buddy that is helping to carry the unfortunate ones down the mountainside. When we threw a dead soldier over the mountain cliff, we did not mean it as an act of disrespect. We were trying to save our strength, because, in combat, a soldier never knew when he must fight for his life. And no combat man wanted to be a burden on another in time of war. We knew that this dead soldier would not mind this kind of treatment, because we would expect the same type of treatment if our positions were reversed. We also prayed for our fallen comrades while we were car-

146

rying them. We also learned not to look over the cliff right after we threw the body over. It was very easy to get splashed with the decomposed flesh and blood and the ever-present blowfly maggots.

16

A Drunk German Officer

One bright sunny afternoon in the winter on Montibelmonti, we were sent on a search-and-find patrol, and we found an abandoned cave in the mountainside, a place of refuge. There were about four or five of us boys who usually made the more dangerous missions and were sent out on this detail. We were in no man's land, as close to the enemy as you get without being in their lines. Actually there are no designated lines and don't belong to either unless one side wants to take it and start a small offensive.

We would have one G.I. stand guard at the entrance to the cave for two hours. Then he would get his relief guard while the rest of us just lay around in the cave, talking and waiting for anything that might happen. There was no time in your duty on the lines that you are completely relaxed and away from your rifle. It is always in your hands or by your side within easy reach. Pfc. John "Buddy" Despot was on guard first at the mouth of the cave. Suddenly he whispered back to us that there was a German coming up the path toward us with his hands over his head, as if he wants to surrender. So we all grabbed our rifles and headed toward the mouth of the cave, expecting some trouble immediately, because he could be a decoy to set us up some way.

"I want to surrender," the German said, but he had not complied with the Geneva Convention rules of surrender. When a soldier wishes to surrender, he must first remove his steel helmet, his cartridge belt with all ammunition, his weapons, and then put his hands behind his head. This soldier had not done any of this except put his hands behind his head and walk toward us. I immediately suspected a trap, that there were other German soldiers waiting to ambush and kill us. But as it turned out, there were no other soldiers involved.

Our platoon soldiers on that search-and-find mission were Pfc. John Despot, Cpl. Joe Buffalo, Cpl. Phillip Braun, and Cpl. Max Rush.

As soon as he got to Pfc. John Despot, with his hands still behind his helmet, he immediately pulled his steel helmet from his head and hit John in the face with it. We all then jumped on him and wrestled him to the ground and held him there while we disarmed him and removed the necessary equipment from him to make him a legal prisoner.

It turned out that he was a German colonel, and after drinking quite a bit of Italian vino, he decided to surrender to us Americans and get it over with. He did not try to shoot us and was fairly cooperative after we subdued him and had him safely bound. We took him back to our battalion headquarters for interrogation. We never heard what information they got out of him.

After we stripped him of his military gear, we divided it up among us as souvenirs. I ended up with his German twenty-seven caliber pistol, holster, and two magazines with eight live bullets. I got an ordnance permit to bring it to the States. I still have it all intact and never fired it. The leather holster has four swastikas on it. It is in the same condition as the day we captured him. It is a beautiful pistol without a scratch on it.

After the war was over and we were headed home, each G.I. was allowed one ordnance piece, usually a souvenir pistol, to bring home, but you had to get a government permit with the serial number in triplicate. I still have my permits also. But no shells or anything explosive was allowed. I put my shells in my pants pocket and was not personally searched. Only our barracks bags were searched. I still have the shells, but I keep them separated from the pistol for safety in my own home.

17

A Winter on Montibelmonti

On Christmas of 1944, we were just off third base on that winding road leading up to Montibelmonti, Cpl. Phillip Braun and I decided to have a drink that night. We had been standing guard duty part of the day a couple hundred feet from each other. I had some hard candy in my jacket pocket, he had some cognac, and we had water in our canteens, so we had all the mixings for a strong Christmas drink. We were in reserve three or four miles back, in case of an attack.

So we fixed each other two or three of these cognacs mixed with water until it was getting late. I decided to walk him to his place a couple hundred yards away. We slipped and fell down a few times in the snow while getting to his bunk. Then he decided to walk me back home to my bunk, and we fell down a few times getting to my bunk, but we didn't feel a thing then, because cognac makes a very good tranquilizer or sedative.

After seeing each other home a few times, we finally split and went to our respective beds. But the next morning when I woke up, my Lord, was I sore! My elbows, and entire body, were black and blue. I either fell down many times or that Italian cognac turned my body black and blue.

In combat, you soon learn not to take a drink if you are going on patrol. Neither will you ever take a drink of wine or alcohol while you are in a combat situation, because it will cause you to lose what little nerve you have left. You will be scared to death and endanger the lives of other American boys if you take alcohol in the foxhole or in any combat. It will greatly affect your effectiveness in regard to thinking and your reflexes while in a dangerous situation that could involve a few other soldiers besides yourself.

That same Christmas week, we decided to have a Christmas

tree, as we were still in reserve a few miles back of the line company front, expecting a German counterattack any day that winter. We were to be sent to reinforce the front at the major attack point.

There were plenty of those little firs that we have here in America, so we dug one up and put it in front of our quarters and started to decorate it. First we used colored paper and ribbons that came on some of the packages that the boys got from home. Then we dyed some condoms with printers' ink that we had found. We blew the condoms up like balloons and tied them to the tree's limbs. That gave it more color. Some of the other companies' boys came by and made fun of it, but we thought it was about the prettiest and sexiest Christmas tree that we had ever seen.

Of our fine and brave sergeant, I cannot say enough things about him because he was one of the finest men that I ever knew. He said, "We are not going to stay out here in the cold snow Christmas day. Since we are not on the front lines and not needed right now, let's go to town." He could have been court-martialed for that, but he always had the comfort and safety of the boys at heart. God bless him, S. Sgt. Barney Allickson.

The rear troops were having a turkey dinner with all the trimmings, and our sergeant put us right in there with them. I also had a fruitcake from home that my aunt had sent me. We stayed in a nice warm barn all night, and the next day, they took us by truck back to our outposts, where we had our beautiful Christmas tree still standing and welcoming us back. It was a great and enjoyable break in our combat days. I will always remember that Christmas.

I think of it quite often. I will never see these wonderful soldier boys again. This is very sad for me. All Christmas days are sad for me.

Most of the boys in the infantry were young teenagers. Most of them, in WWII, made a low grade on their written examination the first day they were inducted into the service. Most of them who made a grade of one hundred and twenty or less were automatically slated for the high-risk infantry. The infantry had eighty to eighty-seven percent of all the deaths in WWI and WWII. The U.S. government said that, "if we have to lose our young boys, let's not lose our brains. Put the low I.Q. boys in a high-risk service, and put the ones who make over one hundred twenty some place where their brains can be used. If we have ones with a high I.Q., let's put them in a training program, where they will be safe, as we will need them to lead America in the future." The United States government may deny this, but I will challenge them to disprove it.

Many of the young boys in my infantry division were so young that they had never had a date with a girl before being drafted. Neither had many of them ever shaved, voted, had an alcoholic drink, or driven an automobile. Many of these boys were killed in action before they had ever experienced any of those that the other boys who were in branches of service that had a lower death rate got to eventually enjoy. I felt so sorry for those young boys, who would obey an order to fight in many suicide missions and were not old enough to know that their chances of coming out alive were very slim. Yet they obeyed, saved our country, and died for it because they were young, had a low I.Q., and loved and believed in America, and were sent to their death. I salute every one of them. God bless every one of them.

We were always waiting for the most dreaded words in the combat infantry, "Okay, boys, let's move out." That means that orders have come down to go on the attack, to get out of your foxholes and start looking for the enemy to kill, or take prisoner if you can without jeopardizing your own life or that of your buddies. The Italian word for move out, or go "forward" is *avanti*." Sometimes, our sergeant would use that word instead of the American words: *avanti subito,* advance right now, or *avanti pronto,* march, quickly.

There is about a five percent loss of American lives as they get out of their places of cover on the words, "move out." And there is a fifteen to twenty percent loss of lives before the attack is finally completed. This does not include a mayday situation, where you may lose eighty, ninety, or one hundred percent of the infantry boys. However, these are rare situations. I went through one at Bloody Gulch just up from Anzio-Nettuno, where I became a reborn Christian and made my three promises to Jesus Christ that if he let me live three more minutes, I would keep those three promises as long as I lived. To this day, I have tried my best to keep those three promises for the gift of life that he gave me. He helped make my healing in chiropractic easier for me as I prayed silently over every really bad case that I worked on.

When you are in combat, directly confronting the enemy, you know that you are there to kill as many of the enemy as you possibly can. But you have inborn, innate hesitation because you have been taught all of your life by your Christian parents and the Christian world that you were brought up in that it is wrong to harm another individual or animal. But the U.S. government says that you have to kill now as the future of your country depends on you risking your life to save millions of lives back home and for other countries also. This Christian conflict will go through your mind all of the time.

This creates some confusion and doubts in the minds of any young American soldier especially when he is confronted by the real enemy soldier on the battlefield, "Do I kill him before he kills me, or should I give him a chance to escape or let him kill me so that his death will not be on my Christian conscience. "Thou shalt not kill."

Many times the enemy has you in such dangerous situations that you are glad to kill him so that you may be alive for a few more hours or a few more days. Then you are glad to kill at that moment because you know that his family will receive that dreaded letter from the government stating that he was killed (K.I.A.) in action. After he is dead and lying there, all quiet and motionless,, then a sense of guilt and often a nausea comes over you. You will probably vomit after your first killing and not eat even a C ration for the next day or so.

The family will now receive the dreaded K.I.A. letter from his country. In my mind, I could always see their family sobbing and crying at the loss of their young son, just as we did here in America over one million times in WWII alone.

The worst part was realizing that these enemy boys are just the same as us. They went to school, and participated in sports and other activities, had mothers, fathers, brothers, sisters, and close school friends, the same as we did here in America. All of this guilt complex comes on you as you look down at this prostrate lifeless human being that will never breathe again or see and hear the voices of his loved ones. Yes, it will make you sick and nauseous and it should—because this is against everything that you have been taught all of our life and you will again be taught this at home if you make it back to the States. And you know that you alone did this killing of a human.

The worst feeling that you can get is when going through the backpack and finding letters and pictures from his home with fam-

153

ily members just like the pictures and letters that you have in your backpack. In fact if you look at him in the face long enough, he will begin to look like you or some friend or member of your family. You also know that in a few hours or a few days you will in all probability be shot by the enemy and will be laying on the ground with a German soldier standing over your lifeless prostrate body wondering about your family and life back in America.

Combat soldiers from all countries are young, healthy boys, about the same ages, eighteen to twenty-two years old. All of us, from all countries, due to our age, had a lot in common in growing up. Their families loved them just as much as did our American families. Their personal loss was as great as our personal loss in wars. If you make it back to the States alive do you think that you will ever be able to forget all of these experiences? I am very proud that I was in combat infantry and lived to write this book from total memory after sixty years of peace time. Although the government tried to draft me again in Korea and Vietnam, I had finished college on the G.I. Bill and had set up my chiropractic office in Lawrenceville, Illinois. I told them that I thought that I had already done my part, and it was now time for someone else to do theirs.

According to the Geneva Convention rules, no soldier from any country in any war is allowed to use a telescopic sight on their rifle. If that soldier does use a telescopic sight, probably as a sniper, and he is captured, he can legally be shot on the spot as a traitor. When you capture a lone soldier at an outpost, you always examine his rifle to see if there is a telescope on it or some shiny metal spot near the rear sights, which would indicate that a telescope had been mounted there but was discarded when the offending soldier knew that he was going to be captured and possibly executed on the spot if the telescope was still on his rifle. You will usually find just a shiny metal spot near the rear sights because the offending soldier would have discarded it any way that he could, it is certain death for him.

Suppose it is you who captured him and you have to decide what to do with him. For a scenario, you have just lost three of your best buddies by this sniper who was also shooting at you. If you turned him loose, he will probably shoot at you again or tell his buddies where you are. Now you have a choice. Do you shoot him on the spot or turn your back on him and let him go back to his lines

154

and probably live to go home to his family, or should you take him as a prisoner back to your lines for interrogation and let him live out the war in an American P.O.W. camp? That is the decision that you must make in a few seconds, as the war is still going on around you? What would you do? This happens to all combat men many times during a long war, as WWII. This is a very stressful decision for a young boy soldier to make, to obey the rules of the war and your country or obey the rules of Christianity, God, and the Bible?

The decision that you make in the heat of battle may not be the same decision that you would have made an hour earlier or an hour later had the same situation confronted you. But put yourself in this situation and ask yourself what you would have done in the same situation and being only nineteen or twenty years of age? Your decision at that time will remain with you the rest of your life.

18

Laying Mines in the Snow

We were still on Montibelmonti that entire terrible winter, when word was sent to our P.A. platoon that the line-company boys had discovered a small, narrow pass in the mountain range nearby that the Germans were sending one or more patrols through almost every night to seek out our positions and possibly capture or kill some of our boys. It was a search-and-find patrol such as we were using all of that cold winter on them.

So our platoon soldiers were ordered to go up into this pass one night and lay antipersonnel mines scattered throughout the narrow pass so as to cripple or kill anyone entering this pass. This was part of our job, as well as to detonate mines and booby traps and sweeping roadways and ditches ahead of the line companies or advance even with them as they would attack a village or just advancing down the road. We also laid trip flares, and went on special details such as taking care of any dangerous situation that the line company boys couldn't handle or did not have the time to handle as they were advancing toward the enemy.

We spent the next day going through our routine of laying the personnel mines. Each man was assigned a specific job to do that night as we were going to lay the mines. Each man had a job to do, and there was to be no talking that night, as the Germans were close enough to hear us. As we reached our destination, each man was to do his individual job and be absolutely quiet about it as the lives of all of us depended on absolute silence.

We had three or four extra boys to go along to form a protective skirting party. A protective skirting party doesn't do the actual mine laying. They lie on their bellies with their backs to us, facing toward the probable enemy approach.

They lay on the outskirts of the working group who cannot

keep an eye out for the enemy while they do their job. This was done on many special dangerous jobs when near or in German territory. Also, we were afraid that another German scouting party could possibly come through that pass at night while we were laying these deadly land mines and we would have had to fight our way back to our lines. And God have mercy on us. A skirting party soldier in this position was supposed to live long enough to fire three rifle bullets to kill or warn of any enemy in sight. This applies to an outpost sentry or any soldier on guard duty who is supposed to live long enough to fire three bullets in rapid succession to warn the main group that there are enemy soldiers in the immediate area and there is great danger of a large offensive attack by the enemy. He knows that he is sacrificing his life and he has about five minutes to live. A line company soldier goes through this same situation many times a year while in combat. This is why even today sixty years later a person should never walk behind a line company soldier and tap him on the shoulder or startle him. Always walk in front of him to talk to him or touch him if you know that he has been in combat.

According to the rules of the Geneva Convention, which all countries at war are supposed to adhere to, any country laying land mines must survey that immediate area and make five copies of all of those mines as to longitude and latitude. One copy goes to Washington, D.C., one copy to Geneva, and one copy to be turned over to the victor. These mines could then be found and safely detonated.

About five of us boys went up that night and took our compass readings and came back and made our five copies of where the mines were to be located. And we laid them, adhering to this exact plan.

The next night, all of the same crew went up to lay twenty or twenty-five antipersonnel mines as we had practiced in our duty run, so that there would be no confusion or noise.

The snow was knee deep and pure white as I ever remembered snow as being. It was a beautiful night. The rear echelon searchlights reflected on the white snow, making it even prettier if only we had not been on a mission of death possibly for us and the enemy.

We were very lucky that night, as the Germans did not send a patrol through that pass. We laid all the mines that night without any incidents, and the skirting party did their job. We waded through the deep snow back to our old peasant's house that we had been using all winter for our headquarters, sharing it with the communications platoon. We were all of the Third Battalion, 135 Regiment, Thirty Fourth Infantry Division. Iowa, Minnesota, South Dakota National Guard units and us, new replacement soldiers for the dead and wounded.

The Thirty Fourth Infantry Division accumulated the most combat days in a war than any other American division in any American war. They accumulated 520 combat days during WWII. In Korea and the Vietnam conflict, the army learned their lesson; they allowed each soldier only one-hundred-combat days, then rotation home. This helped the combat infantry some.

The following night, after we laid the mines, two of our best combat boys went up to the pass to see if any of the German soldiers might have tried to come through that pass, and what could have happened to them if so, did they get caught in our well-laid mines?

And when our two soldiers got to the mine-laden pass, they found, to their surprise, six or seven German soldiers who had tried to go through the snow-covered pass as they usually did. However this time all of them must have stepped on our mines as they were still alive, kicking and screaming with their arms and legs blown off and they were rolling around in terrible pain and crying and screaming for help. It only takes twenty pounds of pressure to set off an antipersonnel mine, so when some of their blown-off body parts would land on another mine, they also would fly into the air, splattering blood all over the pure white snow. I was not on this patrol and I am very glad that I wasn't for it must have been a sight that no man from any country should ever see in his lifetime.

The two soldiers from our platoon who were sent up there to see if any Germans had gotten caught in our mine field now had the gruesome merciful task of shooting the German soldiers in the head to kill them. They had to shoot them in the head as the other body parts: the arms, legs and human trunks would soon die anyway without the head attached to them. This was a mercy humanitarian killing after the soldiers had been caught in our mines. What a terrible thing war is. There can be no wars or wars without killing people. There should be verbal diplomatic wars so that the young country boys would be equal to the more affluent boys.

After our two soldiers came back and told us about the terrible experience that they had to go through, this subject was never brought up in conversation again, even to this day, sixty years later. And at the time of this patrol duty, none of us other soldiers ever pressed these two buddies of ours for any further details. Very sad experience, but this is war.

All wars are a regrettable and an unforgettable experience for the ones who are directly involved in the killings that they will never forget and probably never discuss them with anyone.

I have never told these stories to anyone, not even to my parents. I could not talk about them without choking up and that embarrasses me so much that it is easier to just sit there and think about them and let someone else do their talking. None of us Christian boys were born killers.

I have found it easy to type these stories. I didn't think that it would be so, but I actually feel better after typing these stories than I thought that I would. I think that it has been a welcome form of therapy for me. Because I could never emotionally put them in words in front of an audience or to just one person without choking up and losing my voice and tears coming to my eyes, even to this date.

No one is born a killer. It is just a necessity of fate if your country is at war and you love your country as much as we combat people do and suffer through the sacrifices that we did and still love America more than anyone who thinks that they do. "Great soldiers are made in troubled times." We hate killing worse than you do. We have seen and experienced it. Thank God you haven't and for what we went through in those days you never will know the agony of killing another Christian human being.

Often in the winter, while we were in the snow-bound, static position, we would have to go as a protector or skirting party for the communications platoon, which was a part of our company that we worked with and lived with some times. They were very brave soldiers.

If their communication lines would suddenly go dead, they knew that artillery or mortar shrapnel had cut into them or a shelling or the Germans had come across our lines under cover of darkness and cut our communication lines (commo lines).

If these commo lines suddenly became full of static for no me-

159

chanical reason at their base, then they knew that Germans had probably scratched the insulation off the metal lines and were taped in to listen to our American plans of strategy. This was easy for them to do, as many German soldiers had been to American schools, and some had even graduated from our prestigious colleges with honor but went back to their homeland and were now in the German Army working against us.

When the communication boys found a break or interference in their lines, they would get the line in their hand and follow it until they found the problem. Sometimes it would be an accidental break by a army tank running over it or a piece of shrapnel cutting the fine wire, and sometimes, it was an ambush with two or three German soldiers waiting nearby under cover to kill them. Sometimes, if they were short of men, they would ask for some of us to go with them. I went with them two or three times. Now this was a scary patrol. I don't think that I took a breath nor my heart didn't take a beat the entire two hours that it would usually take to make this important and dangerous run. We would go along as protection while the commo boys would repair the lines. Riding shotgun, as the cowboys would say. I did not care for this kind of security guard because they never sent along enough soldiers to suit me.

During that same terrible winter in the foothills of the Alps, as usual, we were low on food, which was usually C rations in a can. But we were on the front lines, and it would have been very dangerous for the cooks to get any food to us, as the road was under artillery observation by the Germans and the terrain in the mountains was rough and covered with about two feet of snow.

Sometimes we would have the Italian mule skinners load the small donkeys down with barbed wire, cases of mines, and booby traps. When you load a mule or a horse, you have to balance the load on each side equally or the animal will get down. The load must be 50–50 on each side or you will have problems with the animal losing its footing and going down to the ground. If one of these animals goes down to the ground, you must completely unload it and help it up then reload it again, only slightly lighter or they will go down again. Their legs are so small for their body that they cannot rise to their feet with any load on them.

The excess load that the donkeys could not carry was then distributed among the infantry boys to carry to the front lines. We were doing it anyway before we got help from the Italians with their mules. It was very difficult and dangerous to carry a heavy load like that while watching for the enemy and be ready to fire a rifle at a moment's notice. And you are quite aware of the disadvantage that you have while carrying a five-gallon can of water, a roll of barbed wire across the front of your helmet, and your pockets loaded with ammunition. And you are supposed to be ready for a surprise ambush attack from the enemy, possibly with machine guns and a few rifle men. You had better believe that I was scared and silently praying for a few more minutes to live. A combat soldier has a prayer on his lips and in his head all the time he is on the front lines. At no time is he without a prayer in his head and another prayer ready to come up.

We were wondering what to do for food, as we would in all probability be there for a few weeks. We were in no man's land again, so we had to be very careful of everything that we would do such as no cigarettes lit at night and no extra noise of any kind. We were never allowed to build a fire.

The very brave soldiers who went on this very dangerous land-mine-laying mission were: Sgt. Barney Allickson, Cpl. Phillip Braun, Cpl. Joseph Buffalo, Cpl. Max L. Rush, Cpl. Frenchy Dorin, myself, Pfc. John Despot, Pvt. James Keane, Pvt. James Vulanti, Pvt. John DeHore, Pvt. Mike Lipp, Pvt. Max Rotopel, Pvt. Jake Jacoby, and Pvt. George Loechner.

19

Crossing a Raging River

There was another very dangerous search-and-find mission that I was on that bad winter. Sgt. Barney Allickson and seven or eight other of us soldiers were to go and see if we could find some German soldiers to bring back for interrogation. We were in a static winter position, and so was the enemy. I do not know why headquarters wanted us to risk our lives to find a lowly German soldier for interrogation, because they would not know any more about their headquarters' plans than we enlisted men would know about ours. And if G-2 (intelligence) wanted to know about the enemy's plans, they should have come up and captured the enemy so that they could have the bragging rights if they were to learn something from any enemy prisoner.

We had to wade across a small stream going over to German territory to look for enemy soldiers. We walked around for a couple of hours without encountering any enemy soldiers. They must have been smarter than we were and were holed up out of the rain and cold somewhere, as it had rained for a couple of days and nights.

When we were ready to leave and go back the way we came, the small stream that we had waded across had swollen to a raging torrent of swift mountain water coming down from the Alps. It was very swift and very deep now. There was no way that we could cross that stream, as we were on foot without any equipment which was at our supply truck on top of the hill where most of our platoon was staying.

We had a dangerous problem confronting us—Germans behind us and an uncrossable mountain stream ahead of us. It was getting dark and still raining slightly. None of this had been planned on by us. What had started out to be a routine combat search patrol was now a life-or-death situation. But what routine patrol in combat was not a life-or-death situation?

All we had were our rifles and some ammunition; no ropes, no tents, no food, just what we had on our backs and in pockets, which were filled with ammo.

Luckily, we looked across the swirling river on the American side and we recognized some of the other boys from our platoon. They had become worried about us because we were overdue to return to our camp. As usual in the infantry, a search-and-rescue team was sent out to look for us. They knew the area that we would be in, as in this service, you always told your superiors where you will be and about what time to expect you back. This way, no one is left on the battlefield to be rescued without all of us knowing where to start looking. This surely saved our lives this time and a few other times also.

However, we were not out of danger. The Germans were sending patrols out all the time. Eventually, one of them would discover us, and a deadly gun fight would follow and most soldiers on both sides would surely be killed or wounded. Also, the swift mountain stream was still rising, and we didn't know if we were in a flood area or not. Everything looked hopeless for us on this side of the river. We were desperate, but we kept level heads, as most of us had been in a mayday situation before and came out safely, only to get caught in other dangerous situations. But that can be the everyday life of any combat soldier. Support troops and stateside soldiers have no idea of what a combat soldier goes through. There are two kinds of American soldiers, those in combat and those who just put on a uniform and leave home for a short while.

Sgt. Barney Allickson was in charge of this patrol to cross the swift river with Pfc. John Despot, Cpl. Max L. Rush, Pvt. John DeHore, Pfc. Phillip Braun, Pfc. Robert Seyl, Pvt. Jake Jacoby, me, and others.

We found some German wire, and our sergeant tried to throw it across the raging and swollen river but the light-weight wire would not carry that far with the wind blowing against us. Some of our fellow buddies on the other side also tried to throw a light-weight rope across the water, but it would not reach us either.

Sergeant Allickson got the brilliant idea of trying to reach the other side by firing a grenade launcher from his M-1 rifle with a fine

163

German communication wire attached to it. But he didn't want the grenade to explode and the noise to give our position away to the enemy nearby. So he took the detonator out and emptied all the black explosive powder from the grenade. All he had left was an empty steel grenade as a carrying agent for the fine wire across the swollen river to the other side.

I am sure that his heart was in his throat as were the hearts of all of us in ours. Time was running out; it was now about dark, and we were in German territory. This was almost a mayday, mayday situation again for us. He put the grenade launching bracket on the end of the M-1 rifle, and Sergeant Barney put the butt of his rifle on the ground in front of him and fired it almost straight up in the air, so that it wouldn't travel a great distance parallel to the ground. He wanted it almost straight up in the air and almost straight down so our buddies on the other bank could find it. Meanwhile the rest of us had formed a protective perimeter by lying on our stomach in a circle around the sergeant to protect him and the others from a German ambush, which was sure to occur in their own territory.

Sergeant Allickson fired the rifle. It landed in a very good, close spot, and the boys on the other side retrieved it and started to make a lifeline to safety as was the hoped for plan. Our main supply truck was on the hill where we camped, so our buddies went back there and got the necessary equipment to make a pulley system to ferry us back across the dangerous river to safety.

The other boys got the necessary equipment from our truck and tied some heavy rope to the narrow, fine wire and made a two-way pulley system across the river by attaching each end of the ropes to the large trees on both sides of the river. Then they took a litter bearer stretcher and anchored all four ends of it to the bottom rope and used the top rope to pull the stretcher back and forth across the river.

Each soldier, one by one, was laid down on the stretcher and roped down securely so that if the stretcher tipped over, the soldier would not fall into the river and drown. One by one, all of us boys were pulled to safety and saved from drowning or being shot by the enemy. Thank God the Germans did not appear on the scene and discover us, or that might have been our last battle. There could have been some divine intervention here again for me and the rest of the boys. This type of life-saving incident happened to us many times. I wish to thank God for the great sergeants and their guidance in all these life-saving adventures during this war. Many of these missions were miracles.

We had two great men with us then who I think should have been presented with the Silver Star for their exceptional skills and bravery. They were two of the greatest men that I have ever known to this day, almost sixty years later. They are both deceased now, and I think I am still alive today because of their bravery and leadership. I wish to God that I could see them today and thank them personally. It is ironic that these two that led us through so many death-cheating experiences were from the same town and had grown up together and joined the National Guard together. They were without a doubt the two greatest gentlemen and soldiers that I ever knew. May God have mercy on their souls. Second Lieutenant Blake (K.I.A. June 28, 1944) and S. Sgt. Barney Allickson, both from Montevideo, Minnesota, as was this original platoon all from the same town. It must have been a great town to produce such great soldiers.

The supply truck that our boys on the other side of the river used to get the ropes and pulleys from for our river rescue mission was the same truck that the four of us had risked our lives in that suicide mission that we so successfully completed in Bloody Gulch a few months before. They told us we would need it again in combat. T. Sgt. Kenny Blake told us on that first mission that this truck was a very necessary piece of our equipment, and he was so right. That trip not only saved my own life and the lives of the others in that patrol, but a few other of our young American soldiers as well. All the boys of our platoon were great, unselfish soldiers. We all went to bat for each other many times to save each other's lives.

Although we were always afraid for our own lives in combat, we felt that it would have been a personal disgrace to have run from the enemy or to have refused a dangerous assignment in front of the other soldiers in our platoon. We were always afraid, but never a coward. We had too much pride and ego for that. We loved and respected each other greatly. I so wish that I could see all of them again alive, but that is never to be. Many of them are deceased now, and the ones still alive do not wish to rehash old, terrible memories, and neither do I.

There was a great war once, and we did our part. It's over. Let's forget it and move on. What a sad story that is to the ones who lived through it. We are all very proud of America and what we did to maintain its freedom, but we are very sad for the killing part that we had to go through to maintain such luxurious freedom for so many people who do not know what we went through. Every day, I think of the young boy soldiers who were killed in their prime of life and very few of us even knew their names or worried about them as we should. But that would be impossible for anyone who has not been in combat. And it is difficult for us even though we went through it personally. There will be other wars for freedom and other American boys will experience terrible combat the same as we did. God have mercy on them.

The other soldiers in our platoon who came looking for us across the river and supplied us with the ropes and gurney stretcher to save our lives were Cpl. Frenchy Dorin, Cpl. Joseph Buffalo, Pvt. John DeHore, Pvt. Charles Hoffman, Pvt. James Keane, Pvt. Mike Lipp, Pvt. Bill Zimmerman, and Pfc. Freeman James, our wonderful truck driver who had been with me in Camp McCain earlier in basic training.

20

The Italian Campaign

While still on Montibelmonti in January of 1945, we were moved to a new location, and since we were low on replacements, they decided that we needed more protection and ordered us to string coiled barbed-wired entanglements across our side of the mountain to prevent to German soldiers from sneaking up on us. First, we had to get the large, heavy coils of barbed wire from back of the rear battalion C.P. which was about three miles back in the dark, rainy mountains. As usual, I was chosen for that job to lead the Italian mule skinners back up this terrible mountain with their small mules loaded with our supplies in addition to the barbed wire. I was usually chosen for this job because of my knowledge of the Italian language. Most of the soldiers were smarter than I was. They did not learn the language, so consequently, they got out of a number of these dangerous details.

I walked back down this mountain to the rear C.P. and got my mule supply detail and led them back up to our area. But as soon as they got close to our area, their mules started to "spook" and discharge their loads in the cold, snowy mud. The mules were kicking and running wild, dropping all their loads. We did not understand why, until one lieutenant caught one of the Italian mule-skinner soldiers cutting the wire that held the loads and then slapping the mule on the rump very hard. He spooked the mule himself because we were getting close to the German lines, and they were very scared that they would get shot at like us infantrymen.

So our lieutenant caught two of the soldiers spooking their mules and he beat them both. He had been a boxer in the States. He was later court-martialed for striking a soldier of another country. He was a fine officer and a gentleman. We all liked him. He was just trying to protect his men under enemy fire. And all of my platoon was up there in this rain and enemy soldiers.

After we got our barbed wire and the perimeter coiled steel ground pegs that go with the wire, we had to string the wire east and west, between us and the Germans. S. Sgt. Barney Allickson (God bless his soul—he was the finest) took about four or five of us to string the main large center coil out to the end, then put two rows of lower and smaller coils of barbed wire on each side, called a skirt. These skirts had to be anchored with twisted and coiled steel screw-in–type rods into the ground for strength.

As usual, we put a perimeter guard around us, as we were not able to carry a weapon and lay the wire at the same time. It was still raining all this time. We got all of the barbed wire coils laid except through a small pond right near where we were bivouacked.

"It is impossible to anchor the coils and skirts of the entanglement in that five feet of water," I told my sergeant. "And the Germans surely would not cross there anyway. It is too deep, and they would all get dripping wet."

"The Germans may think the same as you are thinking," my sergeant said, "which is exactly why they would come through there. So put the skirts on in that deep water, and we will be a lot safer."

It was just a little above zero that night, but I had to run the wire and skirts continuously or we would have a weak link in the whole system. I was one of the few in our platoon who could swim well, so it became my job. I could swim, but I couldn't hold my breath under water very long. So each time I took a steel peg to screw in the five feet of water, I had to hold my nose. But I did get five or six steel pegs screwed into the muddy bottom of that small pond. I usually get the flu or pneumonia when I get chilled, but I didn't that time. We got the entire barbed wire strung well after midnight without an incident with the Germans.

After we had all the skirts up and all the steel pegs screwed into the ground, our next job was to put up a few tin cans with a couple of rocks in them and wire them to the main coiled wire. The rocks in the tin cans would rattle if anyone was to jerk the barbed wire any place along its stretched route. This would happen if an enemy soldier was to cut the wire and it would snap back, or if a soldier would try to crawl through the wire of if the enemy would lay boards across the wire to walk over the wire to enter our territory that we had just captured from the Germans.

We were here about a week before we were changed to another sector. Our military experts said, "If we keep moving our troops around from one area to another, it will confuse the Germans, and they won't know which American division they are fighting." I think that this was a mistaken strategy on their part, because we had to learn the new enemy hideouts and their main places of defense after we had just learned them from the last move that we had. I think that if the Germans stayed in one place and got to know our hideouts, they would have a distinct advantage by our moving to a different location all the time, which we were ordered to do quite often. It was sometimes quite difficult for us to move at night in the rain on those narrow mountain roads. Those narrow mountain roads also got some of our boy's lives, our vehicles driving over the cliffs and army trucks sliding down the mountainsides at night, unable to see adequately. I disagreed with their plan of strategy completely, but maybe that was why they were the generals and I was a pfc.

During this winter's static position, we were moved out for a few months, then moved back into the same location again. Often, we would use the same house, caves, and roads as before. I still think that it would have been safer for us to have remained in the same area all the time until we advanced on the attack. I think that it might have confused the American soldiers more than it did the Germans. I was there.

The old stone house that we were staying in might have been a two-story house at one time, but now it was a large pile of rubble about six feet high. The stones were so large that when the house was destroyed, there were air pockets in the pile. About fifteen of us in our platoon had found these air pockets, or rat runs, and could crawl into them and make ourselves a small, protective refuge. We lived in these rat runs for about a week, there in no man's land, half ours and half the Germans. We were on red alert at all times, never knew from one minute to the next what our future was.

One night after being on patrol, I came back to our rubble quarters, and as I walked around the corner of our building, I must have startled a sleeping red Plymouth-Rock rooster as he let out a terrible squawk and flew right into me. He scared me nearly to death, as I had just returned from any enemy patrol, laying that barbed wire entanglement, and my nerves were all in my mouth, as was my heart. When this rooster hit me with that weird squawk, I had to sit down because my knees bent and I could not stand up. This panic attack lasted only a few minutes. Then I was able to walk around the building and crawl into my rat run for safety and possibly some sleep if the Germans did not attack us that night, which they didn't. That entire week was one of our platoon's worst since Bloody Gulch. But we did not lose any boys or have any wounded, thanks to S. Sgt. Barney Allickson. We always had very sensible sergeants who had our safety at heart first. We did not have any gung-ho sergeants. Thank goodness. This bettered our chances of coming home. To my knowledge, we had the greatest sergeants and other noncoms in the infantry ground forces. God bless them all!

About this same time and very near our combat area a very sad incident happened that did not involve my platoon. This is a true incident and it happens too many times in a war where everybody is scared and sometimes a little trigger happy.

Sometimes in combat a soldier will shoot before he is sure of nationality of the target. This happens in all wars since the beginning of time. It is just natural to be scared and extra protective of yourself. In the newspapers this is called "killed by friendly fire."

Any time a company of combat soldiers move into new territory, they always set up guards on the highest lookout point to observe enemy movements if possible. This is just good strategy on either side. Even our American Indians did that.

In this particular incident, this American platoon had just driven the Germans from the area after a week of hard battles, so they set up their advantage outlook posts or the entire platoon formed a perimeter, lying in a circle, all looking out with their feet pointing in toward each other; their visual capability was three hundred and sixty degrees, and no enemy could sneak up on them.

These perimeters of guard protection were used by other countries when there was a work detail or special protection needed someplace near the enemy.

A guard on duty or an outpost like this was not supposed to win the war, but in case of a major enemy attack, they were supposed to live long enough to fire three rapid shots into the air as a

170

warning signal to other troops behind them that the enemy was approaching. "Help! HELP! HELP! MAYDAY! MAYDAY!"

On a mayday, or life-and-death situation, an outpost or posted guard like this was supposed to live long enough to give the warning shots. His life span then was about five minutes on an average attack. They were usually all killed in the first wave of a major attack. It was the most dreaded assignment that a soldier got during combat, but it was one that he would draw many times if he lived long enough.

This platoon had just taken the area from the Germans in January 1945 during a very cold and snowy winter on Montibelmonti. The American machine guns were outposted on the highest point, with about four or five soldiers attending the outlook post. They would stay there for a few hours then be relieved by another squad. This would go on for as long as they maintained their position or until the squad leader told them "let's move out," the most dreaded words in combat. "Let's move out." That means that you are going on the attack. You must leave your foxhole or where you were seeking protection and stand and start toward the enemy, who is still dug into his protective cover. You feel like a lonely duck in the middle of a pond, without any protection. There are not words that can describe that lonely God-fearing feeling that each soldier experiences when he believes that each footstep is the last that he will ever make. Yet he keeps making one step at a time, until he's near his objective and the bullets and the mortars begin to get his attention and his mind is refocused on the battle at hand.

You must kill the enemy, fight for your country, don't disgrace yourself by turning and running away. You can get shot and killed that way just as easily. Defend yourself and your buddies with you and be ever watchful for some kind of bullet-proof shelter. You must do all this and kill the enemy as you are advancing forward. After the attack is over, you look to see if you have any blood on yourself. Then you try to find the rest of the squad or platoon and see how many of them are alive. All this time, a prayer to God and Jesus is never out of your head or off your lips. It is hell, make no mistake about it. But you have been in combat many times before, and you know that now somewhere along the line that you have been dehumanized to the extent that you have enjoyed some of the killing. Most of us have some German blood in us, like myself. I am over half of German ancestry and the rest of me is Irish and French, I think.

When the infantry gets the let's move-out order, the generals have figured that when these soldiers leave their foxholes and bunkers on the attack, about ten to fifteen percent of them will be killed just leaving their hiding places.

They are the most vulnerable to the enemy at this time. They have not had time to defend themselves as they are probably walking straight up and have not located the enemy as yet.

In combat the most dreaded words in the English language are "O.K. boys let's move out." As soon as you hear those words you are immediately a different person inside and out because it is now kill or be killed all over again. It was this terrible winter on Montibelmonti that I was to learn that all wounds do not show or heal, ever.

In one such battle, the outpost was secured, a line-company search-and-kill squad of six or seven infantrymen came through this lookout point and said to them, "We are now going out on patrol on a search-and-find mission to see if we can capture a German soldier for the officers to interrogate, to find out what the Germans are planning for this winter and next spring. We will be coming back through here about 0200, so don't fire on us. We will give the password for tonight, which is "Blue snow."And the machine-gun point guard said, "Okay, we will be expecting you, will watch out for you, as you will be coming from our front, which is German territory. Be sure and give the correct password!"

The squad walked down the hill toward German territory, looking for a soldier to capture. It was a cold, windy night, and it had been raining with a light snow for about two days without a letup. Combat was bad enough without having all this winter weather to contend with. The wind whistles around your steel helmet and plastic liner inside, and you often have to tilt your head sideways to hear anything clearly, as the wind makes a whistling noise around your helmet and makes it difficult for you to hear correctly.

The sergeant called his boys together after about two hours of searching for a German prisoner. "Boys, we haven't found anything so far, and since it is getting close to 0200, we had better head back to camp. The guard will be expecting us and we should get back about the time that we told him we would, just to be on the safe side." They all agreed and headed back by the same route that they had come and would be expected. But as they got close to their point guard outpost, machine-gun bullets started to rain in on them like hail from the sky. So they called out their password, "Blue snow."

But the American outpost did not respond with the counterpart, "Snow." The patrol kept hollering, "Blue snow, Blue snow," but the machine gun kept shooting directly at them. Then they started hollering, "We are Americans. Don't you remember us coming through your outpost and telling you that we were going on a patrol and would be back about 0200?" Still no answer from the outpost. They just kept firing their machine gun and rifles at the American patrol. Finally, the patrol got suspicious and started firing back at the outpost. The outpost then asked the patrol to "advance and be recognized," which they did.

The patrol sergeant said to the outpost boys, "What in the hell is wrong with you guys? I told you about midnight last night that we would be coming back through here about 0200 and not to mistake us for Germans, that we would give the proper password. What in the hell is wrong with you guys, anyway. Are you crazy or drunk?"

The outpost sergeant said, "We just came on duty a little while ago to relieve the other squad. They did not tell us about any of our boys being out there that would be coming back through here. We had to assume that you were Germans, as you were coming from their direction, and with the wind and rain, we could not hear you give the password." The first outpost squad had not passed on the word when they were relieved of duty. This is an unforgivable error in the army at any time, much more in combat.

Of the seven men that went out on patrol, two were killed by their own outpost sentry boys and one seriously wounded. Of the outpost boys, they had one killed and one wounded by "friendly fire," killed by their own troops. I am sure that someone got severely disciplined, or even court-martialed, for not passing the word on that they had a patrol out there and to be extra careful and watch for them.

In January or February of 1945, I got a chance to go to Florence after it had been captured a few months. I was amazed and angry to see hundreds of American soldiers walking the streets without a care in the world. They had a girl on their arm and were laughing and having such a good time. These support troops never had to fight a day in their life. But here we combat infantrymen had been up in the front lines for two years without a decent meal or bed. I almost got sick to my stomach as I saw these support troops with almost all the luxuries of home while we were not even sure that we would be alive all day. I would have paid the U.S. government more than they were paying me to have been transferred to the support troops. I could not stand to see these soldiers walking around, without a care in the world, some working and getting off at five P.M. We never heard of such a thing. I had thought that all soldiers were fighting as we were.

It was no wonder that we did not have enough front-line soldiers to launch a major attack against the Germans that winter. Our line companies were down to one-half or one-third strength, with battle-weary young soldiers who were miserable, cold, and hungry. There were enough support troops walking the streets of Florence to have staged an American offensive. And I understand that Naples, Rome, and some other towns were the same way. Those boys never got too far away from the U.S.O. donut and coffee line, I never saw U.S.O. donut and coffee station all of the time that I was over there, twenty-seven months, two years and three months. I was put in the front line the first day that I got there, and so were all other combat soldiers. What a terrible military injustice!

21

Deadly Cherry Pies

During that terrible winter on Montibelmonti, I often compared it to the winter of 1777–8 with General George Washington's Revolutionary troops at Valley Forge. It was a cold and hungry winter, and our soldiers' morale was low just as I have read about theirs.

One of our tasks as special detail platoon was to dig our boys out of the mountainside caves that they had dug in the cold weather. In the frozen weather the mountain dirt was frozen and the boys could dig back into this south side and make a nice two-man cave to keep them warm and protected against machine-gun bullets and artillery shrapnel from hitting them.

On the other side of this mountain, the Germans were probably doing the same thing.

The bad part about digging into the side of the frozen mountain was that when spring came with warm weather, the dirt thawed, and the small two-man caves fell in and smothered our boys to death as they always went in head first; their feet were the first thing that you would see as you crawled into their cave.

In the spring, our P.A. platoon got a few calls to go up and try to pull these poor unfortunate boys out of those caves, as they were completely covered with a couple tons of dirt. We would tie our tent rope around an ankle and then we would all pull to get them out. But we never saved a boy this way. They had suffocated from lack of oxygen when covered by all of this dirt without any air pockets to sustain them while waiting for rescue. When we got them out, their flesh would be completely black from lack of oxygen.

One night when we were pulling some of these boys out of their fallen in caves, we heard, on the east side of this mountain just a few hundred yards away, machine guns rattling away. We all hit the dirt and remained quiet for awhile, until some of the soldiers came from around there and said that their cook (not ours) had sent word that they had some cherry pies baked in large square pans and if they could come and get them they could have them. Well, the only time we would get a rare delicacy like that would possibly be on Christmas or Thanksgiving day feast. So, sure, the boys would send a detail back to the kitchen to get enough for the whole platoon.

They went back and got some of the small Italian mules, loaded the pie pans on them, and headed back up to no man's land which was where we were digging out the caved-in boys.

On the way back to our position, a German raised up and hollered at them: then he disappeared into the darkness. Our boys ran to the other side of the small ravine that they were in to escape the Germans and they fell right into a German ambush as there were quite a few Germans waiting there for them with machine gun bullets and rifles. I think that it was a five-man detail, and three of our boys were killed instantly and two escaped badly injured. The Germans all escaped to a retreat on the other side of the mountain without a loss.

Immediately after the German patrol ambushed our cherry pie detail and killed three or four of our line company boys one of the boys who survived the killing came over to me and said that he had just lost one of his best buddies in that ambush. He further stated that he saw that his best buddy was seriously wounded or possibly dead from the ambush firepower so he went over, sat on the snow-covered ground, and pulled his buddy up on his lap between his legs. His buddy looked up at him and said, "Mama, are you my mama?" and he said, "Yes, I am your mother," and the dying boy looked up at him and said, "Mama, I love you," and his head slowly rolled over toward his left shoulder and the other soldier's left leg, and his whole body went limp and sagged downward never to move again.

He was a young boy about nineteen or twenty years old, like most of us were at that time. I did not know this boy personally, but he was in our battalion. He was a great fighter and an American hero.

I have heard of other dying soldiers asking for their mothers or thinking that the person with them at that time was their mothers. But I have never heard of one asking for their father. I don't know why. I think an awful lot of my father and I am not sure which one I would ask for under the same circumstances. Fortunately, after sixty years, I still have not had to make this decision.

Possibly this is a part of God's master plan of motherhood from womb to dust. Who knows?

It was impossible to carry the dead soldiers back down the mountain for the G.R.O. boys to pick them up and bury them, so we would stick a tree limb in the snow and mud so that the G.R.O. boys could see them from the road and bury them properly. If we had a handkerchief or a white rag, we would tie it to this stick also, so the G.R.O. could see it more easily when they arrived.

I was not able to eat cherry pie for over twenty-five years after the war but I have never told this story and many other stories here to anyone before in my life. You are the first to hear this.

Still when I see a cherry pie, to this date I always think of this night on Montibelmonti and those pitiful young boys. God bless them. They were only nineteen and twenty years old. Some had never shaved yet nor had some ever had a date with a girl back home. What a terrible waste of human lives. There is one thing worse than death; that is suffering.

Our platoon soldiers on that dangerous detail were Cpl. Joe Buffalo, Cpl. Max L. Rush, Pfc. John Despot, Cpl. Phillip Braun, Pvt. James Keane, S. Sgt. Barney Allickson, and myself.

We have all heard the quotation "before you die your life will flash before you." This happened to me twice in combat in Italy. The first time, an armed German soldier had me dead right when he had the drop on me, and I stood there before him about fifteen feet away without any rifle of any kind. We both stood there looking at each other and my innate subconscious mind knew that he was going to shoot me in cold blood right then and there, and I knew it also in my conscious mind that this was *it* for me. But he turned his back on me and walked away. Just then, three pictures of my youth flashed before my eyes, each picture took less than a second and then were gone. They were all three pictures of my youth, I remember that. The first one was of my mother at home in Fairfield, Illinois, when I was in grade school. I do not remember what the other two pictures were about except they were about my youth before service. But he did not shoot me, he walked away.

The second time that my life's three pictures flashed before my eyes, I was in a similar life-threatening situation and I knew that there was no escape for me, and three more pictures of my young life with my family at home flashed before my eyes. They were not the same three pictures that I saw the first time, that I thought I was going to be killed by the enemy gun fire but they were also of my young civilian life at home. Years later, I have often wondered why they were not the same pictures flashing before my eyes each time. I would have thought that they would have been the same pictures that made such an impression on my mind at that impressionable time of my life that they would have been the same identical pictures crossing before my eyes. And I still do not understand the differences in the pictures flashing before my eyes. I understand the pictures flashing at this disastrous time but not the variation in pictures. I would have thought that they would have been the same impressionable pictures.

These pictures did not remain long before my eyes, just a split second then the next picture appeared almost overlapping the previous picture. They were all gone in less than a second, but they were real and I remembered the situations that were in the pictures, although I had never thought of them twice in my entire lifetime. And I cannot tell you what all of them are today. I remember that the first picture in the first flash by was of me being with mother at home on the farm in Fairfield, Illinois where I grew up. What any of the five pictures were about I do not remember now nor am I sure that I could have told you then what they were about. I have often wondered if an incident was so impressed on my mind at that young age why were not the same pictures flashed before my eyes each time?

Now I wonder, if when I am faced with a certain death situation in the future will I see scenes flash before my eyes again, and will they be some of the same pictures that flashed before my eyes when I was in combat during WWII? I find this very interesting to think about.

I was saved twice that I know of this way by a German soldier who had no right to spare my life. He was there to kill his enemy, the American soldiers, the same as I was there to kill my enemy, the German soldiers. But I am sure that we were all Christians and did not want to kill anyone. We were just caught up in a political situation by our own beloved countries. I am sure that he loved his coun-

178

try as much as I loved my country. All residents of all countries love their homeland.

These two experiences in combat could not have happened by the same German soldier as the second incident happened months later in a different battle zone. I am sure that the Germans saved my life four times that I know of, so I am sure that I was in their rifle sights or artillery and mortar range, and they could have killed me any time that they so desired. I think that they were very good to me when a live-or-die situation came down to the final second, thinking against Christian upbringing or be faithful to my country, letting him live because "maybe a soldier on the enemy side will take pity on me and not shoot me, or maybe he has already saved my life, so I should spare his." This is what goes through the mind, and I am sure that it has gone through the minds of millions of other combat soldiers from every country that ever fought a war.

I sincerely think that my life was saved by divine intervention throughout the war, because I barely missed death so many times.

22

The German Who Would Not Kill Me

One night, still on Montibelmonti, we got a call from one of the line companies that there was a suspicious board in the forward observation outpost hut, in no man's land. It was a loose board on the threshold of the entrance door to the hut, and every time someone pushed on it, the board would go up and down, as if it was on a spring. It could possibly be a booby trap. So since that was our specialty, six of us were sent up to investigate and disarm it if it had a detonator of any kind.

The Germans had patrols moving about all the time, so we had to work in silence and to have a perimeter guard near the hut from among our six men to protect us from a surprise enemy attack while we worked.

We had to walk through minefields. We were also within machine gun range and possible attack from an enemy scouting party at any moment, which would mean a deadly skirmish for both sides. This was the last thing we wanted to encounter, because it was hard enough to work on detail and watch out for the enemy or return fire at them to protect yourself and your buddies.

When we got to this lonely one-room hut outpost,. I immediately bent down on my knees in the cold and deep snow to examine the wooden board, a door transom step, to see if I could find any wires or anything that would tell me what kind of a booby trap it was. As I gently slid my right hand under the board very slowly, with my heart in my mouth, I could not feel any wires or object of any kind that resembled a booby trap. Being the only farm boy in our platoon, I often took the initiative on something like this rather than trust a city boy without any rural experience. I spent most of my life on a farm surrounded by woods, creeks, barns, and animals. All that I could feel was grass or wheat growing that had just sprouted from the moisture in the snow. Wheat will sprout and grow in the cold of wintertime. I knew this from my life back on the farm from Fairfield, Illinois, where I grew up. I was a farm boy clear through. I had even taken four years of agriculture in high school so that I could possibly be an agriculture teacher in high school if I came out of this war alive.

I felt very carefully that there was not anything else under the board but enough fresh green wheat sprouts that were strong enough to push the board upward, since there were so many sprouts they were strong enough to do it. The board was not nailed down. I told Sergeant Allickson what it was. He said, "Okay, now, Hammil, go around this building and check the windows to see if there are any booby traps on them."

So I got up from the deep snow on the ground to go around the small hut to check the windows while all the others stayed in the hut. In my hurry to obey this order, I left my rifle in the hut or on the ground, I don't remember which.

As I went around the hut and turned to my left, there, in front of me stood a young German soldier with his burp gun pointed right at me about fifteen feet away. He must not have heard us in the hut, as we always worked very quietly when in or near German lines.

He looked straight at me, with his burp gun aimed right at my belly. I looked right back at him, mostly in surprise, as I was not expecting him and I had five buddies in the hut, which I am sure he was not aware of. He must have seen that I foolishly did not have a weapon of any kind on me. This was an unforgivable error on my part, or of any combat soldier to be near enemy territory and not have his weapon loaded to the fullest. He would have the safety off so that he could shoot at a moment's notice to save his life.

After he looked at me for a couple of seconds, he turned his burp gun to his right, about waist high, and fired off five or six rounds from the gun. He fired at no one, just into the dark night air. Then he looked at me again, in the face, turned around, and walked away, and the last I saw of him was a gray shadow disappearing into the foggy night, his back turned to me in a very trusting manner.

I went back into the hut and told the other boys about my expe-

181

rience. I told them, "Boy, was that German soldier a terrible shot. He even aimed his gun in the wrong direction."

It was not until a few hours later that I put all the pieces together and it dawned on me that this German had turned his burp gun sideways on purpose to avoid killing me. He had deliberately saved my life. It was possible that when I left my rifle back in the hut that he saw that I was not armed and that I could not shoot him, so he would not shoot me as I could not possibly harm him even when he turned his back on me and walked back down the mountain. I sure would like to see him today and thank him. The Germans could have killed me four times that I know of and possibly more that I do not know of. I told my buddies in the hut about my escape from death, but no one said anything. They were ready to leave. God bless that German infantryman and all others like him who did not kill every time they had a chance. Our platoon always tried to take prisoners when possible, as most of us had German blood in us.

I am sure that when that young German soldier got back to his squad, he told them that he had a terrible gun battle with an American soldier but that he finally killed him. He would have to have some kind of an explanation like that, because in the high mountain altitude, a bullet's sound carries a long way. Especially in the still of a cold winter's night when you are listening for them anyway.

I am very sure that he did not tell them that he had refused to shoot and kill an American fighter when he had him at a great disadvantage, as he had me. I think that this would not have gone over with his superior officers or some of his buddies. It would have been considered a weakness, which his country did not approve of. I am sure that he got credit for an American kill. But I sure wish to thank him now for his soft heart. I and many other American soldiers that we do not know about, probably had our lives saved, by the German enemy during this war. We also reciprocated many times by not shooting and killing them every chance we had. I have also done that myself.

But I am still alive at the age of eighty to write this story, and I hope that he is also still alive. I want to thank you, whoever you are. God bless you, my friendly enemy. I am still alive today because of you and God. There is a possibility that you were a Christian boy and that our mutual God intervened again in our lives. I have always thought so, even to this day sixty-one years later.

I think that this was definitely divine intervention. In my mind, I had many of these divine interventions during WWII and later on in my civilian life. As I pray, many times a day, even now, I can see the daily problems solved by prayer and divine intervention. I am a great believer in prayer as is my entire family and close relatives, such as cousins and nephews. They are all avid church goers and use daily prayer to help get them through life's daily problems.

Two thousand years ago, before the birth of Christ, Roman Empire soldiers and gladiators fought in this very country, these very towns and these very hills in defense of their empire. They were taught many tactics in battle, as we were in WWII. From the first day that you swear allegiance to America until the day you are killed or die of old age, you are taught in the American forces, the same motto that the Roman soldiers were taught, "Death before dishonor." That kept many young beautiful boys on the front lines charging the enemy on all our combat fronts until they were killed or badly injured for life. We were all scared, but never a coward to neglect our duty.

It is probably hard for a noncombat person to realize that a serviceperson often knows the instant that he is going to die. When I thought that I was going to be machine-gunned and die that moment, my mind flashed a few pictures of my youth in front of me. I did not personally flash these pictures. They just came there from my subconscious mind. I think that God also thought that I was going to be killed and He flashed those few pictures in front of me to remind me of some of the happier moments that I had at home with my family. Both times, I was saved by a young German soldier by his not shooting me when he had the distinct advantage. I think that God must have intervened in this enemy's soul to not shoot and kill me at that moment.

When I realized that the German soldier had me at his complete mercy, and he turned his burp gun away and fired into the darkness, I matured a great deal. It took a few hours for all this to be straightened out in my mind. But when it all came to me, I wanted to find that soldier and thank him so much for saving my life. He did not know me. Neither did I know him. I am sure that he remembered this incident all his life as well as I do. God bless him over and over again.

It was then that I realized how cheap one human being's life is. Each person's life is about as important as a grain of sand is on the Florida beaches that I was to visit many times in my adult life. I would often think of this analogy as I walked the sandy beaches of Florida. I could see where I should improve my personal life by treating other people nicer and not be so critical of their faults. Even though I am not perfect, neither is any human being perfect. I should be more tolerant of all people and not take life so seriously.

After all, we are put here on earth by God, and our life span is a very brief spell in his master plan. I am just one of his sheep, as is everyone else on earth. I am not the sheepherder, He is. And to think that this was all brought about by my forgetting my rifle on a mountain in central Italy and a Christian German enemy soldier refusing to shoot me as I was unarmed in combat at night on patrol. This was in the winter of 1944–1945, probably Janaury or early February. We didn't have calendars up front, so we did not always know what month it was anyway, nor days of the week. All days and nights were the same. Our morale was always low after spending so many months in combat without much relief and not much of a chance of living much longer, as the enemy was always just a few hundred yards in front of us, shooting machine guns and throwing mortar and artillery at us all the time to just let us know they were there.

During the war, the number of commissioned and noncommissioned officers in a company and a battalion was governed by the U.S. Army Table of Order (T.O.). The infantry had the lowest number of officers and noncommissioned officers per fighting unit than any other branch of service, the Air Force had the most.

During 1945, Sgt. Barney Allickson tried to get some of his best soldiers a noncommission promotion in rank, but to no avail. But about a month or so before the war came to an end, a new T.O. came out and allowed him to promote and upgrade some of his soldiers. He was very glad to do this for his men, because they had been doing upper grade work without any increase in pay and very little recognition for their life-saving work for one, two, and three years in front-line combat without any luxuries at all.

So he promoted Cpls. Joseph Buffalo of St. Louis, Phillip Braun of Bloomfield Hills, Minnesota and San Diego, California, Max L.

Rush of Camden, South Carolina and Pfc. John Buddy Despot of Homestead, Pennsylvania and Manhattan Beach, California all to the rank of sergeants. These were the brave men who were the backbone of our platoon. Their patriotism and bravery is above reproach. Some of them had fought under General Patton in North African Sahara Desert in Tunisia, forty-five combat days in Sicily, weeks at the Abby at Casino, then onto Anzio Beach. America could not ask for a braver self-sacrificing bunch of young soldiers. They were all eighteen-and nineteen-year-old high school age boys to begin with. Then, as twenty-two and twenty-three-year-old war-experienced, mature men, they hadn't had a date, three square meals a day, a bed under them, or a radio to listen to for all of that time. These soldiers all got to come home. God bless them all. They were the finest men and the bravest soldiers that I ever knew. I have visited most of them since the war was over.

23

A German Lady Spy

One night, a week before Christmas 1944, I was walking my post on guard duty in and around a bombed-out house where we were staying. As I turned the corner to walk around the small house next door to us, where an elderly Italian couple was living, there was a young girl squatted down on the ground urinating, and some of her urine splashed on my winter boots.

This was very embarrassing, as neither of us had seen the other in the darkness. We both excused ourselves in Italian, and I continued to walk my post, and she re-entered the small house of the two elderly civilians. This was not unusual. Many civilians continued to live in a combat area with us and also when the Germans occupied the area.

The next day, I heard that there was a young girl staying in this small house with the two elderly Italians, and she was having sex with the soldiers for two dollars a session. This was not unusual. This was the going rate for sexual favors during the war, regardless of where you were. Two dollars or a package of cigarettes.

However, this girl was a little different. She told the men that she preferred officers rather than enlisted men to visit her. So the officers took advantage of this nice invitation, but they still had to pay their two dollars each time.

One officer in our battalion went in and paid his two dollars, but he became very suspicious when she kept asking details about the war and the possible spring offensive attack that we all knew had to occur in a few weeks. So after as he got his two dollars worth, he went back to the officers quarters and told some of the other officers that he suspected that she was a spy because she was not living there when we first arrived. The two elderly people lived alone then, and we befriended them and gave them food, which was greatly appreciated by them. We had stayed there a few months before.

So two or three of the officers went back into the house together. One officer held the young girl's arms so that she could not resist them or possibly shoot them with a gun which she could have hidden.

The other two American officers searched the house thoroughly and found a German short-wave radio behind a curtain in the kitchen. She had been talking with German field officers, giving them what information she had gotten from an officer while having sex with him. I doubt if these officers knew anything in advance that would have jeopardized our positions of future attacks.

She was hand-tied with a small cotton tent rope and taken back to Intelligence (G-2) for further interrogation. I watched them load her into a jeep and head back to division headquarters. But I never told them that we had become close buddies, as she had urinated on my boots. This is the first time that I have told this romantic spy story. She would have never made it in Hollywood.

The elderly couple said that she had parachuted in and threatened to kill them both if they told anyone, and she had the gun to do it with. The Germans knew where this house was and the local terrain, as they had stayed there while fighting us before we drove them out and they had to retreat to the north. We always used their old foxholes rather than dig our own in the hard rocky mountain soil. I never dug a complete foxhole in the two years that I was in combat.

There must have been many spies in our combat areas, because Axis Sally, the German propagandist, would broadcast every evening. Some of the headquarters' officers had battery radios, and they would pick her up on their radios. She tried to encourage American soldiers to come across no man's land and surrender for safekeeping. They would play popular American songs, and often she would say, "You American soldiers who are going out on patrol tonight, do not forget that your password is 'Blue Snow,' " or whatever the password was for the night.

Many times, she would be right, and we on the front line had only received the official password one hour before this announcement. This would result in division headquarters having to change the password, and then confusion arose, as sometimes we would already have men out on patrol, and they would be using the old password, and the answering sentry would suspect that they were Germans using the old password. This caused some loss of lives among the combat infantry soldiers due to two passwords being used in one night. This was called death by "friendly fire."

However, this did not affect the division headquarters, because where they were housed, they did not go on search-and-find patrols as we front-line boys did. Axis Sally was very accurate in many of her radio broadcasts. She must have had many spies on the front lines. Many of the officers who had radios listened to her just to hear the American songs, which she played as part of their propaganda program to make the Americans boys more homesick than they already were.

Front-line combat soldiers were not allowed radios or cameras at any time during the war.

One night, Axis Sally said on her nightly broadcast just before Anzio break out May 23, 1944. "We are going to counterattack you on Anzio very fiercely, and we are not going to take any prisoners." In combat talk, that means they will kill every American soldier they find.

So the American generals sent word down that we were to "Take no prisoners" also. They said that two can play at this game.

Some companies already had German prisoners that they had captured earlier and kept in a barbed-wire compound near Anzio Beach. American boys were Christians, and we did not kill except in self-defense, and we tried at all times to take prisoners if possible. But in a global war, such as with the Germans and the Japanese, sometimes one had to do what was necessary to save his life. One's country and all the people at home were depending on him. Another factor that I very seldom hear about is his not wanting to lose the esteem and respect of his buddies that he had trained with, and let them see that he was too scared to kill and fight when confronted by the enemy face to face. This would be a combat soldier's greatest personal disgrace, regardless of the branch of service that he was in, but I can only describe the conditions of battle of the combat infantryman as that was all that I was.

This German woman spy was not at all like the ones in the movies that I had seen back home. She was short, rather of stout build, no makeup, straight hair, and very plain-looking. She must have been very intelligent because most soldiers would have passed her in a crowd without a second look. I know that I would have passed her up, and I dated a number of young very pretty Italian senoritas in my two years there. I liked the Italian people and I got along with them very well. They liked you if you thought enough of them to want to learn their language. They enjoyed teaching us their language, and we taught them our language.

I learned later on that this woman spoke four languages fluently, German, English, French, and Italian. But she sure wasn't a beauty.

24

A Terrible Winter

The local Italian people often told me that all Americans were millionaires. I told them that if we were all millionaires, money would have no value because we would all be rich and there would be no workers, no producers, and no consumers. In the world today, you must have rich people, middle class people and poor people. Then there will always be supply and demand because of the rich people, producers, laborers and consumers. And it is usually the consumer whose purchasing usually sets the price on products and the value of the dollar. That is the law of supply and demand. Some people say that we live by the Golden Rule—those who have the gold usually rule.

I think that you must almost die many times before you really appreciate life and know how to treat other people. I am sure that I am much more tolerant of other people now than I would have been if I had not undergone the constant life-or-death situations. And do not ever make the mistake of expecting perfection of any person. It just does not happen. Don't take life so seriously, and go with the flow more. After all, over ninety percent of us were conceived and born by accident anyway.

They say that God works in mysterious ways, and I am living proof of that after all of my military life with all of the terrible battles that we all went through. I did not go through any more dangerous situations than did many of my buddies. In fact, most of them had fought in North Africa, Cassino, and had more dangerous combat experiences than I did. So I can write only about the actual experiences that I went through. These are all actual experiences that I went through, without any exaggeration or dramatization whatsoever. Every statement made here is the absolute truth, so help me God.

When we would be chasing the Germans and they were not putting up much resistance but waiting somewhere down the road where they had been set up to stay and defend to slow down the approach to Berlin, the Italian natives would come out to the roadside and welcome us very loudly and offer bottles of wine for us to take a drink from. We were not supposed to take the whole bottle but were supposed to take a toast drink from it and then give it back to them. To them, this was a good luck sign that you were their friend and would remain so. However, most of our boys would take the whole bottle with them and keep it for themselves and their buddies. In Italy, this was considered very rude, and as we went through their town, the man who lost his entire bottle of wine would be shaking his fist at us.

As we would go along the roads and through towns of Italy, they asked for chocolates or chocklates as they had not had any since the German occupation five years previously. But we had very little chocolate to give them, as we enjoyed what little we got from home. Some of our rations contained chocolate bars but not very much. We mostly had hard candy from K-ration boxes. That suited them and us also. Better than nothing. We also gave them chewing gum, which they had never had before in their lifetime. We had to teach them how to chew without swallowing the chewing gum.

Some of our boys had what we considered at that time a very cute trick. They would get a prophylactic condom, and one G.I. would hold it open and another would pour about two gallons of water in it from our water cans and tie a knot in the neck of the condom and as the civilians were waving at us as we were going through town and the local people would be reaching out their arms to us in a gesture of friendship, these two boys would drop this water-filled condom on their heads, and boy, would that splash them. Two gallons of water, when they thought it was something nice the soldiers were throwing to them and scramble to get to it only to be surprised with being showered with water. These combat soldiers were only eighteen, nineteen, and twenty, and some twenty-one years of age. They had just come through the valley of death a few times and didn't know if they would be alive that night, and they were just having some harmless fun.

191

A few other times, we would take a small tree limb switch and switch the girls on the rear end as our truck would pass them on the road, especially if they were riding a bicycle. This made a good rear-end target for us boys who had switches once in a while. However, we were careful not to switch them very hard, just enough to get a little attention and maybe an angry fist shaken at us. We never hurt anyone. Just a little fun from some homesick boys who never had a chance to date girls or go to the hotdog stand on Saturday night like most American boys did. Our generation did not have a teenaged youth. We went straight from high school or the farm into military service.

When we came home, those who did make it home, were grown up, battle weary, broke, and lonely, and most of the girls had gotten tired of waiting and married someone who was still home. I got my Dear John letter while I was on Montibelmonti.

The older men, when they got home, found, after three years overseas that they were the father of a one- or two-year-old child. This of course resulted in divorce in many instances. Many wives never told their husband this while he was overseas, otherwise her military spouse's check would be discontinued. Or maybe she thought that he would forgive her if she apologized enough times. Sometimes it worked and sometimes it didn't.

I had a buddy who when he came home, his fiancé told him how faithful she had been those three years and had not dated anyone in that entire time because they were engaged before he left for overseas. He had changed his mind and did not want to get married, but she put up such a strong argument of how she had turned down dates and he was obligated to marry her because they were engaged when he left for service. So they had a big wedding, and five months later, he was the father of a healthy, full-term baby.

They were divorced a few months later. He remarried another girl and is now a father and grandfather. I still correspond with him after fifty-seven years of friendship.

During the war, there was also a proxy marriage. If a serviceman were overseas or could not get leave to get married, he could legally designate a friend to stand in for him at his wedding (the serviceman's) usually a quiet ceremony with just the immediate family of both present. This was particularly handy if the girl found out that she was pregnant and he was overseas, or if he wished his death benefit to go to someone other than his parents, or in some cases, the soldier did not have a parent or had parents who had abused him at home.

At some port of embarkation towns, they found some girls who were married to a dozen different boys without any divorce and were receiving spousal benefits from all of them.

We always had a lot of vino wine to drink while we were in Italy. The natives gave us a lot and we confiscated a lot more as we liberated the houses or the towns. Most large nice homes or villas had a large wine cellar. We would always take the best that we could find. Sometimes we would find vermouth and cognac, which we always took as much as we could and gave to our buddies.

One time in a small town where one of the line companies had driven out the Germans and liberated the people, one of the soldiers found a cellar full of champagne. He stood at the door of the house and sold the champagne for one dollar a bottle to all of the other line-company boys and put the money in his pocket. When it came to the last of his company passing by he left his post in front of the wine cellar with all of the money that he had taken in, and another soldier from another company took over his place and started selling the champagne at one dollar a bottle.

We drank only when we knew that we were not going into combat on the front lines that day or night. If you drank anything that day, you would be scared more than usual and your senses and responses would be slowed up. So we never drank then. We drank mostly when we were in reserve or on leave.

The cognac that they had over there would burn in their Zippo cigarette lighters for a while but would eventually gum up and not light.

We were never allowed to light fires on the front or the rear lines, as the smoke, curling its way upward, would be a sure giveaway to the enemy. No fires in a building or outside, as they would smoke, especially the wood that we could burn. We were never allowed to build a warm fire the entire time overseas in WII.

In combat there were a number of ways to get out of combat. One was by self-inflicted wounds. The most common for him "to accidentally" discharge his rifle and shoot himself in the foot, usually the left foot for the right-handed soldier.

The next way was for him to crush his arm and shoulder muscles in the right shoulder by backing up against a stone building, holding his rifle loosely against his shoulder and fire all of the .30-caliber rifle bullets from the rifle. If the shoulder muscles were not crushed enough, then another clip of shells was loaded into their rifle and fired all over again. This would usually make it impossible for him to lift his arm or use it for a long time.

The next S.I.W. trick was to make a hand grenade and pull the detonator out of the cast iron shrapnel shell and put the detonator under only the arch of the left foot and pull the pin out. He has five seconds until the detonator goes off and blows a small hole in the arch of his boot and foot. It won't blow the foot off but it will take a small piece of flesh out of the arch of the foot, enough to get you in the hospital for a few weeks and out of deadly combat.

You have to remember that all of the kids or young boys were fighting for their lives while the rest of the servicemen at home were having an almost normal life. I find it very difficult to blame any soldier who has been at least once up on the front lines to try to get out of any more combat. There were too many support troops and not enough combat troops. The support troops outnumbered us four to one. Not once were support troop sent to help us.

Another method that some of the boys would try to get out of combat was to eat the paraffin wax water-proofing on the cases that the C rations and K rations came in. There was a rumor going around that if he ate nothing but this wax, after a while it would give him yellow jaundice. And the way to tell was to look into the soldier's eyes, and when the arteries and veins started to turn yellow, he would be lucky and have jaundice.

We had one boy in our outfit, nineteen years old, who ate the wax by scraping it off the cartons with his bayonet and then eating it. Every day he would go around to some of us and ask us, "Don't you see a little yellow coming into my eyes?" We always told hm no. He gave it up after a few months that winter on Montibelmonti and never got jaundice. I visited him a few years later after the war was over. He died of cancer on my sixty-fifth birthday. He went through hell in Sicily, Anzio, and all through Italy.

Another way the boys heard about was to eat ice and snow all winter on an empty stomach, with the possibility that you might get ulcers. I don't know that any of the boys in our platoon tried that one, and I am not sure it would work any way.

Of course, after a few boys with the same condition would show up on sick call with these same conditions, the doctors and officers would get very suspicious and list them as possible S.I.W. If it was proven, the soldier would get the maximum of seventeen years in prison, in Ft. Leavenworth, the military prison, in Kansas. Most of the boys were court-martialed and received the maximum sentence.

I understand that most, if not all, of these sentences were dismissed against them about five years after the war ended.

I knew of one young soldier that I was in Camp McCain with who was in basic training and winter maneuvers in Tennessee in 1943. When we went overseas, we were sent to separate companies, but we would see each other once in a while in combat in Italy. I heard that during a German counterattack, he had suffered a concussion and was bleeding from the ears. He was a private in a line company, which was the most forward and most dangerous of all positions in the infantry.

After he had suffered the concussion and still bleeding from the ears, he became disoriented and walked toward a German tank and began pounding on it with the butt of his rifle. Before the Germans saw him, one of the other American soldiers saw what was going on and grabbed him and dragged him to safety and back to the American lines.

He was later court-martialed because, the judge said, "it looked like he was going to the Germans to surrender when he pounded with his rifle on the German tank." He, of course, denied it. But military courts are the opposite of civilian courts in principle. In the military court, you are considered guilty until you prove yourself innocent. He was unable to prove to the court that because of his concussion, he was innocent.

He was sentenced to seventeen years of hard labor at the Ft. Leavenworth, Kansas Military prison. I think that he was released, as most of the other convicted WWII prisoners, after the war was over a few years later. God have mercy on all those boys.

Even if any of them were guilty, their crime was no more than the single boys who rushed to the justice of peace to get married and have children right away, or they escaped to Canada or Mexico and then came back to their beloved America after the war was over and were later pardoned by our president, Richard Nixon.

Or the ones who were married started having children to avoid the draft or get a deferment.

The next day after the war was declared, the newspapers carried pictures of the long lines of young men waiting in line in front of the courthouse in their hometowns, waiting to get a marriage certificate. They are all proud Americans, walking around free today without a blemish on their record, while the soldiers that served time in Ft. Leavenworth got a dishonorable discharge (D.D.) And were unable to hold many jobs, including Civil Service and any public office. Isn't that a shame?

If you have ever served in combat, especially the infantry, it will either kill you or ruin you for life. No wonder everyone wants to avoid it and join other branches of services. The army now says that they have two hundred and twenty-two careers to learn if you sign up and enlist. In the infantry, there is but one trade to learn—kill, kill, kill.

We were told to do our jobs, and we did them with very little grumbling. There is some pride in doing a job well even if it's killing. We should all do the best we know how, even in times of war.

We have an old saying in the infantry: "If you have been in combat in the infantry, you are guaranteed to go to heaven, because you have already had your hell on earth." I believe this is true, as I have been there. "We are not heroes, just survivors, those of us who came back." A very small percentage of actual combat boys made it back. Many overseas soldiers claim to have been in combat but weren't at all. They must have the Combat Infantry badge to prove it. I have mine.

The Germans had a few small biplanes that looked just like our American Piper Cub. They used them to fly over our lines at night to see where we were so that their artillery pieces could fire on us. When the observation plane would be first noticed somewhere on our front lines, a yellow alert call would go out to the entire Allied front. All of us combat soldiers were to stay close to protective cover and be alerted to the code red, when the plane would be immediately over our positions. Then you were to move about as little as possible and absolutely no cigarette smoking or flashlights, as you would give the position away of many hundreds of front-line combat soldiers. This could be disastrous to our cause. Poor line-company boys don't have flashlights.

These red alerts would last only five to ten minutes as the small plane flew over. We often could see the German pilot in his cockpit, looking down at us. I knew that he could see us often, but he very seldom called artillery shells in on us. I think they just wanted to know where we were for their military strategy for future use. We often thought about shooting him down, but the army said no. Then this airplane pilot got to dropping surrender leaflets over our front lines, offering immunity to any American soldier that would defect and come over to the German side and surrender. This was meant mostly for our boys who had enough combat and were ready for anything that would get them out of combat and possibly make it home alive after the war, because the longer that you remained in infantry combat, the less chance you have of coming home.

If the secretary of the army and defense had put twice as many soldiers in the front-line battle zones, we could have won the war much quicker with no greater loss of men. There were plenty of support troops and U.S.O. warriors in the States to have done this. Instead, the U.S. Army intelligence relied too much on too few men. Consequently most combat men came home crippled or battle weary.

Not many Americans or boys from the other Allied branches of service took these surrender pamphlets seriously at that time. In war the German word was not to be trusted. The pamphlet had lines on it for you to write your name, rank, and serial number. A few of the boys filled them out in some of the other platoons and went over the lines to surrender at night in groups of two, three, or four soldiers at a time.

If four soldiers went over to the Germans to surrender, we would wait. In about twenty minutes, you would hear four single German rifle shots ring out in the night as they had just shot our boys who in good faith had gone over to their lines to possible surrender and live to go home. But very few were honored by this supposedly humane gesture. I think that it depended on the attitude of the particular German soldiers at that front-line post. Maybe they had lost a buddy to us a few days earlier or, possibly, had too much combat themselves. But this was war. It wouldn't be war if no one was killed. And all of us hoped that it was someone else not me or any member of my family that would get injured or killed.

Some of the boys still wanting to surrender got together and would send one of our boys over their lines with the surrender leaflet in his hand. He would tell the Germans that if they didn't hear a rifle shot and he was not killed, there would be three or four Americans come over in thirty minutes to surrender also. So the Germans didn't shoot him, and in thirty minutes, they would soon come crossing over, the other soldiers who were going to defect and surrender safely to stay alive for the remainder of the war in a P.O.W. camp somewhere in Germany.

But the Germans were too crafty and smart for this plan. They waited until the rest of the boys went over to surrender then they shot all of them together instead of taking them prisoners as the leaflets guaranteed them. Not all defectors were treated this way, but most of them on our front were. I have no idea of how many boys were killed this way or how many boys did this and made it home after spending months and years in one of those terrible German prisoner of war camps. (P.O.W.) Most P.O.W.s were taken in hard combat fighting or shot down in airplane or made parachute jumps into battlefields, and only God and each one of these soldiers know what they went through just to stay alive. In combat, as long as there is a sense of breath in your body, you will continue to fight for your country and your belief that this was a just war.

Even when a soldier is severely wounded and could lie still and possibly live, if he sees a chance to kill the enemy, he will rise and keep shooting until the enemy finishes him off completely. This is combat infantry any place in the world where they are fighting, and all combat troops do the same thing. If you have not been in combat, no explanation is possible.

You see many freak things during combat. A bullet hitting inside a soldier's helmet in front, then traveling around the top dome of it and coming out the back of the helmet, making a hole in it as it exited without even scratching the green plastic helmet liner inside that fits over the head, and not even injuring the soldier, or in the heat of battle he might not have even been aware of being hit there.

Sometimes a small Bible or New Testament in the front pocket of a G.I.'s shirt would stop a bullet and save his life. I kept a New Testament there in my left front shirt pocket all during the war, but

198

it was never hit. However, my reading it did improve my life and might have saved me in other ways, then and now. I have always said that I was a born-again Christian on Anzio and all of Italy. I still have that New Testament at home.

I have often been asked where was I born and grew up? And I always answer, "I was born in Fairfield, Illinois, and I grew up on Anzio, Italy, in 1944, when I was twenty and twenty-one years old."

Gen. George Washington once said, "They purchased our liberty at the price of their blood, the loss of their sight and hearing, and the loss of their legs. Such is the cost of freedom. Psychological problems and physical health ruined forever. Freedom is not *free* to many people"—The year 1779.

These German soldiers were just young boys, like us, and should have been home with their loved ones, finishing high school, buying a used automobile, and trying to get a date with girls their own age.

Most of us American boys had European ancestral blood in us that was the same blood as the ones we were trying to kill. I have German, Irish, and French blood in me, and so did a large majority of our American boys. We also had some second generation Italian boys on our side fighting in Italy. The government tried not send soldiers of the same ethnic group in to that same country as they might not want to kill people of their own ancestry.

Most of the foreign boys from our infantry divisions of European origin were sent to the South Pacific to fight, rather than fight their own ancestral relations or family friends.

However we did have one soldier in our P.A. platoon that was born in Germany, then as a young man, with his parents, came to America and took out citizenship papers. As soon as he became an American citizen, when he reached eighteen years old, he had to register for the American draft, which he did as a patriotic American citizen. Then he was drafted into the American army infantry and fought against his home country with us in Italy. We used him a lot for captured German soldiers as an interpreter. This most of us did not approve of as he should not have been sent to fight and kill against his natural born homeland. He should have been sent to the South Pacific or at least as a member of the noncombatant support troops or work as an interpreter in G2 Intelligence in one of the headquarter companies.

We had quite a number of second-and third-generation Italian boys fighting in Italy, as well as on other fronts in Europe and the South Pacific. Most of them were from the east coastal cities and a few from the Chicago area. Most of them had never been away from home overnight before being inducted into the Army or any other branches of service. They had never been a Boy Scout member, had never walked or worked in the woods or country, like a lot of us midwestern farm boys had done all our lives.

But these boys made great soldiers and learned to put up with the rough army life very well. I admired them very much. Some of these Italian-American boys were killed in action.

These boys all spoke Italian at home and they were glad to help us non-Italian boys learn the Italian language while we were over there.

In the South Pacific, some of the island natives would spy on the American soldiers and report their position to the Japanese for a cash reward. But not so in Italy. We never had to worry about these people reporting on us to the enemy. They were so fed up with the sacrifices they had to make for our five years of this war that they were glad to help us out. We always rewarded them with chocolates, cigarettes, chewing gum, and anything else that we had. They had almost nothing and anything that we gave them was usually something that they didn't have or had never heard of or seen before. We grew to trust the Italian civilians during battles in their local towns and villages as to where the Germans could be found hiding.

All was not serious on the front lines. Often it was a humorous incident that we were not able to enjoy or make light of at the time. It sometimes was a very serious incident that almost got us killed. But a few days later, someone would bring it up and make a crazy remark about one of us, making it quite funny now, but almost got us killed at that particular moment.

When a new replacement came into the platoon and asked us what to do when the German artillery shells start to come in on us, the standard stock answer to that was, "Sit down, put your head between your legs, and kiss your butt good-bye, because it now belongs to God."

Another answer was, "Crawl up into your steel helmet and don't let any part of your body stick out but your elbows and your feet, then pray. But get into the helmet first before you take time to pray."

One time, while we were in reserve, one of our soldiers went out to the slit trench latrine and came back in with a small piece of shrapnel in his hand, the metal still warm from the explosion, which none of us heard. It had broken his skin a little, and there were a few drops of blood which made him eligible for the Purple Heart.

He didn't want to go to the aid station to get it treated because it was such a small wound, but we all walked him down there and made him report his wound. He was awarded the Purple Heart Medal which he and all of us took in a frivolous and joking manner.

Another time, one of our boys decided to walk quite aways from our old, bombed-out, stone house to have a bowel movement. He took a roll of white toilet paper with him and squatted down in the open field to have a bowel movement. About the time he got through, a German airplane spotted him and started to buzz him. Our boy took off, carrying the white roll of toilet paper with him, the further he ran the more the white paper unrolled and left a very clear white streamer behind him.

Two of our corporals called to him and told him not to come to our hide-out but to keep on going and lead the airplane pilot away from us. By then the white paper streamer was about forty feet long and was very easy for the German pilot to follow him, but the soldier never heard our boys hollering at him to go away. He came straight into our building, where all of us were and our supply trucks as well.

So we all got behind rocks and stone walls to protect ourselves as best we could. The German airplane pilot would now know exactly where we were and could now bomb or strafe us at will.

The airplane pilot made two or three passes over our building, but he never dropped a bomb or fired bullet to strafe us. He was either out of ammo or felt sorry for us, because then he left and never returned. I think that he took pity on us and just wanted to have some fun. Many times during this war the Germans could have killed me and some of the others, but they didn't. Many times they were sympathetic toward us and did not kill us when they could have. I think that they were kinder and more sympathetic toward us than we were toward them. They refused to shoot me a few times

201

when we were not over twenty feet apart and they had the drop on me with their burpguns.

Later on, the services went to olive drab toilet paper. Toilet paper and underwear were the last items to go olive drab for camouflage purposes instead of the white.

In one building where we were staying, two of our soldiers found a little brown-and-white puppy just about three months old. They would pour some beer that they had in one of the their helmets and the puppy would drink it and get drunk. Its little front legs would cross, and he would fall over, drunk, on the floor. I didn't think much of the idea of giving the little innocent puppy enough beer to get it drunk, but most of the boys laughed and enjoyed it, so it was good for their morale.

However, later on that night, when we all went to sleep on the floor in our new sleeping bags (fart sacks), that same little puppy remembered who had given him the beer to drink and they had bonded together, so he decided to sleep on the sleeping bag at the feet of his new-found buddies.

When these two guys awoke the next morning, they started cussing and blaming the puppy that they had so befriended the day before. He had urinated during the night on the foot of their sleeping bags. I thought that they got what they deserved, and I enjoyed their little escapade for the first time.

Our platoon had a very congenial bunch of young soldiers. There was never a fight or much verbal disagreement between any two soldiers. We were all American draftees in a very dangerous wartime situation. We were all in this mess together. No one tried to take advantage of anyone else. We were comrades in distress. When on the front lines, we were all business, very serious about our assignments when put to a dangerous job. No one argued or disagreed with our sergeants' or officers' orders. We were serious about staying alive and also looking out for our buddies as they were doing the same for me. While in rest areas, we would often play little tricks on each other, but nothing serious enough to offend. Your life still may depend on him again the next week.

Another unusual incident happened to one of the boys not in our company but in our division. This line-company infantryman, was shot and received nine German .31-caliber burp gun slugs in his face at one time. He immediately spit out three or four of them in his hand, telling his buddies about it. They took him to the first aid station and evacuated him back to our nearest tent city hospital for treatment and surgery. He returned a few days later, almost well, and had to return to front-line combat because he could still walk, shoot a rifle, and pee in a bottle. He could have been sent home with a monthly pension.

The above story and others like it are what might have made me a little bitter about not having fair and equitable training and rotation for all service men so that the burdens of combat would not be so terrible on so few. The multitude of home-front U.S.O. warriors and support troops did not see one day of combat, while the poor wounded infantryman are wounded and sent back up sometimes as many as three times after serious wounds. These poor soldiers should have been sent home with a medical discharge and a pension for life for what they went through before their twenty-first birthday. A regular service person who had never been in combat did not even know what the war was all about. There isn't any way that a movie can build up the tension, fear, hunger and life-saving tactics that you have to go through to survive. God bless America and all combat service personnel. Most soldiers never saw combat until they saw the late movie, *The Saving of Private Ryan*. Most combat infantrymen could write a movie with much worse in it than that one. That movie contained everyday occurrences for a front-line enlisted combat soldier.

All during the war if an American soldier was killed and left on the battlefield when there was not much fighting in that immediate area, Italian civilians would go out at night and strip all his clothes and shoes off, except his underwear, to keep or to sell to another civilian.

They could sell a G.I. shirt for about thirty dollars, pants for about forty dollars, and the shoes for about forty dollars, depending on how much rubber was left on the soles and heels.

We sold our cigarettes for about two-dollars-fifty-cents, and they were twenty cents a pack in the U.S. I never thought that in my lifetime that I would ever see cigarettes in America for $2.50 a pack. But due to the lung cancer scare they are now $4.00 a pack. I never smoked, so I always sold mine on the Italian black market. My worst problem was to keep my combat buddies from stealing them and selling them before I had a chance to.

We in combat, if we knew that we might get a two-day pass some time soon, we would save up our hand grenades and sell them to the Italian fishermen who would take them out on the ocean in their fishing boats and pull out the five-second pin and let the grenade explode a few feet below the surface of the water, and kill the fish which they would then sell to the markets and grocery stores. We would get seventy-five cents apiece for each hand grenade. There was a very good market for the grenades.

Prophylactic condoms also sold for seventy-five cents each. Even though this was a very strict Catholic country and the Church did not approve of birth control there was a very good market for them in Italy.

All during the war, some American soldiers had the disgusting habit of looking into the mouths of the dead Germans hoping to find gold or silver teeth caps. When they would find one, they would hold the mouth open and, with a rock, hit a stick that he placed on the gold or silver tooth and knock it out to save and take home to possibly sell for precious metal. They usually had a small Bull Durham or Golden Grain roll-your-own sack in their pocket to put the tooth in. I understand that some of the boys had eight or ten teeth saved up when the war ended.

You must remember that these soldiers were depression boys who were not used to making over a dollar or two a day for their labor back home before the draft and now were receiving $55.00 to $65.00 a month.

I always looked for German hand guns, but that was about all. I could usually find a small pistol in the inside of their black leather boots. Most souvenir-hunting soldiers usually overlooked this place. This was particularly true of the S.S. panzer troops. They always had a small pistol inside their boot.

Some of the boys also would cut a notch in their wooden M-1 rifle stock after every German that they killed. I didn't really care for that either.

Back home in Illinois, I would go rabbit hunting with my older brother and two of our cousins, but it bothered me to shoot and kill a rabbit. I always felt sorry for the rabbit when I would pick it up and it was still warm and kicking. I eventually got so that I would go with them with my twenty-two rifle that my brother had given me for Christmas, but I would not shoot at anything. After the war, I never went hunting again even though our farm had plenty of deer, rabbits, quail, and foxes. My dad and I later on turned the farm into a wild game reserve, which we kept for about fifty years.

During the entire war if the dead American soldiers were not able to be removed soon after their death for three or four days during the hot summer months, it was very sad to see a young American boy, who had given his life so bravely, now to see him lying there, on his back rotting away, with the maggots crawling out of his nose, mouth, ears, and from any place on his body that had open wound and the flesh and blood showing. This will really get you the first time that you see this horrible sight. But after your first and second battle and you see about twenty of them lying there like that, you will learn to look at them, walk around them, and take off for another hill or town to liberate. You also always imagine yourself lying there.

It is much worse on you if you had known or met his parents as they visited him at camp. Now you can just see them getting that dreaded telegram from Western Union, "We regret to inform you that your son was killed in action in defense of his country. Please accept our sympathy and condolences." That is the worst thing that can happen to a parent, especially if it is their only child.

In the winter months, the bodies were usually frozen hard and covered with snow. They are frozen stiff and do not smell. One time I sat down on a frozen body thinking it was a rock, as it was completely covered with snow. When I realized that it was a dead American soldier boy, I apologized to him, "I am very sorry, buddy." I was sorry for many things.

Dead soldiers make a very good protective shield. When we are being machine-gunned or straffed by airplanes, we lay down on the ground and pull one or possibly two of these dead soldiers over on top of you to take the thirty- or fifty-caliber bullets that will probably be coming at you very soon. When it's over, you always said, "thanks, buddy." If you had been carrying him back to the rear echelon, you put him back on the stretcher and continue down the mountain. You are going to live another day.

All during the war as we advanced the entire length of the continent of Italy, we would often live with the poor mountain peasant people. They had lived a rural life for generations and they were en-

205

tirely different from the city dwellers who had lived in town for generations.

We soldiers in combat spent most of our time with the rural, peasant people because that is where most of the combat fighting took place. However, noncombat troops spent most of their overseas time in large towns where buildings for the supplies were available and restaurants, drinking water, and electricity was also available. This was the ideal way to fight a war. Also there were plenty of girls or senoritas available in the larger towns like Naples, Rome, Florence, Montacatini, Milan, and Bologna.

In the rural areas, when a man became engaged to a local Italian girl, she would usually go and live with her fiancé and his entire family in their house that probably had up to three generations already living there. The young couple would usually get married by the priest sometime before the first child was born. But there was no hurry to get married just because the girl was a few months pregnant.

When the baby was born, there was no use putting diapers on him because they would just get dirty. We were staying in one house in the mountains north of Rome. The mother was carrying around a small baby in her arms, and the baby was having a bowel movement that was running down the front of the mother's dress as she was carrying it across the room. I asked her where were the baby's diapers or pantaloons. And she said that she doesn't need any pantaloons, that she is only one year old and won't need any pantaloons until she gets older. With that settled, she put the baby down on the hard, dirt floor, and the baby finished having its bowel movement. The mother took a small shovel of wood ashes from the fireplace and swept the ashes very deftly around the fecal matter, then all into a dust pan and threw it outside. Then she wiped the front of her dress off of the child's feces and sat down to talk to all of us. Not a word was said by the rest of the family. I assumed that this was the normal procedure for such things and had been for a few hundred years. Personally, I found it a little sickening. I guess that is the reason that I have remembered it all these years.

They also had another custom quite different from ours. It was their sleeping habits in the mountains. They city people slept much as we do. Husband and wife together and the children in another room in separate beds. But not the peasants. They had one large, white, heavy cloth mattress on the floor in one back room. This large mattress was filled with fresh corn shucks each year at harvest time. The mattress was about one foot high or more. It was usually set in one corner and took up a large part of that back room. We slept on these when we got a chance to in combat.

All of the family slept on it each night. Men, women, and children, all together and each with their own cover. The only heat in their house was the fireplace, which usually sufficed as a cooking stove as well if they were very poor. If they were not that poor, they would have an outside kiva oven made from clay dirt. This was mostly for bread. Sometimes, a whole small village would have one kiva, and they each would have a day to do their own baking. It was heated by wood gathered nearby.

If we were not on the line and were in a rest area, and if the grapes were ripe at the time, a lot of us helped the local Italians gather their grapes by cutting the bunches from the vines. We learned never to pull the bunches off, as that would sometimes strip down the bark on the vine and let insects and disease get started. We would fill a bushel basket of grapes and empty them into a large hopper situated in the middle of a wooden wagon that had been pulled into the field. There was a man turning a handle to grind the grapes, stems, dust, and bugs all together and make a very good pulp juice. When the tub was full, it would be removed and another tub put in its place to be filled the same way. The local people enjoyed showing us how to do this. Also, they were glad that we took an interest in their country and their language. Most of us came back with quite a bit of knowledge of the Italian language, as I did.

They cut their wheat crop as it had been cut for hundreds of years, with a sickle about six feet long as our grandfathers used them to mow grass before lawn mowers were invented. They would carry it by hand and make a wheat shock as we did here. Then if they had a team of oxen, they would carry it to a shed to finish drying. There were no tractors or combines in Italy at that time. I think that some of their harvest methods went back to the days of Christ as they still used the sickle with a cradle behind to catch the wheat. We would then flail the wheat grains from the chaff and straw by a flail made from two six-foot-long sticks tied end to end with a rope so that we could beat the grain heads loose from the straw.

Then we would hold it all up in a box and pour it slowly down into another box and let the wind blow the chaff away and the wheat grains would fall straight down into another box, as they were heavier than the straw and chaff. Then we would sweep the straw and chaff to one side and the wheat grains to the other side to be kept for food and seed for the next year. The women and children worked in the fields doing this the same as the men and boys. Their rural peasant life was very primitive, with a scarcity of food and absolutely no luxuries. No running water. They carried their clothes to the nearest creek or river and rubbed the clothes on the large rock. The women had their own day to wash their clothes and their own large flat rock in the cold river bed. They did not have any soap or detergents of any kind. Just pound and rub vigorously until the clothes came clean. They had very few clothes to change to. Possibly one change only in most homes. They had homemade straw brooms they either made themselves or were made by a relative nearby.

When they married, they very seldom moved away from their families. Each family of relatives was a very close knit, small world. That was how many different dialects started. Nobody moved away from an isolated area for hundreds of years, and they gradually used certain words to mean certain things that they used in everyday life until it became common usage. There were very few roads, no money to buy with, no automobiles to travel with, so no one left their immediate area.

I have talked to many elderly people in small towns who have never been outside their city limits of, possibly, ten to fifteen blocks long.

Early in the war, the army was very liberal with their cigarettes. They had all brands, but most of them are not manufactured today. I did not smoke, since I had asthma and could not inhale, but I often carried a package of cigarettes and some matches for my buddies. When our foxholes would get water in the bottom of them from the rain or melting snow, we would field strip the paper off the cigarettes and dump them on the ground like straw to soak up the water, which they did very well. It would take three or four cartons of cigarettes to soak up the water, but we had plenty of them until the second front opened up. Then most of the cigarettes and everything else went to them including ammunition and replacement personnel.

The officers of the D-day invasion forgot that it was we who had held off the entire German Army for three years before the invasion. This is when we were known as the *forgotten front.*

Often when we would leave our foxholes and other places of hiding when we were in battle and advancing to the north, chasing the enemy, we would leave many packages of cigarettes behind as well as empty C-ration cans, scrap metal, paper and anything else that we did not want to carry. When we left an area, it was very messy, and the Italians would swarm to that spot to see what they could find.

This was not true of the English or the German Army. You could never tell that they had been in an area when they left. They left a clean battlefield. They picked up everything, including their cigarette butts off the ground. I have looked into the concrete machine gun bunkers where the Germans had been firing at us, and I could not find any trace of a piece of paper, graffiti on the walls, cigarette butts or anything that would indicate that anyone had ever been there. They left a perfectly clean battlefield.

I will never forget one bright summer day when we were helping the line-company boys in an attack, and I was riding on an M4 tank, I got off to look after a wounded soldier that I saw on the ground with one of his legs cut off by German artillery shrapnel. Just a few yards away there was a German soldier to my right who was lying dead on the ground. A young girl ran out of an Italian farmhouse and grabbed him in her arms, hugged him to her chest and began crying and holding him very closely and dearly. I watched this with great sorrow. I figured that he had probably been staying at this family's house during the German occupation and evidently, they had fallen in love with each other. They were both about seventeen or eighteen years old. But war is war. Everyone loses.

However, I am sure that this household welcomed the American soldiers with open arms as did all the Italians. We always did say over there that they told the German soldiers good-bye at the back door and then hurried to the front door to welcome the Americans. Then they would say the *tedischi* (Germans) were *bruta* (mean) and *i tedischi presero tutti via* (the Germans took everything with them).

We in America cannot even have a bad dream and know of the terrible living standards that most of these countries went through even before the war, much less during the combat days when their homes were completely destroyed and they had to live in caves (*il rifugio*) for months at a time and had to eat green tomatoes, green onions and buckeyes and chestnuts off the trees and glad to be able to eat that. A lot of these people had malnutrition sores on their arms and legs where they had bumped themselves and their body did not have enough tissue strength to repair itself. This was very common throughout the European countries during the WWII days. We saw a lot of it.

Many of the Italians had first aid bandages on their arms and legs, so I asked a lady one day what was wrong with her that she had on three or four white bandages. She said that they were malnutrition sores. They did not have enough vitamins and minerals in their diet since the German occupation five years earlier and now if they bruise or cut themselves, their body is not healthy enough to heal and repair with new tissue. These open sores will continue to weep until we are able to again tend our fields and harvest our crops. Our bodies are barely able to sustain our lives, and it is not able to manufacture new replacement cells to heal a wound with. This condition I noticed was very common throughout Italy. I had never heard of it.

Many fairly well-to-do people had a bird feeder on top of their houses. It was a large wooden box about three feet square with louvers on all sides so that the birds could enter and exit at will. When these people wanted some meat to eat or had special company, they would feed the birds then close the louvers, trapping the sparrows inside. Then they would reach up from inside the house and swat them with a flat board to kill as many as they needed. I have been with them when they did this. They never killed more than they needed. They would swat a few times, then count the number of sparrows killed. When they had the amount they wanted, they would open the shutters and let the rest of the birds out so that they could raise more young birds and keep a small supply of meat for the house. I have helped them do this.

They would then dip the little birds in boiling hot water to loosen the feathers, which would then slide off with a pull of the hands. Then they would clean and gut them. The birds were not cut up into pieces. They were baked whole. They would put the flat pan into the oven or kiva to bake the sparrows for a few minutes.

The bird was put on its back, its feet sticking straight up in the air, with about twenty or so other sparrows on one flat baking sheet. This flat pan was then inserted into an oven and baked until they were brown and thoroughly done. They were then taken out of the oven and put on a large plate and on the table. These birds were killed and eaten only on special occasions for their honored guests. Meat was so rare and expensive that this delicacy was not eaten every day, otherwise they would kill off all their birds and not have anything special to feed their guests for lunch. If this was served to you, you were a very honored guest.

When you eat baked sparrows, you picked off the legs and drumsticks first by picking them off whole in one piece and eat it whole, bones and all. That is one reason that they bake them well done. It crumbles the small hollow bones of the bird so that they are as digestible as the red meat is. Besides, they needed what little calcium they could get from the birds' bones. Heat destroys vitamins and minerals, so I doubt if they received many vitamins and minerals from these birds.

The bones of birds and fowls are hollow so that they may fly with less weight than our four-footed animals that only walk. God made sure of that in his plans to make each species able to take care of themselves.

I ate baked sparrows only once while in Italy, and if we had salt, bread, and butter I think they would have been very good. They were all right though as they were. I don't see any difference in eating them from eating pigeons, quail, or doves. I have eaten them all during the depression before I went to service. I liked them.

I cannot think of the Italian campaign without thinking of a young eighteen-year-old soldier who I will call "Little Joey." We were in the same barracks at Camp McCain in the winter, spring and summer of 1943. We both arrived there in February of that year. We were in M company, which is a machine-gun and eight-mm-mortar line company, one of the most risky companies in the infantry front lines. The life of a machine gunner in an enemy attack is estimated at five minutes. Since it is the most dangerous weapon in battle, it is the first that an enemy wants to knock out. I was in this company for one year in the States before being shipped overseas.

Back to "Little Joey." I wouldn't see him for weeks at a time, then all of a sudden, while street fighting with the Germans, someone would holler, "Hammil," and I would look up and there would be Joey with his rifle going through a house, looking for Germans. He was a brave and great fighting soldier.

One day during an attack we were spearheading against the Germans, I was riding on the back of a Sherman M4 tank with some other infantry boys, and I could see German 88-mm artillery shells exploding and hitting the ground from the dust they made when they exploded, but I could not hear them explode. The fumes from the tank's diesel motor soon made a person nauseated, as we had to sit on top of the motor in the rear. I did not like riding them into battle on the attack. We hit a big ditch once, and I was thrown off.

I decided I would be safer if I got off and walked so I could hear the shells. Also, the Germans were firing more shells at the tanks than they were at the infantry boys on foot so I would be safer walking.

I got off and had gone only a few feet when I saw an American soldier lying dead on the ground in front of me. I looked at him as I always did to see if it was someone we knew, and it was Pvt. Little Joey. I examined him and assumed that he was dead. A piece of shrapnel from an artillery shell had cut off his left leg halfway between the knee and the hip. Some other soldier before me had taken his belt off and tied it around the bloody stump and made a very good tourniquet to stop the rush of blood from the severed thigh to keep him from bleeding to death.

I stayed with him a few minutes and put his green summer jacket over his severed leg and went on with the platoon, which we all had to do, as the Germans were retreating and we must not let them have a chance to stop and dig in again.

I never saw or heard of him again, as he was not in my company then. About two weeks later, while we were in a house in Barbarinno for a short rest, a jeep with a trailer with two dead bodies in it stopped in front of the house that we were holed up in. Pfc.

John Despot and I went out to see who the dead soldiers were because, often, we would recognize one of them.

And there was Little Joey lying there with his leg off. I questioned the jeep driver as what had happened.

"Joey was not dead when you saw him. He was unconscious from shock and loss of blood. The medics put him on a stretcher and took him to the front-line emergency first aid station to try to save his life. The medics had shoveled out shallow fox holes about one-foot deep and put a wounded G.I. in each one. However, the Germans started shelling the first aid station, and every time a shell would land close to Joey, he would rise up in a coma and when he did, the blood would rush out of his severed leg, and after four or five times of this, he eventually bled to death."

I thought a lot of this boy. He was seventeen or eighteen when he entered the service and about nineteen or twenty when he died. We slept in the same barracks in the States for a year.

He was like so many young draftees in WWII. He had never had a date with girl, never shaved, and never driven an automobile in his young life. God bless you, Little Joey. He was brave.

You have to be eighteen years of age before the army can legally send you overseas. But so many young boys lied about their age to get into service, the army didn't always know the true age of many of these boys. These same boys ran into trouble with the Social Security office when they reached sixty-five years of age and wanted to retire. Many of them did not have legal proof of their age.

The local draft boards and recruiting offices particularly encouraged the young boys to lie about their age so that they could meet their government quotas, which was set very high during the war. The local recruiting offices even helped the young boys fill out their enlistment papers, even though they knew the boys were lying, in order to meet their quota and receive a promotion in rank. Everybody has a boss.

In all battles and all wars, the main objective is to outsmart the enemy. This can be done in many ways. It can even be the deciding factor in any given battle. The German soldiers were masters at this. Even though they outsmarted us many times, we admired their military strategy and envied them every time they pulled a new trick on us.

One of their very effective tricks was when we were on patrol and firing at each other one of the German soldiers would holler as if he had been shot. Then they would throw a dummy down on the ground that was booby trapped and run back to their own lines.

Our patrol would then go up to the dummy, thinking that it was a wounded or dead German, to search him for souvenirs. When they turned the dummy soldier over, it would explode in their faces. A booby trap would go off and kill or injure some of our soldiers on that patrol. Then they would immediately throw artillery and mortar fire in on the rest of our patrol. It was very effective for a while, until the entire front of our infantry got wise to it and quit going up to a wounded patrol that hollered and left a soldier on the ground.

When we would leave an area to follow the retreat of the German line companies the Italian civilians would rush toward it and scavenger every thing that we Americans left behind. To them almost every thing that we left behind was worth something; most of it they had never seen before.

They were still plowing with oxen when we were there. I would compare their life style in 1942 to 1945 to the American Civil War days about 1865. Italy was a very backward and poor country but the people were always very nice and cooperative to us Americans. We here in America do not know what poverty is until you have lived in a foreign country. We here in America had more during the Great Depression 1920 to 1943 than Italy ever had on their best year. I know I was born in 1923 and lived here nineteen years before going to Italy for twenty seven months of combat. I have been in these situations of hard times and poverty. Maybe that's what made the WWII boys great soldiers and to be called THE GREATEST GENERATION.

I call our generation the SURVIVOR GENERATION. Also it could be called THE GREAT SURVIVOR GENERATION.

Another effective trick that they pulled on us was when the American forces sent some dogs to us to take on patrol so that the dog could sniff out the Germans before our knowing that they were around. This would give the line company boys time to hide and ambush the Germans before they knew that we were near them. The dog's hair would rise up on his neck and he would go on the attack when he smelled them in advance of the American soldiers on patrol.

This canine scout worked pretty well until the Germans captured or killed some of our patrols and then used the canine dog to work against us and for them.

The Germans took the dogs on patrol to find the American soldiers, and soon as the canine smelled the Americans, his best friends, he would really whine and give us away, as he wanted to come back to his original buddies.

When the army asked us if we wanted one, we told Sgt. Kenneth Blake no. He might betray us if we ever lost him. He could lead them exactly to our hideout position. So we didn't get one. But some of the other battalions got them, and regretted it later on. The dogs were wonderful scouts as long as we had them but when the German soldiers got ahold of one the tide turned on us.

When the line companies are in a static position, that is, dug in their foxholes and will be there for a few days fighting, we in P.A. platoon have the job of taking ammunition and drinking water to the boys in each of their individual foxhole or hideout.

When an ammo bearer approached a foxhole or another soldier's position, he approached from the rear, which was the American side. He never approached them from the front or side, as you can easily be mistaken for a German by a nervous front-line boy. And he can't be blamed for that because we are always to approach from the rear and make yourself known possibly with the night's password. Always be recognized before approaching another soldier in combat. He is just as anxious to save his life and come home as you are. And never startle or make an unusual noise before being identified. Make very sure that he knows who you are! Loss of your own buddies from this type of carelessness has happened and will continue. There are always accidents of killing by "friendly fire" as it is called at Washington, D.C.

If he knew the soldier's name he was taking ammo to, he never called it out because a German soldier might be lying in ambush and hear his name. As soon as he left that German will call out his name again, and the American will let down his guard and possibly get killed. So take your time and get well identified, answer any question that the other American soldier asks you before approaching him.

He usually carried three .30-caliber bandoleers around his neck, a pocket full of .45 shells, and a can of water and his own rifle.

215

Also, possibly a can of C rations, but never any mail to the front line boys, as the Germans would often get the name and address from the mail and demand a large ransom for his release from a P.O.W. camp even after he was killed in combat.

On the front lines you never carry any mail that has your name on it. Germany has been known to send $50,000.00 ransom letters to their home.

During combat, when on a search-and-destroy patrol, often the soldier is close enough to the enemy that if he were to sneeze, cough or let off gas, it would give away his position.

So if he has to sneeze, he is supposed to take his thumb nail on his right hand and press it up against the bottom of his nose very hard to cause a slight pain, which will prevent him from sneezing most of the time. If he thinks that he is going to cough, he presses his forefinger against his Adam's apple until it hurts enough to stifle the cough. This is due to the neurological theory that the brain can only interpret one stimulus at a time, and it will be the major stimulus, or the one that hurts the most.

If he has to let out loud gas, he had better slide it out very quietly so as not to startle his own buddies, because when under pressure near the enemy, everybody gets trigger happy and jumpy.

If he is going to make a slight noise or do something that might startle his fellow soldiers, then he raises his hand and gets their attention and motions to himself that he is going to make a movement of some kind so don't get jumpy.

If he were to violate any of these procedures, he stood to catch a lot of hell from his buddies when things eased up, and, if it was of great endangerment, the sergeant might dress him down and give him extra details for awhile. He must have the safety of the entire platoon at heart. No unnecessary risks are allowed by any one individual. You are a family huddled together for the mutual life-saving security of all.

During the entire war if the dead American soldiers were not able to be removed for three or four days during the summer months it was a very sad sight to see a young American boy who had given his life so bravely, now to see him lying there on his back rotting away with maggots crawling out of his nose, mouth, ears and any flesh wound that he may have received. This is a very sickening and sad sight especially if you knew him when he was alive and can't understand how such a vibrant and good-looking boy could now be in this final condition.

You also realize and can see your self in that same decomposing condition some time possibly in the near future. That can make you vomit if you have a weak stomach. But after a while in combat you get used to seeing such horrible things. You get used to it but you don't have to like it or approve of it.

In the winter months the bodies are frozen and terminate in a better condition. They usually freeze in a couple of hours and get covered with snow in the Alps mountain area. They look much better and don't smell. A couple of times they were so covered with snow that I sat down on a stiff thinking it was a snow-covered rock. I got up immediately and I apologized to the corpse "I'm sorry old buddy." I can just see his parents getting that dreaded telegram. Dead soldiers make a good protective cover if you are being strafed by German aircraft or the artillery shells are coming in very fast and close by. To protect yourself is to lay down beside a dead soldier and then pull his body on top of yours, and if you are lucky there might be another dead body nearby and you can pull his body along side of yours. That is not a lot of protection, but it helps some as the 30-caliber bullets will penetrate the dead soldier's body as well as yours.

25

Saving a Trapped Soldier

There was a very sad and dangerous mission, which I was not on, that winter of 1944. It was the digging out of a line-company soldier trapped under tons of rubble when a stone farmhouse in a desolate area had collapsed on him during a heavy wind and rainstorm. He was in no man's land on a patrol with his squad when one of the heavy stone walls collapsed and pinned him under the rubble. No soldier ever wants to get caught in no man's land, but it is inevitable if you are in combat very many months. All soldiers must advance through no man's land to search and kill the enemy, who are also out there looking for them to also search and kill them. It is the most dreaded area in a combat zone. If you live, you will grow to maturity very fast out there in no man's land.

This rescue squad was made up of our four best men. I would have been the fifth man if any of them got killed. All five of us soldiers always worked together as a team in combat situations. Sgt. Allickson said, "I need only four men to work side by side on this suicide mission." These four were all seasoned combat soldiers, and we had faced many dangerous situations similar to this in no man's land. This kind of work was part of our regular duties as pioneer and ammunition platoon, to do the tasks that the regular linemen did not have the equipment for or the time to stop and do, as they were chasing the enemy to keep them from digging in at a new defensive location. All these jobs were in the advancing front lines, all within German shell range. At no time can a soldier let his guard down and not be watching for the enemy while he is doing his dangerous job.

These four great soldiers, Sgt. Joe Buffalo, Cpl. Max L. Rush, Cpl. Braun, and Pfc. Despot, waited until dark to start their mercy mission. Most of our work was done at night so as not be seen too easily by the Germans. When they arrived at the tumbled-down stone house, they leaned against the cold wet bricks and whispered his name. "Bob, Bob. Are you there?"

"Yes, I am," he answered back. "But I'm in a lot of pain. Can you give me any morphine?"

"No, we do not have any morphine. We're not medics. We are combat infantrymen, just like you, so lie still, and we will dig you out tonight."

"No, do not try that. I am severely wounded, and the Germans will hear you digging and will possibly come and kill all of you. I do not want you boys to get killed trying to rescue me here in no man's land. Please, shoot me, and kill me and you guys can go back to our own platoon. It's hopeless for me here, so save yourselves, but kill me first, please."

Our brave soldiers dug all that night with their bare hands only, as a metal shovel or metal tool of any kind would have surely been heard in the quiet of the night and given away their position. It started to turn light, and the four soldiers had to leave before fully daylight and return to our old house without rescuing the wounded soldier. They told him, "Lie quietly, and we will return tonight to dig."

They waited until dark the second night to go on their rescue mission again. Again they whispered his name to see if there was any live response, and he answered.

"Please kill me now, and quit your digging, there is no hope for me, but there is for you. Please kill me and go back to your unit. Don't dig anymore. Save yourselves. There is no hope for me."

And then he said, "There was a German patrol that went past here last night, and I could hear them talking, so they will probably come by here tonight and find you guys, and you could all get killed. So please, shoot me and go back safely to your own unit."

"No way will we leave you here, and no way will we kill you. So just lie still, and we will dig you out of this mess."

They dug for a few hours, again only with their hands. A German patrol of four or five soldiers did come by. They had heard the Germans coming, so they all four crawled in among the stone rubble and remained very quiet until the enemy passed by without noticing them. As soon as the enemy patrol was out of sight, they continued digging with their bare hands to free the injured soldier.

Daylight came, and they had to leave the soldier again in the rubble without rescuing him. They told him that they were leaving and would be back the third night to dig him out. Again, he begged them for a mercy killing, and that they not risk their own lives by coming back for him.

But again, our soldiers refused to shoot him, but they promised him that they would come back the third night to resume their life-saving digging.

The third night that they went to the site to dig him out, they whispered his name.

"Bob, Bob, are you there?"

But no answer came from within the pile of rubble where he was trapped. Then they noticed that another stone wall of this large house had crumbled and covered him up a lot more with stone and bricks. He was now in deeper than ever, and after their digging for two long, rainy nights, he was covered with more stones. It was now that they realized that any further attempt to dig him out with bare hands was useless; only a bulldozer could free him now. So they whispered his name, "Bob," again without any answer coming from inside the stone pile.

When the four soldiers returned to our platoon and told us this sad story, we all hoped that he was dead now and out of his misery. I am sure that his soul went immediately to heaven, as he was such a brave and good soldier, and he gave so unselfishly of his own precious life. I still remember his name, but he was not a member of our platoon and none of us knew him personally. However, he was one of the bravest and most unselfish soldiers that we ever dealt with. God bless.

I have often wondered if on the third night of the rescue mission, it was possible that this soldier boy was still alive and refused to answer so that they would leave and not further risk their lives for his impossible rescue attempt. We all discussed that possibility, but the rescue squad said no, "there was no way that he could have lived through that last stone wall collapsing on top of the already heavy load on him." But I have always wondered about that awful question. But we will never know, and I don't want to.

Later on, all four of our brave soldiers were pinned with the Bronze Star for bravery and valor above and beyond the call of duty. These medals were all pinned on them in a private ceremony by Gen. Mark Clark, who replaced General Patton as our general. We all watched the presentation, with an army photographer who took their pictures and mailed one to their hometown newspaper. The soldier who died was presented with the Purple Heart and Bronze Star for his heroism and valor in combat. They were all well-earned medals. The dead soldier's medals were awarded to his parents posthumously.

Being afraid and being scared is not the same as being a coward. All combat men are afraid and scared in combat, this is very natural unless you have suicidal tendencies and want to get killed to get out of your personal and war time mental situations that you are harboring in your mind. And I am sure that a few of the soldiers from all the countries in this war had a few suicidal soldiers that were extraordinarily brave, that were soldiers with a suicidal mission on their minds, we will never know which ones these brave soldiers were and I personally do not want to know.

After the war was over and all the combat soldiers were home, there were a lot of suicides among them. The army said, "We have no idea how many suicides there are with our discharged veterans, because so many of them chose to die in automobile accidents by hitting another car or truck head on so that their insurance would pay double indemnity on accidental deaths rather than suicide. Companies do not pay on a suicide." Other than the GI Bill for education or on-job training programs, nothing was done for the discharged WWII veteran until recently. The government started to give us medicines at a nominal cost per prescription.

I think by now two-thirds of us are dead who did make it home. Records show that eighteen hundred WWII veterans are dying in America every day. The local V.F.W. and the American Legion are busy every week doing Honor Guard for our deceased, as the government says that each honorably discharged veteran is eligible for a military funeral, and a folded American flag presented to his next of kin with great honor and respect. And this is being done daily by all our veterans' organizations all over America. God bless every one of the dead and God bless the living veterans who are burying them because their time is next, just like mine. Soon, all this will be modern American history. About sixty percent of people now living were not even born when WWII was over in 1945. I hope that this book can somehow contribute to the history of that terrible war.

221

26

Battle of Leghorn

There are so many losses in the infantry and marines that during the war, the U.S. government put out the word to all law enforcement agencies that when a young seventeen-, eighteen- or nineteen-year-old boy was in trouble, give them a chance to enlist in these branches of service and all criminal charges will be dropped against them. Many of them took the police up on this plea bargain and were sent to the army ground forces, infantry, or the marines. Most of them made good soldiers and some were killed. Many of these problem boys were decorated and came home and made good citizens. But the point that I wish to make is that it was a very poor morale booster for us. It made us feel like jailbirds. We were regular army inductees and very proud of our military station in the war. We were very proud of our achievements through deadly and impossible conditions. No other branch can say that. We took a licking but kept on kicking butts of the enemy. You don't know what proudness really is until you have risked your life for your country many times. And you don't know how to live and enjoy life until you thought that you were going to be killed many times. "Don't sweat the small stuff" is what I learned. "You have beaten death so many times that little things are very insignificant. It will solve itself if you leave it alone long enough."

The fact that we beat everything that the enemy threw at us and we survived gave me the confidence that I needed when I graduated from chiropractic college and went into a new town and opened up my first chiropractic office. I wasn't afraid of anybody. I was only twenty-four years of age and very healthy and confident that I would succeed at anything that I set my mind to. And I sure needed it for the next thirteen years when I was involved in the Illinois State political war to license doctors of chiropractic.

During WWII, Germany and America agreed at Geneva Switzerland that they would not destroy any of the great historic buildings in Italy, such as the famous churches, leaning tower of Pisa, the Coliseum in Rome, and also many of the old historic and religious buildings in Venice and Milano.

These cities were called "open cities" (*città aperta*) in the Italian language. Many of the civilians that lived in these towns had a sense of false security. The open city police was adhered to fairly well but not perfectly. The Germans would defend and hold the edges of those towns, and we would have to bomb and fight and destroy those fringes of towns and, as common in war mistakes are made. Many people were killed or crippled and injured in these perimeter bombings. But on the whole, most of these famous buildings were not used by the Germans, and we did not destroy them. They survived the terrible war. You can still visit and enjoy them today.

One slight violation of that rule was that as we entered Pisa, our infantry scouts discovered two German soldiers running out of the leaning tower of Pisa. The leaning tower's construction was started in 1174, but it was not completed until 1350 because it was leaning so badly that the architect was afraid of its collapsing. It is 170 feet high, 40 feet across at the base, and has 294 steps for visitors to climb if they so wish. The reason that it leans 13 feet out of plumb line is the construction fault. The west tower base is extended into the sand and gravel soil adjoining the Arno River. The east side was built on the regular soil ground of loam and clay, which held up under the enormous weight of the tower with its very heavy eight bells at the top floor.

The leaning tower must have been used for some time by the Germans because when I went over to look at it, the first floor had been used as their toilet. It was so filthy that a person didn't want to really go through it to see this very structure that scientist and astronomer Galileo used for some of his experiments with gravity and also invented the thermometer that we still use today.

When I got there, during the heat of the battle, I talked to two infantry linemen. They said, "We ran two German artillery observers out of there. They were not supposed to use this historic landmark in any military way, but they were using it as an observation point for their artillery to fire upon us." They didn't tell me if they killed them or not, and I had too much to do myself to worry about that.

There was only one bridge in town leading north to follow the enemy, and they had blown it up. We had to wait for the engineers to come up from the rear to build a pontoon bridge out of row boats lashed together and then planks laid lengthways across them for the jeeps, trucks, foot soldiers, and tanks, all to cross over on that one very unstable pontoon bridge that was built very hurriedly under German shell fire. But we made it across. I understand that a tank or two got too close to one side and flipped over into the cold, deep Arno River, and all drowned before they could get out of their tank. I didn't know any of the tank drivers personally, but I had ridden on the back of their tanks a few times in our attacks. These were the Sherman M-4 tanks. I had personally worked on and helped build the hull or large body part of many of these Sherman M-4 tanks at Continental Roll and Steel of East Chicago, Illinois, for about five months before I was drafted. As I rode on the rear of these tanks, I would always wonder if this could possibly be one that I had personally worked on in East Chicago.

I was a jeep driver for an infantry company in the States, and the one thing that they always told you not to do was "never shift gears of your vehicle on a small pontoon bridge, as it will jar the bridge too much, and it will possibly fall apart. Always put your vehicle in the gear that you want to leave the bridge with and to climb the exit road that you see ahead of you, but never shift gears on a small bridge." I learned later that this was very good advice.

I was on foot alone as I crossed the bridge. I had a very dangerous job to do. There were irrigation canals extending out from the Arno River into the farm ground nearby, and the Germans had thrown antitank mines into these canals. It was my job, because I was a fair swimmer, to dive down in the canals, feel for the mines and bring them up to the surface and lay them on the bank to be detonated later.

This mine-removal job I did all by myself, but I did not dive into the seven- to eight-foot-deep irrigation canal. I dropped into the water feet first and felt around on the bottom with my feet to locate the mines. I found five or six mines, which I deposited on the canal bank, then I had to mark the cleared spot with white engineers tape which all of us mine sweepers carried inside the front of our shirts against our stomach.

After I had done this, I signaled for all the infantry men and all the vehicles to cross over where it was marked. It was deep, but most of the advancing forces made it across at that time. I was dripping wet. I did the job with all my clothes on except my shoes, which I had removed so that I could feel for the mines better. I sure didn't want to set one off or miss one and let someone else set it off and kill them. I was a little proud of myself for having completed this dangerous mission all alone. It was an extremely dangerous job, and it was necessary for our forces to advance. I would like to visit that spot again. It is right beside a large house. The occupants had all been evacuated at the time.

On the way back from the irrigation canal, where I had cleared a safe passage zone of about twelve feet wide, I was headed toward the newly made pontoon bridge that I had crossed on when I saw two infantry boys that I did not know walking around something on the ground. So I went over to them and said, "What's up?"

"It looks like this soldier stepped on a German antitank mine and it blew him all to pieces."

I looked down at the ground at a hole that had been blown, and there was a piece of red human flesh that would weigh about four or five pounds and, close by was a hard black rubber heel of a shoe or an army combat boot probably.

I asked "What makes you think that it was an antitank mine instead of an antipersonnel mine?" He said "It takes 250 pounds of a man to set off an antitank mine and only 25 pounds of pressure to set off an antipersonnel mine."

"I think that the Germans used a unique trick here. They first buried an antitank mine then put an antipersonnel mine on top of it so that the lesser mine would set off the larger mine. This would blow any vehicle up including an American army tank and any soldier standing nearby." We looked around, and all that we saw was a piece of his liver and that black shoe heel.

Since the war, I have talked to many army and navy combat boys. After a person had been blown up, the most common piece usually found is a black shoe heel and possibly a piece of flesh that resembles the liver. Maybe all flesh after it has been destroyed by concussion looks like the liver. I don't know. No soldier wants to die, but if he has to, "Please, God, make it quick. Don't let me linger and suffer, and tell Mama that I love her." This is basically the same thing that dying soldiers say if they are not killed instantly. "Tell Mama that I love her."

I don't want to imply that only the boys from North Africa and Italy had these terrible combat experiences. The combat infantry and marines in the South Pacific and the infantry boys who invaded Omaha Beach and Normandy Beach on D Day, June 6, 1944, and other boys who fought in combat for any length of time went through all of these horrible experiences, and more especially if they were prisoners of war (P.O.W.). God and each individual prisoner alone knows the hazards that they went through. But I can write only about the experiences that I have personally experienced. They were bad enough, and I want all the world to know what a few of us had to go through so that others can brag about this great country, America the beautiful. Freedom was not free for a lot of our boys and girls. They gave their lives or suffered and then came home, some to continue to suffer the rest of their lives.

The reason that you didn't hear much about the death and suffering of our boys then was due to many reasons. First, all during the war we were told not to mention our hardships because we were to keep up the civilian morale at home, as they had been told to keep up the military morale of the boys overseas.

Second, everyone had had enough of the four years of war, and no one wanted to hear any more about it: "let's put it behind us and get on with our lives."

Third, the boys who went through actual combat and winning the war were too emotional to talk about it without crying and consequentially feeling ashamed and sick about what some of their buddies went through and of those who didn't come back. No one wanted to hear about how bad it was for them and how easy for most of the others.

Whenever we saw a dead German or a dead English soldier, we would always go through their pockets or field sack, looking for food and other items. We especially looked for their food, as it was usually canned fish of some kind, like our American canned sardines. I am not much of a fish eater, but it was different from our C rations and anything was a welcome relief. And we never got much out of our own C rations.

226

Once in a while we would find an Italian family who would sell us a chicken for ten dollars. The chickens were small ones, like our game bantam chickens. They would always ask for the intestines, head, and neck back for free, as we Americans never ate those parts anyway.

They would take the intestines and strip out the two inside linings and throw them away. However, the outside lining they would chop up real fine into chitlins and make barbecue sauce for their spaghetti. I have also helped them make their spaghetti. They would make a very dry bread ball pasta, and run it through a machine like our meat grinder and the dough would come out in long dough strings like spaghetti. Then they would let it dry for a day, then cook it in boiling water and then pour the chitlin sauce over it. Due to the German occupation, they had very little salt, if they had any.

We would help the civilians who lived near the ocean carry the ocean sea water to their house. They would build a fire under the large iron kettle full of water. Since water evaporated and salt doesn't when the kettle boiled dry they would scrape the salt residue out of the kettle into a small pan and have some salt seasoning. A very poor but effective process to extract salt.

27

Innsbruk/Brenner Pass

One of the young American sailors found out that his brother was in an infantry division in Italy fighting the Germans near us. This sailor got permission from his ship's captain to go and visit his brother in the infantry division, which at that time was on Montibelmonti. But neither he nor the ship's captain knew of the dangerous positions that infantrymen were usually in when in combat.

The young sailor got off the ship and started hitchhiking toward the front. The American supply trucks and jeeps would stop and give him a ride as far as they could as soon as they recognized his American Navy uniform.

He finally made it to the infantryman's rear battalion C.P., where he made himself known to the colonel and other officers. The American officers were glad to see him come and visit his brother, whom he had not seen for almost three years.

So the officers sent their company runner to the front lines to contact his brother. He located him in a foxhole surrounded by about two feet of snow, which we had had all winter. He told this boy that his brother was back at the rear battalion C.P. and that he had permission to go back and have a short visit with him.

A foxhole infantry buddy of the soldier said, "You are not going back there alone. It is too dangerous a trip for you to go by yourself. I will go with you." At the front, at that time, artillery shells were coming in and machine guns were firing away just to let you know that the enemy was there and ready for anything you might want to throw at them.

As they were both climbing out of their foxhole, the army brother was shot and killed by a German infantryman. He died instantly. Now his buddy had the grim and terrible task to go back to the rear C.P., through the snow, woods, and German patrols all by himself to tell them that his brother who he came to see was now dead and lying in the snow. I would think that this could be one of the worst things that this boy would ever have to go through.

When he got back to the rear C.P., he told the officers and the navy brother that his Infantry brother was now dead. I was not there, and I did not know them, but the sad story soon made the rounds of the front-line combat soldiers. This was a terrible truth.

After that very sad incident, Gen. Mark Clark, our commanding general, gave orders that this type of visitation was never to happen again.

I felt so sorry for his brother and his family and friends because they will always remember this, and the sailor especially will always blame himself for his brother's death.

In the front lines that winter at Montibelmonti, an infantryman had about a fifty-percent chance of coming out of that winter without being killed, injured, or crippled with frost bite so badly that they would lose one or both legs to the knees. It was such a terribly cold winter that those who made it back will never forget. One could not dream of what an average day was like on that mountain those three miserable months, January to April 1, 1945.

We often said that it's no wonder a lot of American boys got themselves sent to prison on purpose rather than go into service. This is a true statement that America does not want to admit, as with the boys who went to Canada and stayed until the war was over. They lived much better than we did. They worked in factories and made more than our fifty-two dollars a month. There were times that a combat soldier would gladly have traded places with the worst criminal in the worst jail in the U.S.A. We were not born killers; we were born Christians. But I think that our love for our country was just greater in our hearts than theirs. But no one remembers our personal death-defying sacrifices now, sixty years later. No one except the unfortunate boys who had to endure that terrible war as combat soldiers in action around the world on every one of our fronts, not just in Italy.

I can write only about Italy because that was where I was, and I can write only about what I knew and experienced. Everything written here is the absolute truth without any imagination thrown in. I have not tried to glamorize anything about combat. In fact, I

229

have deliberately left out some of the more gruesome facts because I am sure that the family and friends of some boys in combat will read this. Most of the adults who were personally involved in WWII will all soon be dead, as I will also. General MacArthur said that the war will never be over for the combat soldier until the day he dies. How true that is. He saw thousands of them die in defense of their country.

I don't think that there is any greater honor than to say, "*I was a combat soldier for America.*"

I know that I will put my patriotism for America and the American flag up against anyone living. I so love America. I would not advise any one person to question the patriotism of any combat soldier to his face or even let him hear about it second hand.

We had to stay in one small town just south of Leghorn until the Germans left or we physically captured Leghorn. When we arrived in that town, some people living there came over to me and said that Johnny, the midget, of Phillip Morris cigarette fame was their cousin. He and his family lived in New York, and they had not been able to correspond with them for the five years of German occupation, and would I write them and tell them all the news for the last five years?

I said, "I will do better than that. I will get a war correspondent, who is standing right over there across the road, and let him do it and write up your story if possible."

I went and talked to the war correspondent, a civilian, and he agreed to contact their relation in New York and the famous midget, Johnny (Giovanni Roventhini)—"Call for Phillip Morris."

About ten years later, Phillip Morris had about three or four midgets traveling throughout the United States posing as the original Johnny for publicity purposes. He came to Lawrenceville. I was the program procurer for that month, as I was vice-president of the local Kiwanis Club. I had him as my guest, and I told him this story. It made a very good program, and I was awarded a certificate for the program of the year.

In another town, not far from there, we entered, looking for Germans. The local people came out and told us that all the Germans had left a day or so before. They also said that their name was

DiMaggio and they were related to the famous baseball player, Joe DiMaggio. This is a common name in Italy.

During the battle one winter, for about three or four days, we stayed in a house that must have belonged to a wealthy family, because in this very neat, cement cellar, there were about ten large wooden barrels of good red wine on wooden platforms built in a perfect row against the south wall of that very nice wine cellar. Each wooden barrel would have held seven or eight of our fifty-five–gallon drums.

The Germans had evidently stayed there, because when they left, they sprayed the fronts of all the wooden wine barrels with their .38-caliber burp guns and the red wine was still spurting out from the bullet holes so they could have been gone only a few hours.

When we stepped down into the basement, our feet immediately got all wet from being about six or seven inches deep in delicious vino rosa. We didn't bother to drink the vino that was on the floor. We put our helmets under the wine that was gushing out of the bullet holes. We all filled our helmets about full. Then we had to go outside and make sure that all the Germans were gone and not lying in ambush for us. We didn't see any Germans, so we went to the first house north and stayed there a couple of days while the American artillery was going to try to bomb the enemy off a certain mountain. We had not had any food for a day or so and did not know when we would get some, so I drank only about half of my helmetful of wine, and I think that the rest of the patrol did likewise. But we did all get a headache. Most of the time, we had vino on our three-quarter-ton truck. In those war days, it would have cost a lot to fill that many large barrels with wine in that nice cellar that we just left.

That afternoon, some of us heard a commotion at the south end of town. There was rifle shooting, and hand grenades going off. Something was not right. Our line-company boys had run out or killed all the German soldiers in Leghorn that we knew about, or we would have been notified and called in to assist them.

So we went down to the south end of town, and there were our line-company boys shooting their rifles at buildings and throwing

231

hand grenades down the street at imaginary enemy. The enemy had been cleared out for almost a full day, and we could see no reason for this mock skirmish.

Then we were told to stand back and not get caught in the movie film crew standing around, as Gen. Mark Clark, our general, was having a news film for the movie theaters at home to show that he was entering the city of Leghorn with our victorious front-line troops instead of entering the city some time later when it was safe to do so.

The boys who had taken the city the day earlier were brought back in trucks to create a combat scene as if the general was entering the city at the actual time of the combat liberation. These scenes looked real and dangerous when shown as a movie.

But I think that even today, most combat scenes are staged at a later time when most of the danger is past. I know that everyone who ever goes overseas likes to brag about being in the front lines, but most of them never see the front lines or even the rear lines; not photographers, entertainers, high-ranking military officers, or any personnel other than the privates, private first classes, corporals, sergeants, and very few second lieutenants were in the front lines, and even they don't want to be. It's dangerous up there, and you could get killed! The army does not allow anyone except authorized combat personnel on the front lines.

As soon as these staged scenes were shot on film, these boys were trucked back to the front lines to fight again. They never even got a hot meal or a Coke, just loaded back up, dirty as usual, because in Italy, there was always one more town or one more mountain to capture from the Germans. We joined them at Pisa a couple of days later to go into some very heavy combat again.

We were now called mountain fighters, not gorilla (guerrilla) fighters. We in the infantry did not like the word gorilla. Maybe it was because we actually looked like them and lived like them, as sometimes we had to forage for our food, and we could seldom shave or take a bath, so we would be hairy and dirty and stink like a gorilla. Years later, I saw that we really lived the life of a gorilla in many ways. We also had a great bonding among us, like most primates have.

This was a life that most cannot accept as the truth. They will think that we must have had a bad dream, all two million of us during the same four years in combat. It must have been a dream because no human being would do all these atrocities and killings in real life. Now we who were in this terrible combat are old and partially disabled cannot even visualize that we were once young and strong enough to handle those terrible situations that arose in our everyday service.

That must be the reason that they use only young, strong and "gung ho" kids. I think that if there is another world conflict they may choose to draft sixteen and seventeen-year-olds. It is always easier to send someone else's children, than send your own. "War is fine and I am very patriotic as long as they send someone else—that's the American spirit. Someone should do something about that,—but not me or my family. Go get them somebody."

Soon after we took Leghorn, June 18, 1944, the day that Lt. Kenneth Blake was killed, some of our line-company boys got into Leghorn. They discovered a beer distillery owned by the Italians and promptly liberated it. They opened the spigots on the large tanks and took turns holding their helmets under it until they were full, then went off a short distance and got a hideful of beer on an empty stomach. I don't know how many tanks of beer there were, but it took a few hours to empty the entire distillery of all of its valuable contents. But they did.

Meanwhile some of our boys went to the kitchen supplies and poured all the cooks' water out of the five-gallon water cans and took the cans to the brewery and filled all of them with fresh golden beer. When our mess T. Sgt. Bruno went to the cans to get water from the five-gallon cans to cook supper, he found them all full of beer. He really got mad, because he could not cook a meal without water and we had not had a hot meal for weeks. So all that he could do was to heat up some more cans of C rations, the same as we had been eating mostly for a year or more. Then he poured out the delicious beer from the cans on the ground that the boys had saved and then refilled them with water. He said, "If I ever find out who filled those cans with beer, I will court-martial them." He never found out who did fill them with beer, and I never did either, except that it was not me. I just had one helmet full. But it got very quiet around there for a couple of days!

The first night in Leghorn we stayed in a tin building, the first tin building that I had ever stayed in while in combat. I did not feel at ease in it, as I usually stayed in the old Italian stone buildings, which offered very good protection from artillery shells and airplane bombings.

In this tin building, we would often hear a large boom as a German shell passed overhead. This shell was from the largest artillery gun used by any country in any war. It was called the "Anzio Express." It was approximately 280 mm in circumference; an average-sized soldier could stand upright within the empty shell casing. I have seen this done. The base that it was mounted on was two railroad flat cars welded together and it could travel only on railroad tracks with less than a seven-degree turn. If this Anzio Express was very near a stone building when it was fired, the concussion would collapse that building to the ground.

After we left Leghorn and started toward Pisa, we found one of these large guns abandoned on the railroad tracks, so we examined it as well as we could in a forward attack. The railroads had been damaged by our air force so badly that the trains could not move and the large gun had to be abandoned where it was while the main German infantry retreated to another position.

The Anzio Express was a two-stage shell. That is, when it was fired and still in the air, it would explode again, like rocket. This was to send it further in the air toward its target. The only thing worse with that second propulsion was that there was no guide to keep it on its original target and could land anywhere forward. It very seldom hit its target and was very demoralizing to our American forces.

America made one similar to it, not to be outdone by the Germans. I saw it set up behind a large, two-story Italian house so that the muzzle blast of fire could not be detected by the enemy. This was always a problem when firing artillery or large armored tank guns. The fire from the muzzle blast always gave away the position to the enemy, and they would immediately start firing back, which is the last thing that you wanted.

When our large artillery gun fired its first shot, the entire house, which was about two hundred yards in front of it completely collapsed and crumbled to the ground. What was a twenty-foot-tall building was now about six or seven feet of rubble and dust. The officers and artillery observers there were very embarrassed and I do not know if it was ever fired again. When this took place, I happened to be there and saw it all with a few of my buddies that I had trained with the Eighty-Fourth Infantry Division.

The Germans had another effective weapon, called the "Screaming Mimi." It was a form of a rocket that fired five or six shells at a time at the same target and made a weird sound, like a wild animal screaming in the woods. If you were in a valley when it went overhead in the dark while you were on patrol, hunting Germans, it would scare you almost to death. I have dropped to the ground on my knees many times when hearing this terrible scream in the darkness of night, not knowing where the shells were going to land.

While we were still staying in that tin shed in Leghorn, I walked outdoors early the next morning, and there were two Italian civilians having a very heated argument. When the Italians get mad and argue, they get right up in the other person's face and shout very loudly.

These two civilians were really having a verbal disagreement when two of the First Armored Tank Division, which always fought by our division's side, had two of their tank drivers go over to them and explain how they settle arguments like that in Texas. The two tank drivers took their .45-caliber pistols out of their holsters and explained to them how to put each gun in each person's hand, stand back to back, take ten steps forward and turn and shoot the other person with their pistol. The two tank drivers stood them back to back with the pistols in their hands and told them to take ten steps forward then turn and shoot at the other one.

They lined up back to back, and they each took about three or four steps forward, threw the pistols down on the ground, and took off in opposite directions as fast as their legs could carry them. We never heard from them again, and I am sure that they never came near that area as long as the tanks were there. The two tank drivers just about fell to the ground laughing. I heard that one of them was actually from Texas. I enjoyed the incident very much myself and have not forgotten it in sixty years. I had also lived my first twelve years in the panhandle of Oklahoma and Texas near Guymon, and

Optima, Oklahoma, and Hereford, Texas, during the dust bowl years, or the dirty thirties, as they were later called.

In October or November of 1944, we were first to experience "Third base," the only road that could eventually take us to Montibelmonti for the entire winter months. It looked like a very good place for the Germans to dynamite; it was a very narrow place in the mountain road with a very deep valley below. If this road was destroyed, there would be very little chance of our engineers rebuilding it this winter. It would have definitely put our American forces at a disadvantage all winter, giving the enemy a good chance to shoot at us and pick us off one at a time while we were fighting, working, or on patrol. We could have possibly lost that winter. So our Sgt. Barney Allickson sent two of our best soldiers out to walk along the deep ravine under the narrow road to see if the Germans had indeed left a soldier there to dynamite the road as soon as all German vehicles were through passing over it and before the Americans started to pass over it.

A couple of hours later, these two soldiers came back with a German backpack full of souvenirs that they had taken off the lone German soldier that they had to shoot and kill. He was sitting alone, under the narrow road ready to blow up the narrow road in this valley, later to be called "Third base." They did not want to kill him. They would have much rather taken him alive and back to our camp. But they could not afford to take any chances, as this was the only road that we could use all winter.

They did not want to startle him or surprise him as he might have set off the dynamite accidentally. So they had to shoot him immediately.

We all went through his backpack, looking for souvenirs, and became very sad when we found a letter from home from his mother and family with a picture in there with all of them together. We had a boy in our platoon who had lived in Germany as a young boy, so he read this letter to us. We were all very sad to hear him read the letter from his mother, and we could hardly look at the family picture because he looked just like all of us and about the same age nineteen, twenty, or twenty-one. We also felt very sorry for our two corporals who had no choice but to shoot him. I still remember his name and the town in Germany that his mail was from. But we had to save that road. It would have devastated our forces for months that winter. We were in the foothills of the Alps and it seemed to have rained or snowed about two days out of three all winter. We sometimes referred to the Italian campaign as "the battle of the mud."

It was such a sad act of war that had to be done that this killing incident has never been brought up in our conversations fifty-seven years later. I felt so sorry for his family in Germany. I am sure that under different conditions, all the German soldiers in that terrible war could have been friends with any of our American soldiers that they were fighting against. I thoroughly believe that. Most of the boys in our platoon had some German ancestry in them, the same as I did.

All wounds do not show or heal!

One night while we were still on the mountain, three of us got an order to go down to a certain house near German territory and see if there were any Germans there. This was a very dangerous, risky detail for just three of us. There should have been seven or eight of us sent on that dangerous a patrol. We had just spent the night before laying barbed-wire entanglements in the rain and mud, then had to find some small tin cans and put a few small rocks in them to rattle and warn us if the enemy was crossing the barbed-wire entanglements. We were pretty tired from that dangerous job, and now we were being sent out, looking for some Germans to start a possible death gun fight.

But we immediately obeyed, as we had two of the greatest sergeants that any combat man could want. I would have walked through fire for either of them. In fact, I probably did many things more dangerous than walking through fire for them.

We three soldiers went down to this small house, looked around, and did not see anything suspicious. However, we did not go in the house, as I thought that the sergeant might have wanted us to do, but he didn't say so. When we got back to our camp, we gave the sergeant the negative report. He said, "You guys did not go down to that house. Now turn around and go back and check it out again." Our sergeants very seldom talked to us that way, and we were surprised. So we went back to that same house, and with my bayonet, I pried the number off the front of the house. We went back, and I gave him the house number and told him that we did go all the way to the house the first time also. But he gave us the fish eye again.

I was very sorry that he did not believe us the first time. We had so much respect for our sergeants. I would not have his responsibility in combat for any amount of money. I was just where I wanted to be, a private first class, in the middle of the pack, not the first in line or the last in line every time.

That was S. Sgt. Barney Allickson, one of the greatest soldiers that I ever served under. He and T. Sgt. Kenneth Blake (later 2d. Lt. Kenneth Blake). The other two soldiers that went to the house to investigate were Cpl. Max L. Rush and Pfc. John Despot. We worked together on a lot of details with Cpl. Phillip Braun, Sgt. Joe Buffalo, Pvt. Charles Hoffman, Pvt. John DeHore, Pvt. James Vulanti, Pvt. James Keane, Pfc. George Loechner, Pvt. Red Thompson, Pvt. Jake Jacoby, Pvt. Bill Zimmerman, Pvt. Max Rotopel, and Pvt. Mike Lipp. These men were all great soldiers and did more than their share for our country, America the Beautiful.

In the winter of 1944, we were still in a static position on Montibelmonti, and there was still only a winding mountain road leading to this mountain that we all had to use to get to and back. A few hundred yards of this road went past a valley between the mountains that gave the Germans a plain view of our troops or trucks going along this road. The 91st Tennessee Volunteers Infantry Division had given it the name of third base. They said, "If you made to the 3rd base, you should make it all the way home."

There was supposed to be some irony in this saying, but it did not prove true, because we spent the next seventy-five desperately cold days and nights up there and lost a few hundred beautiful and brave boys. I am sure that some of them found relief in death. Before the winter was over, I personally think that most of us probably considered death many times as a relief to this fear, cold, hunger, and loneliness. No human being should have to live like this for even a day, much less a year or two. This is one of the reasons that I am so strong on all soldiers rotating and not always depending so much on so few combat men.

We were all fighting for the same country, same freedoms, and same objectives, so let's all fight evenly for the same cause, not get a few boys down and keep on kicking them until they are dead. That may not seem like a correct parallel, but that is the way most old combat men feel when they hear about the lives of the boys at home and the U.S.O. warriors' antics without fear of death or injury of any kind. A beautiful way to fight a war any time is to not go to battle. Let someone else do it!

During these terrible combat days, all of us would have gladly traded places with the worst criminal in the U.S.A., in the worst prison in the U.S.A. This is the honest to God truth. We would mention this many times when on a break from battle.

Our P and A platoon was told one day that the Russians were driving cattle in front of their tanks while fighting the Germans on the other flank. The weight of a cow's hoof would detonate the mine, kill the cow, and save blowing the tracks off their tanks. So our officers got the word that we were going to get some sheep for us to drive in front of our tanks and boys so that they would be safer. They told us to build a small sheep corral to keep them for the spring offensive, which would start about April as soon as the snow started to melt in these mountains and our vehicles could finally all move out.

So the entire squad built a fence with the barbed wire that we always had, and we were sent about a dozen sheep to put in it. I think that I was the only farm boy, who had been around sheep and knew something about them. We had about forty sheep back on our farm in Illinois, and I had helped deliver new-born lambs, fed and watered sheep, and helped my dad shear their wool and roll it up for sale at Fairfield, Illinois.

We had to keep two of our boys on guard all night, watching over these sheep, because the partisans and other deserted Italian soldiers loved to eat mutton and considered it a great and rare delicacy. They had less to eat than we did, so I am sure that it looked very selfish of us not to let them have one once in a while.

We did let them steal two that week that we were guarding them. Soon, the order came down that we were moving out on the spring offensive and we would not be using the sheep, so turn them loose. We did not turn them loose. We left them in the barbed-wire corral and told the Italian soldiers that they could have them. They could have many feasts with ten or eleven sheep. It must have been a happy day for them to see us leave and give them permission to take all that they wanted. They deserved and needed it for their salvation also.

In December of 1943 or January of 1944, during that terrible winter on Montibelmonti that we spent seventy-five days without relief, the army brought us a small, two person personnel carrier that was built low to the ground, which was covered with a few feet of snow, sometimes waist deep being in a high altitude. They told us infantrymen that this vehicle was for us to use to move our ammunition, booby traps, heavy boxes of mines, and barbed-wire rolls so that we would not have to carry them and fight the enemy at the same time.

Boy, were we glad to see these little machines, which they called the "weasel." It would not set off an antipersonnel mine, as it had only a two-pound per square inch of weight on the tread, which propelled it along on the snow. What a wonderful machine for us to use in the Alps, having so often to carry those loads. We had been using some of the deserted Italian soldiers and small Sicilian mules to pack these loads up to the line-company boys. We all worked as Italian interpreters doing this, as some of us had learned a lot of Italian survival language after two years. I led an Italian pack-mule team to the front lines many nights. But our happy expectations were very short-lived, as the commissioned and noncommissioned officers kept the weasel a few yards behind the front and just used it in the mountain terrain for joy riding. We could see and hear them enjoying their fast ride down ski slopes while we were still carrying the loads on our own backs just as before. This was the only time that I can really say that the officers and noncoms did us a dirty deal. None of us privates or privates first class got to ride in that vehicle. It is now sold all over the world as a "snow mobile."

Many years after the war was over, all of us original combat boys from Anzio remained close and respected each other's feelings. There were sensitive subjects and circumstances that we would not mention to a particular individual. Each of us had his own sad and regrettable incidents. Those were very sad and deplorable years of our young lives. Sometimes any combat man will get a little bitter and remorseful of what he went through for so long a time.

Half of this entire world was not even born when we were making all of those life-threatening sacrifices for them. I hope we

240

did not waste our lives for nothing. And many combat soldiers were worse off than we were. Noncombat support troops do not really know how lucky they were.

Montibelmonti means beautiful mountain, but it was anything but beautiful to the combat troops, American and German. It was the most miserable time for all combat personnel who had the misfortune of being sent there. It was a high altitude mountain range without any village or year-round inhabitants due to the extreme cold and deep snow drifts for over three months every winter. We were kept there three months that winter of 1944 and 1945, but so were the German infantrymen. Many soldiers from both sides were killed there and left in the freezing snow to wait until spring so that the G.R.O. could then pick them up and identify them, if they could find their dog tags nearby.

I want to mention again all the infantry soldiers in our platoon that spent all that terrible winter on Montibelmonti and other battles while I was with that platoon: S. Sgt. Barney Allickson, Cpl. Joseph Buffalo, Pvt. John Red DeHore, Pfc. Charles Hoffman, Pfc. John Despot, Cpl. Max L. Rush, Cpl. Phillip Braun, Pvt. James Keane, Pvt. Maab, Pvt. Bill Zimmerman, Pvt. Max Rotopel, Pvt. Mike Lipp, Pfc. Freeman James (our good truck driver), Pvt. James Vulanti, Sgt. Frenchy Dorin, T. Sgt. Bruno our mess sergeant, 2d Lieutenant Kenneth Blake, Pfc. George Loechner, Pfc. Robert Seyl, Pvt. Red Thompson, and Pvt. Jake Jacoby, and me. They were all great and brave soldiers that America should be proud of. God bless all of them.

We left that terrible mountain April 1, 1945. We went up on it in December 1944. I will always remember it as the worst winter that I have spent in my now seventy-nine years. I have often compared it to the winter that Gen. George Washington spent at Valley Forge before the end of the Revolutionary War, as we were both cold, hungry, poorly fed, no money to buy anything with, and very low morale prevailing among us combat men who had to suffer and sacrifice through it.

I am sure that our support troops that year, living on level ground in Florence, Rome, and Naples had an army bunk and three meals a day. We went three and four months at a time and never knew breakfast or a warm meal. We could always depend on two warm meals a year for sure on Christmas and Thanksgiving, and sometimes we were not sure about them.

When we arrived in Bologna, we were wearing two hand grenades strapped to our field-pack shoulder straps, two bandoleers of .30-caliber rifle bullets around our necks, and bayonets fixed on our rifles. I was a mine sweeper, so I was issued a .30 caliber carbine. I took two extra rifle shell magazines and reversed them, one on each side of my regular magazine and filled them with shells. That gave me three magazines, or about forty-five shells. Man, they loaded us up for some terrific fighting.

They loaded us up in trucks, and we entered the city of Bologna without ever seeing a German soldier. The civilians said, "Where have you been? The Germans left two weeks ago." They had evidently anticipated our major attack and left for the Po River valley in retreat. We thanked God for that.

When we got to Bologna, I went to see the university there. It was one of the finest universities founded in Europe, in 1494, about the time that Christopher Columbus discovered our America. No wonder they called it the new world.

When I entered Bologna, I saw an American soldier that I had basic training with, at Camp McCain, the year before, and we had become good friends. He was now in a different company, and I hadn't seen him for about a year. I went up to talk to him. I soon saw that he was dead drunk and could barely walk or talk. I saw an army M-4 tank on the street in front of us, and I put him on the rear of the tank, where the motor is. I took my tent rope from my backpack and tied him on the rear of that tank. Then I went on my search-and-destroy mission, never to see him again.

However, I heard that he made it home. I sure hope so. There was no way that he could have had any recollection of how he came to be tied down on the rear of a tank. I hope the tank drivers found him and took care of him, because I have ridden on the rear of these tanks and its exhaust fumes would make you sick even if you never had a drink. I am sure that my friend found some wine and drank freely of it on an empty stomach, as we never could depend on being fed regularly.

Before I was drafted, I worked in East Chicago, Indiana, at Continental Roll and Steel as a burner, helping to make these M-4

Sherman tanks. Little did I know that some day I would ride on one that I possibly might have helped make in East Chicago.

We were very low on food, which was mostly C rations, but once in a while, a box of dry K rations made it our way. The cooks and cooks' helpers were supposed to bring us food of some kind on a regular basis. It was a very dangerous drive for a jeep driver to drive all the way up to us at the forward C.P. (command post) and communications center. But that was their job. They drove at night: no lights on the jeep, steep curves in the winding roads, and occasional enemy incoming mail (German artillery shells). We lived with that and worse every minute that we were up there.

We decided that when food and candles became very low, one of us would walk back to the kitchen, where the motor pool, chaplain, mail orderly, cooks, and some officers stayed in a warm tent and even ate three meals a day, even breakfast, although it was canned, dehydrated eggs most of the time. Line-company combat boys didn't get any of that. The second night of these trips was my time to go look and steal from our mess tent some food and candles to take back up the mountain to the boys who were really doing the fighting. It was about two to three miles over rocks, snow and trees, and possibly, you might see a lone German running through the fields, fleeing from his own army to surrender to the Americans. We usually let them go, as we did not have enough time or food to take care of them, and they might turn on you at any moment anyway.

When I got to our mess tent, I saw a soldier walking guard. I was disappointed, because now, I had to avoid my own company soldier as well as the enemy. I had taken a gunnery sack, which we use to fill with sand to build a safe bunker, so I could carry any goods that I could steal from our kitchen that should have been brought up to us in the first place on a regular basis.

As soon as the guard got on the other side of the tent, walking his post, I slipped under the canvas and bent over very low so that I would not make a shadow and he would not shoot me, thinking that I was a German soldier instead of one of his own company boys.

I felt around in the dark for canned food and candles. I was given very strict orders to get plenty of candles, as we needed them to read or write letters with at night, with a blanket pulled over our

243

heads so as not to show any light. That is the way some of the boys smoked cigarettes at night if there was not much fighting going on. If there was any fighting to do or go on a search and kill patrol there was no way that any one could smoke a cigarette or take a drink of wine. We never drank before going on patrol.

I filled my sack full of things that I don't remember what now except I did get some candles and three cans of something to eat. I almost got caught by our guard as I left the tent though, as I had to carry the gunnery sack and run stooped over at the same time. But I did make it safely behind a jeep in time to avoid being seen. Then I had to wait until the guard went on the other side of the tent on his rounds. I was almost as scared then as I was in combat about being shot.

This was not a very successful attempt to get food, so I don't think that we ever did it again, mainly because we couldn't get any of the other boys in our platoon to make this difficult, dangerous, lonely trip back to the mess hall by themselves. Actually, it was very stupid to try it. We had enough dangers without this extra risk so we did not do this food salvage errand again.

In daily combat, if you had just gone through a dangerous life-threatening incident, for the next few days your hands would shake whenever you would try to hold something. If you were going to take a drink of water from your metal canteen, you would stand alongside an army truck or the side of a house and lean your ride arm against the solid object to steady your arm and shoulder, then you would take both hands to get the canteen to and in your mouth. You could get it in your mouth, otherwise you would either miss your mouth or hit your front teeth with the metal canteen and maybe chip your front teeth. This was embarrassing even to yourself, because while you were under fire, you were steady, controlled, and usually made your best decisions under pressure or in life-threatening situations. That is what it takes to make a good combat soldier. You only find this in about two out of three soldiers.

You would not shave during these shaky days. We did not have to shave regularly in combat anyway. Some of us even went a month without shaving. There were no spit-and-polish officers up front. They were too scared to be up there where the real fighting was. They could be found back at the rear echelon: hospital area,

U.S.O. and entertainment areas away from any danger of a shell coming in on them. They loved to find a young wounded soldier coming in from the front lines with a backpack full of German souvenirs. They either bought them very cheaply or just took them for free when he went to the hospital for surgery and was unconscious most of the time.

When we got a letter or newspaper from home, we had to lay the paper on the ground in front of us and bend over and look at it standing up, because our hands shook too much to hold it. If you tried to hold it and read it, the letters would all run together.

We would read other soldiers' newspapers just to have something to read and find out how we were doing in the war. The war news was amusing.

If a dead soldier had a rifle that was cleaner than the one we had, we would exchange them so we would not have to clean our own so often. We would also take his ammunition and any food that he might have on him, as he would not need it anymore. Some of the surviving soldiers would erect wooden crosses on that mountain. Then they would move on to another mountain that day or night, and so on to another and another for the duration.

Sometimes we felt like we were more like rats or gophers, living in such a nonhuman way to fight for our country and save our own lives so that we could come back and enjoy it like everybody else was. We did not feel like Christians, doing all this damage and killing. We could only pray and hope that God was on our side. In the bible, there are many battles for Christianity. I hope that ours in WWII history will also be considered a Christian battle, a Crusade. "That which is bad will eventually destroy itself. That which is good will eventually win out and survive."

Since Adolf Hitler and his Nazi party banned all churches and religious groups from meeting, and he persecuted Jehovah Witnesses as well as Jews, with a little imagination, this could be considered a war for religious freedom for any church, any place, in the free world. Could Adolf Hitler have been the Antichrist of this century, and should we expect a different Antichrist every century?

Sometimes it was easy for us to get a little bitter, having to go through so much when the rest of the world was as comfortable as we used to be. But this only endowed us with more love and respect for America. Nathan Hale said, "I regret that I have but one life to give for my country." Combat infantrymen felt this way as did every boy who was ever wounded, captured or killed.

Most of us who made it back home safely were not heroes. We were just lucky survivors. There were a few heroes that lived to come home but most of the heroes are still over there, dead silent, never to have to fear or kill again. We often wondered which soldier is the lucky one, and which, the unlucky one. We used to discuss this in the foxholes and bombed-out buildings when we were waiting for the enemy to attack. To my knowledge, none of us ever reached a definite decision on who was the luckiest.

We did all agree on one thing; all combat soldiers would go directly to heaven when killed because we already had our hell here on earth. We all agreed on this many times. I think that this discussion helped our morale some. I have always been strong on the benefit of prayer, and I used it extensively in my chiropractic practice later on with amazing results.

It was very cold and had been snowing for about three months in this high altitude mountain range. Our Gen. Mark Clark had given the infantry strict orders that no one was to go on sick call and to the hospital until both legs were frozen blue to the knees, not just one leg, but both legs blue to both knees at the same time.

All the infantrymen coming down that mountain road had both legs frozen and split open like a fast grown radish or tomato on the vine. The legs split first along the frozen track of the arteries and veins the length of the leg from the ankle to the knee joint. You could see into the leg muscles on some of the worst ones. Of course, they would lose both legs to the knees or higher according to the length of time with no blood circulation in those limbs.

Most of these boys were not able to talk to us as we helped them into the back of a rescue truck. Some were unconscious and almost dead, some were hypothermic and semiconscious, not lucid enough to talk sense to us. Some of those would die before their leg amputation took place. Their chances of a normal life after this winter's experience would be very slim.

I saw one soldier come down the mountainside on that road, but he had only one leg blue to the knees, so he was sent back up the road to his foxhole to fight again in the cold and snow. I recognized him a few days later, crawling on all fours coming back down for mercy.

Do you still wonder why I harp on troop rotation instead of keeping the ones in the dangerous fighting until he is crippled or dead? In WWII, being put in the infantry was a sentence of death. In most of the other branches of service, you were almost guaranteed to come home alive. It was not hazardous at all.

The first evening that the crippled young infantry soldiers came crawling down that lone mountain road on Montibelmonti, we could hear the most spine-tingling, soulful, human moaning that I or any of our platoon had ever heard in combat. We could tell that it was coming from human beings, but we did not know if it was coming from our American or the German troops.

Then we looked up the road about a mile and half toward German territory, and in the dusk, we could see brown uniforms spotted in the snow and frozen ground crawling on all fours, on both hands and both feet—none were standing up, walking. We did not know if they were American or German infantrymen. At first, we thought that they might be German soldiers trying to play another trick on us, so we got our rifles ready and waited nervously for them. But as they got closer, we recognized the American uniforms, so we eased up some. But it could still have been a German trick in American uniforms, so we watched them very suspiciously until we were able to examine them.

Their moans were not loud cries. They seemed to be stifling their pain and cry for help and mercy. None of us had ever heard that sound before in combat, and we hoped never to again. After sixty years, I can look to the north and still see and hear those boys coming down that mountain road. I rate this as one of the most pitiful sights of WWII. I saw many pitiful sights in this terrible war, but I rate this one at the top.

Every soldier was groaning, not just one soldier. As they crawled down that road, their heads were hung low and almost none of them were able to speak coherently to us. They were all line-company soldiers from our battalion. Their heads were drooping so low that their heads almost dragged in the frozen dirt road, unable to look up or ahead of themselves because of pain and fatigue. Most of them had been in combat for more than a year without any humane treatment, just surviving one hour at a time without any thank-you from anyone.

The reason that Gen. Mark Clark put out that order regarding both legs turning blue to the knee was because some boys were taking a shoe and sock off one foot, then standing in the icy melted snow water so that they would lose just one leg and get to go home right away with a small pension after the war was over. They said, "At least I will be alive, and you other guys may get killed today or tomorrow. One leg is better than death." As a form of self-inflicted wound, any soldier who did that could get up to seventeen years in the military prison at Ft. Leavenworth, Kansas. But their response was, "Seventeen years in prison is still better than death."

In my combat-experienced mind, I would say, "These boys should have been rotated home before this condition developed. Most of these boys were combat weary from being up on the front lines too long already. Most of them had been in battle too long. They were battle weary. Their nerves were shot from being up there one to three years in death-defying circumstances. They had already seen most of their original buddies killed, and they had to keep on the attack without being able to tell them good-bye or help tend to them in any way without further exposing themselves to the same deadly end.

You were taught to kill, kill, kill from the first day you were put into the infantry, so life became very cheap, even your own, after a few months of life-surviving combat. You wonder why there are about six to seven million soldiers in the States who are not being sent over to replace you and others who have been there too long. We are all fighting for the same country. Why can't they all experience some of this? I have had about as much fun as I can stand. Most soldiers never saw the enemy or fired a rifle in anger or had to save their own life. How unfair our draft system is!

28

The Day My Lieutenant Was Killed

Our infantry line companies fought long and hard to get to Leghorn (Livorno). They fought two years without any R and R. We had never heard of R and R until the boys kept hearing that the infantry boys and other troops were getting it in the South Pacific fighting. We did not know what it meant at first. But it didn't make any difference to us because we had lost so many boys by death and injury that there was not any way that our Fifth Army would start rest leaves from combat. So forget it, you are here until the war is over plus another six months or until death do you part.

We were staying in a small village just south of Leghorn, when we got a call to sweep mines in front of a line company that was to attack down a certain road that led directly into Leghorn, an old city that had been used in medieval days as a very busy and rich seaport. The Germans were still using it as a supply seaport. We were on a small mountain, and the seaport town of Leghorn is sea level, of course.

On our way, riding in the back of a truck with our land mine sweepers by our side, we met a couple of truck loads of line-company boys that I had known in Camp McCain a year earlier.

"Why are you turning back? Has the town of Leghorn already been taken?" I asked them.

"Heck, no, they want us to advance straight down that dirt road in plain view of the Germans and act like we are the main attacking force on that city" and then he added, "There was another line company sent here before we were, and they refused to be slaughtered, walking down that suicide road."

But our line-company boys did walk down that suicide road a few minutes later, with terrific loss of life.

The march down that road in plain view of the Germans was to be a perfect decoy for the Germans to think that this was our main

249

attacking force. But the American Japanese, Nisei, boys were to be the real attacking force, to come from the east out of the woods, where they were hiding, ready for the word to attack.

This plan worked perfectly. The Nisei soldiers attacked the large seaport of Leghorn very quickly, but the group walking down that suicide road suffered great loss. Artillery and mortar shells were coming in so heavily that a soldier could not count fast enough to count all of them. I tried to count them in the air by their whistling noise before they landed and hurt some poor young soldier near me. I could also hear some soldier hollering medic. Our job as P. & A. platoon soldiers was to sweep the roads and ditches with a land-mine sweeper alongside the line-company boys or, sometimes, just ahead of them in an attack. That day we did not get to finish the job as they advanced ahead of us.

Some of our line company soldiers had already started down that terrible suicidal road towards Leghorn. When we arrived to sweep land mines, a terrible artillery and mortar barrage came raining in on us. The worst enemy barrage that I had ever been in. It was as heavy as a hail storm. We all jumped behind a large rock near the road to seek some protection from the enormous amount of shrapnel that was flying all around us. Many of the line company soldiers were hit and killed before they could find what little shelter there was in this area. We watched them in horror as they were hit and killed while running past us.

Our large rock was about the size of an automobile but it only protected us from shells coming from one direction. Due to the umbrella effect of shells when they explode, we had to seek a better place of refuge. 2nd Lt. Kenneth Blake and the other soldiers in our detail took off back toward our truck and to safety. How they got through that hail of artillery fire I do not know as they ran right through it like it was no more than rain drops. I did not leave with them because I did not think that a human could safely run through that fire power without getting killed. So I stayed at the rock. It soon become apparent to me that this was not enough protection from the enormous amount of shells that they were throwing at us.

I looked around and saw that all the other infantrymen had gotten into ditches, culverts, and old German foxholes, as we had not had the time to dig our own foxholes. Actually we did not have enough time to dive into the old German foxholes because this Ger-

250

man shelling came on us so strongly. Most of these German foxholes had been dug by German prisoners of war from other countries while their soldiers were fighting the Americans a few miles further up front.

I looked around for some place to crawl into, when I spotted an old German foxhole that was empty of anyone using it for shelter from the artillery. So while the shells were still coming in very heavy on us, I ran for this empty foxhole to possibly save my life temporarily. I did not know for sure if I could get to the foxhole alive or not, but I did make it.

I think the shelling stopped when the Nisei soldiers surprised the Germans from their flank and made them surrender. However, we did not know that the Germans surrendered until an hour or so later.

There were many young American and German soldiers killed that day. The Germans that did not surrender retreated and headed toward Pisa to fight us again, with our soldiers right behind them without any rest, food, or water. "We must destroy the Germans as soon as possible so that we can go home. This is a terrible way to live our young lives," we kept thinking to ourselves.

Soon as the heavy shelling eased up, I left my life-saving foxhole, which was in an Italian peasant's garden, probably dug by the German slave labor forces. I did not have time to dig my own foxhole.

I was in this foxhole for a few minutes, when I saw a young line-company soldier come running my way. He jumped into the foxhole with me and stayed there silently, not speaking a word to me while we were both praying to stay alive. Soon as the artillery shelling eased up enough that it was halfway safe to get out and join his unit, he left, going forward to catch up with his platoon who were chasing the Germans to keep them moving so that they could not get dug in too well in another defensive position, which they did at Pisa. He was a young Hispanic soldier who I had never seen before or since. We never spoke to each other the entire time that we were together in that one foxhole—no words were necessary. I hope he made it home. He was having his hell on this earth that year if he lived that long.

As soon as the shelling eased up some more, I knew that it was time for me to return to the large rock where we had all started from to see what was going on. When I arrived at the rock, no one was there. I decided that I should try to return to the small village where our platoon and supply truck were. I looked all around at the dozens of Americans soldiers lying dead, quiet as if they were just sleeping on the ground in the afternoon sun. They had all been killed by mortar and artillery shrapnel.

As I looked at one dead soldier lying there dead he looked like our 2nd Lt. Kenneth Blake. I examined his face and uniform and at that instant I knew that it was our beloved Kenneth Blake. I examined him all over and I only found one small wound, a small piece of shrapnel had entered the base of his brain just below the back of his steel helmet. I could not find any other wounds.

I could not believe that this wonderful soldier who had been with the division all through the war—first in Ireland for a staging area, then in North Africa, where he was in charge of our platoon, then into Sicily for forty-five days of combat, and then on to Anzio beach, Rome, and Florence—and then this happens to him. It was impossible. He could not be dead. He didn't deserve this. I could not comprehend it.

So I left him there and went and got some of the other boys in our platoon to come with me to verify that it was him. We all feared that it was him as he had not returned to our supply truck. Two other corporals went with me to where I showed them where he was lying and they immediately recognized his body. We then picked him up and carried him out of shell range.

We then went through all his pockets and took his personal items and put them in a box to mail to his widow. In combat, fellow soldiers always take the dead soldier's personal items and give them to the chaplain, as it is his job to mail them to his family along with a letter of sympathy. The U.S. Army headquarters sends the death notice by Western Union Telegraph.

In the army, when you receive a battlefield commission from a noncommissioned officer to a commissioned officer, you do not receive it immediately. You must wait twenty-four hours between ratings, in which time you are in limbo, neither noncommissioned or commissioned. When he accepted this commission, he had twenty-four hours in nonstatus; he was killed during the non-status, twenty-four-hour period. This was unbelievable. He was the heart and brains of our platoon. No high-up officer ever questioned his decisions. He was above reproach. His commission went through anyway, and he was highly decorated for this act of looking after his men and trying to save them. He deserved every medal he received posthumously and every word of praise spoken of him. God bless him. We all loved him very much.

He was the greatest. He always had all of his men foremost in his mind. He knew exactly what men to send on certain details because some of us were better at certain jobs than others. In the year that I was under him, I never heard him raise his voice one time, nor did I ever hear any soldier disagree with him and have an argument with him. We respected him that much, and he deserved every minute of it. After his death, our platoon had another staff sergeant from his hometown, S. Sgt. Barney Allickson, also a great leader of soldiers.

But there was always a void after his death, and worst of all, the void was in our new sergeant's heart and mind. He had grown up with him, and they had joined the National Guard together; just as all the original boys in our platoon were from the same town. The town had a lot to be proud of, the 34th Infantry Division, 135th Regiment, Third Battalion Hq. Co. P.A. Platoon. They lost a lot of boys, but they all contributed very much to the war effort. Without them, I think that the war in North Africa, Sicily, and Italy would have lasted much longer and more boys killed. I salute you. The day that 2nd Lt. Blake was killed was the saddest day of my life.

He was later awarded his 2nd lieutenant's commission, the Bronze Star, Silver Star, and the Legion of Merit. The only medal next to be awarded to him would have been the Congressional Medal of Honor. These medals were all awarded to him posthumously of course. He was killed June 18, 1944. I remember it with great sadness every day of my life. I would have gladly given my life to have saved his life, then and now. The other four of us soldiers who were on that suicide mine-sweeping mission are still alive. We are all near eighty years old now, but we very rarely see each other, and then, we do not speak of this terrible incident and our great lieutenant's death. It was too sad a loss for us to discuss.

Second Lt. Kenneth Blake was very ably replaced by his best friend and boyhood chum, S. Sgt. Bernard "Barney" Allickson, also from Montevideo, Minnesota. Sergeant Barney had also fought all through North Africa, Sicily, and Italy with this platoon. He was also a great, fearless leader of a combat platoon. He knew all the ins and outs of combat strategy in fighting the Germans. We all liked him very much also. Lt. Kenneth Blake and S. Sgt. Barney Allickson were very much alike in all respects in combat. They could have been twins the way they handled combat situations. Our division was lucky to have those two great soldiers. They were the brain and heart of our platoon. They always gave "above and beyond the call of duty." Sgt. Barney Allickson and all the rest of the platoon made it home.

I examined him very carefully and carried him back out of shell range, then went to get some of the other boys in our platoon to verify his death. He was the greatest man I ever knew. I am sure that all the others in our platoon thought the same way that I did about him. I would easily have given my life to save his. He was that great and brave and unselfish a person and model soldier. He had joined this National Guard Infantry Division during the final years of the Great Depression. God bless him in Heaven, from me and all of the many people's lives that he touched and influenced during his short life. I am sure that he saved my life and the lives of all the other soldiers in our platoon many times.

Lt. Blake was very safety-conscious of the lives of our boys in our platoon. He never sent us out on a dangerous mission unless he had scouted it out first, alone, to see if it was too dangerous a mission for another soldier to attempt. His platoon boys' life and safety were always paramount to him. I never heard him raise his voice to a soldier or ever heard a soldier argue with him. All his superior officers in the battalion and regimental headquarters wanted him to take a 2nd Lieutenant's commission and serve in their unit, but he refused twice.

"I will never leave the boys that I started with. If I take that commission, you can transfer me out to any unit, I will not do that. I will stay here as a sergeant and be with my boys," he told his superior officers.

However, after about two years of talking to these other officers, Washington, D.C. army headquarters finally said, "All right, if you will accept this battlefield commission, we guarantee that you will never be transferred from your present platoon." With this promise, he agreed. He was killed the very next day.

The three other boys had gone back to the platoon, but I stayed during all the terrible shelling attack by the Germans.

As I helped carry the lieutenant back out of shell range, I noticed a concrete wall about six feet high surrounding a nice villa at the junction of the road that we had come down on the way to suicide road. All along this wall were pieces of German artillery and mortar, metal shell shrapnel pieces still sticking into the villa wall. I went up and looked at them; most of these shrapnel pieces had hunks of red, human flesh hanging from them, fresh blood still dripping down the side of this wall. Then I knew that these were pieces of German shrapnel that had torn through some young American boy and had taken with it a part of his brave, wasted body. This was a very sad picture that I did not have a camera with me to photograph and save it for posterity. I can see it now, and every day I have seen it thousands of times whether I am at work or laying on my pillow at night. That stone wall with the flesh and blood running down the wall is always there in front of me. That one picture could tell you all about war, without a word spoken. God bless every soldier who ever fought in combat at any time in any war. As Gen. Ulysses S. Grant told a reporter who asked him what combat was like, "If you have never been in combat, no explanation is possible. If you have been in combat, no explanation is necessary." "Combat is HELL."

Today, sixty years later, this battle seems impossible to have taken place. We have so many luxuries today that are available to the entire world because of the great sacrifices made in our wars by so few Americans in combat. Over one-half of the people living in the world today were not even born when WWII was going on. I cannot blame them for not knowing much about our wars or why they should even worry or care about old wars or old soldiers, dead or alive. Let's get on with our lives with something that they understand and need. It was necessary then, but then is not now. We did what was necessary, and the sun has set on a lot of us, and waiting to set on the rest of us. I hope there is life after death so that I can see all these soldiers again without any combat.

Soon after we took Leghorn and Lieutenant Blake was killed, we had an unusual incident. This incident was not in my division. It must have been in the 91st or the 88th, not my 34th. We were usually side by side or replacing each other during the entire Italian campaign.

As the navy was now using the port of Leghorn as a supply depot, American sailors were there, unloading our infantry supplies.

29

The War Is Over

The war ended May 7, 1945, at about 2:30 that afternoon. The German Thirty-Fourth Infantry Division surrendered to our American Thirty-Fourth Infantry Division in Biella, Italy. I was there. Our division lined up in front of the German soldiers with burlap sacks in our hands, and the German soldiers stood at attention and put their guns in our sacks one at a time. Very impressive.

All of us Americans were allowed to keep the guns that we received and we soon sold them to the Italian civilians for about $25.00 to $30.00 apiece. Which we soon used to buy wine and cognac to drink and celebrate in our own way. About 15% of our unit was left. America said we need an extra day to prepare for the end of the war, so we will use May 8, 1945, as the end of the war. They didn't ask the real combat veterans what we thought about that one day change. We didn't have to read it in the paper when the war was over, man we knew, no more killing, freezing. The night after the German army surrendered to the American Allied Forces and the German 34th Infantry Division surrendered to our American 34th Infantry Division all of us old combat soldiers went out and tried to drink all the wine that there was in Biella. We did not get to drink all of it, but we did get more than our share. I can personally guarantee you that.

Most of the Italians held their own private parties that night, also celebrating the end of the war. We went from house party to house party, drinking and eating what we wanted to without invitation. Some Italian people came up and spoke to us.

"This is a private party. You soldiers are not allowed here."

"We left our home and country to liberate you, and many of us were wounded and killed. If it was not for us, the Germans would still be here and you would not have anything to celebrate and

256

throw this party," we responded and just kept on drinking their wine and then went to another party. We were told at two or three parties that this was a private party, but that did not bother or stop us. We kept on celebrating a victory day that most of us never thought we would see, and many of our buddies did not see.

About 0200 in the morning we all started to go back to the large, three-story house that we were billeted in. A few of the boys were vomiting and a few were still hollering about our long-delayed victory. It was a glorious day to celebrate for those of us that were left to see it. But our minds kept going back to the buddies who we had lost and they too wanted to live to see this day. I hope that there is life after life so that they got to see it also. God bless them wherever they are and I hope that they saw the end of their war.

Another thing that I do think America should be ashamed of is the way the army pressured the recruiting offices in all the counties in the states. They would raise the monthly quota every month during the war and award them with extra days off with pay if they met or exceeded their monthly quota.

This pressure that they put on them caused most of the recruiting office men to encourage the young boys to lie about their age, many only sixteen and seventeen years of age, under the mandatory eighteen years. They encouraged them to drop out of high school and enlist by lying about their age. They told them, "You will have a better chance of getting into the branch of service that you want." This was all a lie so that his office could get recognition for meeting their quota of enlistees.

I talked to some of these kids after they were put in the combat infantry. They said, "I never heard of the recruiting sergeant again after I got in the service, and what he told me had nothing to do with what I am doing now. He outright lied to me."

But he would have to be put in the infantry. Where else would you put an underaged, poor, uneducated, high school dropout, and healthy gung-ho boy? He had to be put in a cannon fodder division.

I have often wondered if those recruiting office people who committed those crimes ever kept track of those boys as to how many were killed and wounded, or were they just a monthly quota number on a sheet of paper?

Most of these boys regretted lying about their age when it came to signing up for their Social Security. There was a lot of confusion then as to the actual age of that person. I have heard this tale of woe many times after the war was over and the boys were older.

No history of the 3rd Battalion, 135th Regiment of the 34th Combat Infantry Division would be complete without some mention of a soldier from Tennessee. He was a little older than most of us. He had been one of the original 34th boys going overseas in early 1942 or late 1941. I am not sure which year, as I was still in high school at Fairfield, Illinois, and graduated in May 1942 and entered service at Camp Grant, Illinois near Rockford, Il.

The 34th Division was the first American Combat Division overseas in WWII. Even when Franklin D. Roosevelt made one of his famous radio addresses in which he said that "our American forces will never serve overseas in this war," the 34th was on a ship in the Atlantic Ocean headed for Ireland then to North Africa near the ports of Oran and Casablanca.

The 34th fought against the German Army led by the German General Rommel. Many historians claim that he was the greatest and smartest general of all fighting forces in WWII. I agree with this statement.

He was in all the early fighting in the Sahara Desert in Tunisia and was captured by the Italian Army, which was an ally of Germany at that time, and put in a P.O.W. Italian concentration camp for a few months as a P.O.W. early in 1943. However, about that time, Italy decided to leave Germany as an ally. They gave up their P.O.W. camp and no longer fought for Germany, or the U.S. and its allies either. They just left their units and were on their own to do as they pleased.

Many formed small guerrilla attack groups, partisans, or "Patriots of Italy." I was to meet and know some of them later on in Italy after Anzio beachhead was established.

The infantrymen that had been captured in the South Pacific and escaped were sent to the European theater to fight in combat again. I love America with all my heart, but I am ashamed of this manner of treatment of a combat soldier, when there were nine million soldiers out of sixteen million who never saw one day of combat. I will say again, this is a national disgrace for the representatives of our country in Washington, D.C. Shame on them.

I am in no way trying to slight the U.S. Marines. They live and die in the same miserable way that all combat soldiers do. My hat is off to the marines as well as any special forces, such as the SEALS and paratroopers. But I did not live their life, so consequently I am not able to write about them. But they were all great soldiers and brave men. God bless each and every one of them.

There were two groups of soldiers in the U.S. Army: those, particularly in the infantry, who were trained to kill on the first day of being inducted, and the majority of soldiers who just put on a uniform and left home never to see the enemy or fear for their lives. They would never know the fear of death, feeling cold, hungry, and being shot at, sometimes for twenty hours at a time. I understand that they even had breakfast, lunch, and dinner. We never heard of that in combat infantry.

During the five years of German occupation, the Italians were not allowed to write letters to their friends and relatives in other towns, nor were they allowed to travel and visit them either. When people in one town that we had liberated found out that our next objective was a town where they had relations or friends, they would often give us their name and address to tell them who was still alive and who was dead.

We did not always get to deliver these messages, but we tried to the best of our ability. It was when or if we had the time. Many of these people that we were supposed to find were either dead or their homes destroyed, and no one could find them. There had been no communication between the civilians for five years under the German occupation and restrictions.

They also had all the sugar, salt, candy, and meat taken away from them so that the German soldiers could be better taken care of and be better fed.

I visited a young girl in Montecatini, near Florence, a few times when we were in rest, also after the war was over. I stayed in that town, which was famous for its hot mineral water baths and which the Duke and Duchess of Windsor often visited from England. When I got home, I mailed her a nice box of perfumed soap, which she had told me earlier that she missed very much during the German occupation years. During the war, she wrote my mother a very nice letter in English, as she was of a well-to-do, educated class. I still have the letter here at my home now. However, I remember the few times that we got to sit in her parlor during the terrible war and discuss world events at that time.

They told me that at the end of WWII, there were many parades in May for the victorious soldiers. We, who were sent overseas had to do another five, six, or seven months of occupation and wait on the point system before we could come home after two, three, and four years overseas in terrible combat, arrived back in the States too late to see any parades.

The parades were all over when I got my honorable discharge December 11, 1945, over seven months after the war was over.

All of the parades, victory marches, and welcome home hero feelings were all over, and life was back to normal for the stateside soldiers, but not for the real heroes who were killed, disabled, and nervous. The real heroes never saw a victory parade. They were still overseas doing army of occupation duty. The parades were for the home-front working people and stateside soldiers. All the parades were over with by December 1945.

30

San Remo, Italy

After May 7, they sent us to San Remo, Italy, right away for a much-needed rest, as we had been on the front lines most of the time for the last three years, however, I had only been with them for two years. Some of the original National Home Guard boys who had joined them in the States in 1940 and 1941 had been in combat and in the infantry front lines through North Africa, Sicily, and the rest of Italy, and had accumulated over 520 front-line combat days. These combat days do not include days in rest or reserve. Combat days are only those days that you are within small arms fire (machine gun, mortar, rifle, and artillery).

Somehow the armed services infantry learned a lesson from us WWII boys, because they said that in Korea and Vietnam the soldiers in the front lines would be limited to one-hundred combat days only, as that was about all that the human mind could take and still be normal when they go home and back to living with people who did not know anything about war and wouldn't understand some things that they would say or think. They were also limited to one year overseas.

I would like to say a few words of praise for the combat sergeants in all combat areas. They are the brains and guts of any platoon. A platoon is just as good as its sergeants; they make the great successful platoons and enemy details that we use every day in combat. They are our Golden Boys that we obey even though we know that we will in all probability be killed in fulfilling our assigned duty, but we believe in the old Greek Spartan motto, "Death before dishonor."

Our sergeants have to pick each soldier to go on each dangerous mission, even though he knows that a few of them will proba-

261

bly not return again to that platoon. They will be silent and unafraid forever. All combat men go through this, sometimes every day. But I always felt sorry for the sergeants whose duty was to pick out the ones to go on each dangerous and suicidal mission. To a combat platoon most of the time the sergeants are more their leaders than are the commissioned officers. They surely were in my platoon. God bless our army sergeants.

While we were staying at the Astor Hotel in San Remo in June, word came out that there was an American soldier lying dead on the beach just one block away from our hotel. One of our officers and some of our boys went down to the beach to investigate. The American soldier had his throat cut and had bled to death on this Riviera beach.

He had been dating an Italian girl, and the local Italian men didn't like it, so they killed him. He had come through all of the war and never got a scratch. Now he was dead from a jealous ex-lover or possibly just an acquaintance.

Our regimental officer then took all the enlisted men and put them in the back of one of our army trucks and went around the town of San Remo and had our soldiers jump out of the truck and grab every young man that was on the street and put him in the truck and hand-tied him and took them all to our hotel.

The officer figured that these were the boys that were going around town looking for American soldiers dating their local girls. They were going to scare our soldiers out of dating them so that they would again date the local Italian boys.

Our boy that was killed made the mistake of going out on a date without a buddy with him, as was recommended by the army at that time.

That night, about midnight, that officer and some enlisted men held a kangaroo court for these local boys that they had rounded up and judged and convicted all of them of the murder of our American soldier on the beach. This kangaroo court was held in the lobby of our hotel just after midnight that night.

Some of our boys held the Italian boys while the other American soldiers beat up on them very severely. They even deliberately broke the arms on some of these Italian boys. Then they took them outside the city limits and made them walk back to town suffering

262

as they were. From my third-floor room, I could hear them screaming.

I was not one of the boys who did this brutal retaliation, but I did hear the screams from the local boys as they were being handed down their kangaroo court justice, which was similar to the old western vigilante hanging party.

On hearing these boys scream, I left the hotel room and I asked one soldier in the lobby what was going on.

"It's best that you don't know anything about this, " he said.

These young Italian boys complained to some army officer, and they subpoenaed all the American boys involved in the kangaroo court incident, including the officer in charge, who was the ringleader.

The officer in charge was court-martialed for striking a civilian during wartime in a foreign country. What his court-martial sentence was, I never heard. And what sentence the enlisted men received, I don't know either. But I am sure that they were reduced in rank and fined a few months' salary, which is the usual sentence for an enlisted man.

I soon left beautiful San Remo for the University of Florence for one semester of psychology, agriculture, old English literature, conversational Italian, and football. I played on the Fifty Army football team there, and we won seven out of eight games. We had three all-Americans on our team and played in the Spaghetti Bowl and won the Mediterranean Theater of Operations championship in November 1945.

While we were staying in San Remo, the enlisted men stayed in the large, beautiful, three-story Astor Hotel, with its marble floors. This was the only time that the infantry did us a favor, but Lord knows we needed a favor when the war was over.

In this hotel, we slept in beds with sheets and pillows, the first ones that I had slept on since February 1943, when I was nineteen years old. I was now twenty-two years old. We had an inside toilet and shower between our two rooms. We had almost forgotten how to use either one of them. There was also a room bidet, for the women but we didn't know what they were. We thought that we had two toilets. We didn't even know how to pronounce the word much less that we were not supposed to use it or a male soldier could possibly wound himself very badly.

Most of the soldiers had gotten themselves a steady Italian girl-friend after just a few days there, because in the mountains, in combat, we very seldom saw a girl at close range. Most of the girls stayed in the hotel with the boys at night.

It was not safe for them to go home at night because of the local boys beating up on them or cutting off their hair completely.

One night, after about three weeks there, the officers came down from their hotel to our hotel and pulled a sneak inspection about midnight that night. They went into all of our hotel rooms on all three floors and rounded up all the Italian girls who were in the rooms and put them in the hallway of the second floor. There were about forty of these girls for about sixty-five to seventy-five boys. The officers told the girls to go home and not come and stay in the hotel again. Then the officers left, and most of the girls went back to their new found American soldier friends. And some of the guys went back to their rooms without their girls.

As soon as the officers and most of the soldiers left, we who stayed around for a while got our pick of the girls left and took them to our rooms. My regular girl, had already gone home, as she lived in the mountains and had to leave before dark to get home. She usually came to the hotel about 4:00 P.M. I had met her previously as a partisan, a guerrilla, in the resistance. I met her as she was hitchhiking on the road from Monte Carlo to San Remo, her home. She and all of the other partisans were given one thousand dollars from the Italian government for their work in the resistance.

After everything quieted down from the midnight inspection, there was one little Italian girl sitting on the second floor steps with just a cotton slip on and she was crying loudly. So I asked her in my best Italian language what she was crying about.

She said that no one wanted her. All the other girls had been chosen to go back to the rooms with the soldiers, but no one had asked her. It was two o'clock in the morning and "I cannot possibly go home at this hour. No soldier wanted me."

She was very sad and I felt very sorry for her just sitting on those cold marble steps.

I said, "Come with me, I will fix you up and give you a place to stay all night." So I took her to a room on that floor, opened the door, and hollered out the names of the two soldiers in my platoon that were staying in that room and told them "I have a present for you," and I pushed her in there on one of their beds and went out and closed the door behind me. I never went back until after breakfast to see the two boys. The girl was gone by then, so I never got to question her about her last night's love affair with my American buddies. I have often wondered, though?

These two boys were known to us as virgins. They were both seventeen years of age when they joined the army and neither of them had had a date in his life or had ever shaved. Now they were twenty years of age and had over three hundred combat days and had lost their virginity. I think that they did, because this girl would have to have been experienced in love-making, or she would not have been staying in our hotel with soldiers all night.

I never got to see the girl again and the two boys would not give me a civil answer to my question, "Did you or did you not?" I still correspond with one of them today. He was married and has children of his own now. But I have never again mentioned the subject, and there is a possibility that he does not know that it was I who put the girl into his room that night. I will ask him some year at the convention or on the telephone, as his wife is now deceased.

It was a very beautiful break from combat and the only favor that the Infantry ever did for me in three years of service. San Remo we love you! I would love to go back there again, as that town is in my thoughts a lot.

After the war had been over a couple of weeks, while we were in rest at San Remo, they had all of us line up, and the officers read off all the names of the soldiers that had ever been in our battalion that were killed in action (K.I.A.). I talked to the surviving boys, and we remembered a few and had forgotten a few also. This was one of my saddest days of the war. It was a long list of the K.I.A. It was so sad that I wished the officer would come to the end of the names. I saw this done once on a television movie, and I had to get up and leave the room, thirty years after we had gone through our own death list. Our officer read off 1,023 names of the K.I.A.

Incidentally I think that San Remo is the most beautiful town in Italy that I was ever in. It is like Miami, Florida, is to us. It is just down from Porta Fina, Italy, near where Benito Mussolini had a summer home which is now a museum for sightseers when it is open if you travel about ten more miles on the only highway there, past the border customs station and enter into Monaco and their town of Monte Carlo, where I went twice during my stay in San Remo. San Remo is lined with palm trees, which the Pope in Rome uses on Palm Sunday each year during the great Catholic Mass held in the great square in Rome.

If I ever return to Italy, I wish to return to Florence, Montecatini, and San Remo. I do not wish to revisit my old battle-fields, too many bad memories that I have spent sixty years trying to forget but can't, no matter how hard I try. But it was for a just cause, to keep America as it is today. I only wish the dead heroes could come back to life today and see it as it is now, if only for one day. Would they be proud of America as it is now, and say, "It is worth the sacrifice that I and so many other Americans made?"

At San Remo, a month or so after the war was over and the boys with the most points started to go home for their honorable discharge, some openings came up in the noncommissioned ranks such as corporals and sergeants.

S. Sgt. Barney Allickson came up to me and said, "Hammil, you are going to be made a sergeant next week."

"No, I am not," I said. "I have already talked to the mess sergeant, and there is an opening in the kitchen for me. I have always wanted to be a commercial chef, and since I will going to chiropractic college in Davenport, Iowa, I will probably have to learn a cook's trade to put me through college." We were all three years older now than when we were drafted.

Then he said, "Don't you think that you should have talked this over with me first?" and I said "Yes, but the war is over, and now I have to think about myself more." This was the first time that I ever turned down a sergeant's rating in three years of service.

I was in the kitchen about six weeks, and the mess sergeant went home on points and for his honorable discharge.

So the officer in charge said, "Hammil, you will be made the mess sergeant next week, a tech sergeant." And I again said "No, I won't either. I read in *Stars and Stripes* that some U.S. soldiers would be eligible to enroll August first for entrance to the University of Florence, Italy. One of the most prestigious colleges in the world. I have sent home for my high school diploma and grades, and I have been accepted in that college as of August 1, and I am going."

He wished me well and I left my favorite infantry division, of which I had so many memories, never to see them all together again. God, I miss them. The finest and bravest human beings that I will ever know, and I was with them through it all. God bless all of them, especially those who didn't make it back home to their families. It was the second time that I turned down a sergeant's rating within a two months' time.

I was promoted from a private to a private first class, the first promotion that was issued at Camp McCain, Mississippi, in March of 1943. It took six weeks in basic training to do that, and I remained at the private first class rank until the war was over, three years later.

As soon as the war was over, our battalion was sent to San Remo, Italy, near the Italian/French border, just about twelve miles from Monte Carlo, Monaco and Nice, France. That was the most beautiful area of any country that I had ever seen. I loved this area.

We were put in the Astor Hotel, which the Germans had used as a hospital during the war. Our hotel (albergo) was just one block from the ocean. We swam in it daily, and most of us had girlfriends who went to our hotel rooms with us on a regular basis. To a young infantry soldier who had lived in fear and misery for over two years, this was better than heaven. We would often say, "I'll take San Remo now, heaven can wait."

At this hotel, we slept in real beds, real beds, which we had not seen since we were drafted three years or more earlier when we were just young innocent kids. Now we were experienced killers. That was the only trade that the infantry taught then. I don't know how it is now, and I probably wouldn't believe what a recruiting sergeant told me. It is hard to find a soldier in service now who has had any combat experience except the small skirmish in 1990 in Saudi Arabia. Then very few soldiers really got combat experience, since the Iraqis surrendered by the thousands as soon as they saw the Americans. These combat soldiers were very lucky to have to serve so few days and nights in combat. I am so glad that they did not have to go through two to three years of combat misery as we did in WWII, Korea, and Vietnam. Those wars were hell on wheels, that no soldier who was in combat zones can ever forget.

Every town we first arrived in to drive out the Germans, the people loved us, gave us wine, and hugged us. But after a few months of liberation, and the war was over they were ready for us to go home. We had changed their poor country forever. The girls

267

would not go with the poor Italian boys. They all wanted an American G.I. for his food and cigarettes and possibly a trip back to the U.S. by marriage.

After a soldier had dated a local girl a few times, she would always ask, "You take me to America, no?"

Many of the large buildings had signs, "Go Home Americans." Others had signs up, "We can stand another war, but we can't stand another liberation."

After the war was over, the local men whose girls had dated German soldiers would grab these girls and completely shave all the hair off their heads, completely bald.

Just before most of us combat troops left in December 1945, these same men were starting to shave the heads of the Italian girls who had been dating the American soldiers. This caused some minor scuffles between the Italian men and our men. From then on, we went out only at night with no less than two of us men at a time, and we all carried a small pistol in our pants' waist, the bottom button of our shirt unbuttoned so that we could get the gun out quickly if necessary. I personally never had a fight with any of them over this matter, but I knew some of the boys who did.

The last week that I was overseas, we were all sent to Naples, Italy to wait for the ships to return from America to take us home. There were so many of us that the navy could not haul all of us back immediately. They had a point system. Five points for being married, five points for having children, and one point for each month overseas regardless of combat or days as a truck driver or a cook.

A soldier that was over there about one half the time that we combat soldiers were would probably go home before we young, single, combat-weary soldiers would, especially if he had a wife back in the States. Just another instance of discrimination against the young uneducated school boys that the entire fighting of the war depended solely on. I am not selfish enough to be speaking of myself alone, but for the two to three million young boys out of the sixteen million five hundred thousand who were in the armed services. This was not fair and just classification of our draftees and enlisted men. There should have been a compulsory rotation of jobs, as I have mentioned before.

I understand that the army improved on this rotation system during the Korean and Vietnam conflicts. I understand that each soldier in combat was allotted one year or one hundred combat days, whichever came first. When I was called up again for Korea and my profession was not necessary to the security of America, the infantry offered me a second lieutenant commission or an appointment to West Point officers school. I told them that "I had always wanted to go to West Point, but was too late now. I don't think that I could keep up with those younger boys. You should have made me this offer in 1943 instead of putting me in the combat infantry."

When I was in Naples, awaiting my turn to board the ship, *Wasp*, to come home, I was put on fire-guard duty at an abandoned U.S. Army depot that had probably been used during the war as a replacement depot like the one in Naples that I had been in a year and a half earlier, before going up to Anzio and Bloody Gulch.

The entire camp was abandoned except for me, walking fire guard. I had a bad gut feeling that I was not alone, that there was something unethical going on around and near me. The bunks still had all their pillows and army blankets lying on them. In the entire camp, there could be thousands of these bed items left unguarded in open canvas tents with board floors.

As I made my rounds, I noticed a one-horse pull cart sitting next to a fence that had a hole cut in the fence near the ground, large enough for a man to crawl through if he so desired. The two buggy staves that go on each side of the horse were pointed upward and the bed of the box upside down on the ground.

I walked my guard duty route about three times, and each time the buggy was pointed upward toward the sky. So I decided to use my combat experience and change my route. I came by another route and changed the time. This I did and as I came back by the carriage, this time the wagon staves were pointed down toward the ground instead of upward as it was before when I made my rounds. My suspicions were now confirmed in my head that there was some stealing going on with a well-organized group. So I went over to the hole in the fence where the wagon was reversed and looked around, just then a young Italian boy rushed past me, and I hollered at him in Italian to stop. He did not stop but he did thrust about thirty dollars in American bills in my hand and crawled through the hole in the fence with an armload of army blankets worth about thirty dollars each on the Italian black market. I just stood there in utter amazement at what was taking place. I finished my night watch about daylight and I watched him carry armloads of army blankets and other items from the abandoned camp. These boys had evidently all gone back to the States on the point system, and the army didn't have any soldiers to use this many blankets. A blanket like these would bring $30.00 to $40.00 on the street and they might even bring more money than this with the large black marketers with a truck to transport them to some of the poverty ridden European countries as many of them were doing then after the war was over and civilian crossing of the borders was again permitted.

During the war, civilians were not allowed to cross the border of any German-occupied country to another, nor were they allowed telephone calls or sending of letters from one town to the next, even to relatives. It was incommunicado for everyone under German Nazi regime.

I reported my guard duty experiences to the superior officer of this camp, and he told me "not to worry about it." So I didn't worry about it, as I had made thirty dollars, which was equivalent to my three months' pay in hell in the infantry. This is the second time that I have told this story. We left for home a few days later, about the twenty-fifth of November 1945. I was discharged December 11, 1945, at Camp Grant, near Rockford, Illinois. It took me all day to hitchhike home to Fairfield, Illinois, where both of my parents were still living on a rented farm and had put my tan, 1936, four-door car on wooden blocks during the war. I was ready to kiss it and drive it around. The car was all paid for when I gave my last two weeks' check at the used car lot for it: total of $125 in 1942 before I was drafted into the infantry in February of 1943.

If you were fortunate enough to be one of those American truck drivers who had the "misfortune" of losing one, two, or possibly three trucks or just helped in the stealing of the trucks or just furnished the black market boys some keys to the trucks, then you probably had more money than you could get home. All black market people were not Italians. Many were American soldiers who had been involved in these illegal operations all three years during WWII. Some of these were American soldiers that for many reasons one of them being for the rich rewards of the black market. Most of them were in supplies of some kind and could get their hands on marketable goods even without truck drivers to move their goods.

Most of these black marketers were regular American support troops.

If you had more money than you could get home, there were a few good ways to do it without being caught, and you could keep on adding to your account as long as you were over there.

Number one, you could get engaged to a single Italian girl and put the money in a savings account or certificate of deposit in her parents' name or even in her name, and they could not withdraw the money until after you got back to the States. Then you marry the girl, and you both have free passage back to the States when your time for the point system rotation comes up.

You have to deposit this money in a Bank of America, which had a branch in all large Italian towns: Rome, Florence, Venice, Naples, and Milan.

When you were home and discharged from the service, the Italian family, on the due date of the deposits, signs over to you your money in one of these banks that is negotiable in America in a few days. You can mail them their share or deposit it in a Bank of America in their name, and they can draw on the account in Italy.

Now under the WWII soldier marriage act, if a foreign bride gets divorced within two years of her arrival in America with her new soldier husband, she will automatically be deported back to her home country. This was enacted to keep some wealthy Italians from paying an American soldier so much money to marry their daughters just to get her to America. However, this was not foolproof. A few soldiers did marry foreign girls who had relatives in America, and who, as soon as they reached our shores and unloaded they just disappeared, separated by previous agreement before they married in Italy. They both go their separate ways, never to see each other again, so there is no divorce on record to deport her with and they both have some money to start life anew.

This marriage scam was also worked by the black marketeers quite often. But there were many true love marriages that were on the up and up, and they lived happily ever after, as far as I know.

Some black marketeers put the money in their names in the Bank of America or had it transferred to their American bank. It was possible that this could be done from home, without going back.

There was a lot of American money on the streets over there. On board ship, we would often see a soldier or two carrying a can-

271

vas overnight bag or small suitcase all wrapped and covered with white medical tape. This was a sure sign of a bag full of money. If it was Italian lire, it could be exchanged at any Bank of America in the States. These bag-toting fellows usually had another soldier with them at all times to guard them and keep other soldiers from robbing them.

When we had time to sit around we would often discuss which was the better way to go, get killed the first day of combat, fight for a year or two then get killed or wounded, get wounded early and sent home if possible, be taken a German P.O.W., or go through this hell for years and then go home to your family a nervous wreck. Most of us decided it was better to get wounded early and sent home on a medical discharge,.

But being an enlisted or draftee noncommissioned soldier, we would probably be sent back up to the front lines again to fight all over again regardless of the wound as long as we could walk. A lieutenant, captain, or colonel could get sent back to the States, but it was very difficult for a private, private first class, corporal, or sergeant to get sent back. Officers got preferred treatment on discharges. Many of them got a pension for life with a very slight disability, such as flat feet, hearing disability, bad knees, injured hand or foot, nervous stomach, or many other minor things that an enlisted man could not. And their doctor bills would be free for the rest of their life for that particular condition only.

Due to so many records using May 8, 1945 as the correct day of the surrender on V-E Day it was changed back to the correct day, May 7, V-E, meaning victory of Europe (and V-J Day meaning victory in Japan, August 14, 1945).

Those of us who came home are not heroes or victors. We are only survivors of a horrible war. It was a *just* war, as far as defeating Hitler's reign and the Japanese atrocities. But there were too few of us involved in the actual combat, and we were kept there too long while eighty percent of those in uniform never saw battle or an enemy. The only time that they fired a rifle was on the rifle range, and some of them did not do that.

I knew a U.S.O. officer that fell down drunk in an elevator entrance in Cincinnati and got a good pension for life, and was never overseas. We who were in combat—a living hell—for one to five years, came home and have not received a dime in pension. The United States is the only country in the world that does not give its combat soldiers a small pension unless they have a wound or more. But all wounds do not show.

Most soldiers who were not in combat but contributed in other ways, such as motor pool, ordnance, or support troops of any kind can have very good reunions and renew old friendships, but not many infantry-line companies can have a good attendance at their reunion because most of the original boys that they started basic training with are dead, wounded, or won't attend the reunion because they are afraid that someone will mention a bad incident, or the sight of a combat veteran will bring back too many bad memories. A line-company man has more bad memories than he has good memories, while it is just the opposite for the noncombat soldier. He only went through loneliness and restrictions, not death, starvation, freezing weather, no bed or pillow or radio.

Cameras and radios were not allowed to overseas troops, especially front-line boys, as the enemy might capture them and recognize some of our military installations.

In the 1950s, I started getting letters from the army draft board, which I could in no way understand why because I had served my full three years of WWII plus six months, as we were told we would be doing. I had also accumulated almost three hundred combat days. I had been in the front-line infantry in some of the worse fighting in the European theater of war. I had failed the regular army physicals three times at the Chicago examination station, but they took me anyway and said that I would "be in armed restricted services."

I was never in restricted service. I was put in the highest risk category of all military services, the combat infantry. I must have disappointed them by coming back alive, and they now had a legitimate chance to get a shot at me again.

They kept sending me threatening letters that they could not make me re-enlist, but they could make me wish that I had.

I told them if they sent two military police after me, "I could probably take both of them, so they had better send the Home National Guard unit."

Then I said that I was "not eligible for overseas duty because in

273

Korea and Vietnam, the soldiers were allowed only one hundred front-line days. I already had almost three hundred, about three times their allowable amount."

Then this army officer on the telephone said that they would give me a second lieutenant's rating or appoint me to West Point Academy. I said that I always wanted to go to West Point, but not now, as I had finished chiropractic college and now had my own office set up in Lawrenceville, Illinois and was five thousand in debt for my office equipment. So I was mailed my Korean 1-A draft card and never had to go due to my repeated refusal. Many WWII boys went again as retreads, but not me. A few years after the Korean and Vietnam conflicts were over, the army said that taking in the retreads was a mistake. They should have used all fresh young boys for combat service.

Leaving the soldier buddies of mine while we were still in San Remo was one of the hardest things that I ever did. It reminded me of my high school graduation exercise when we were told that "never again would all of us see each other again in our lifetime." And I knew this was a turning point in our lives when "never again would all of us see each other again in this lifetime." And we haven't.

All the young soldier boys that I left there had grown from a teenager to mature manhood of twenty-one, twenty-two, and some even twenty-three years old. But mature and experienced far beyond their birth years due to this unfortunate WWII conflict that disrupted nine-tenths of the inhabitants of this world. But that will soon be just a few paragraphs in our history books, because time does not march on, it is we who march on. Time is an infinity: no beginning and no ending or changing (Albert Einstein).

May god bless each and every one of you for giving above and beyond the call of duty so many times in your young lives. You deserve the best in life after what we all went through.

So with this my final page in this book I wish to say to all of my combat infantry buddies, "Thank you, and good-bye. I love all of you. Have a good life, and I have enjoyed the ride."